Clinton and Japan

Clinton and Japan

The Impact of Revisionism on US Trade Policy

Robert M. Uriu
University of California, Irvine

OXFORD
UNIVERSITY PRESS

OXFORD
UNIVERSITY PRESS

Great Clarendon Street, Oxford OX2 6DP

Oxford University Press is a department of the University of Oxford.
It furthers the University's objective of excellence in research, scholarship,
and education by publishing worldwide in

Oxford New York

Auckland Cape Town Dar es Salaam Hong Kong Karachi
Kuala Lumpur Madrid Melbourne Mexico City Nairobi
New Delhi Shanghai Taipei Toronto

With offices in

Argentina Austria Brazil Chile Czech Republic France Greece
Guatemala Hungary Italy Japan Poland Portugal Singapore
South Korea Switzerland Thailand Turkey Ukraine Vietnam

Oxford is a registered trade mark of Oxford University Press
in the UK and in certain other countries

Published in the United States
by Oxford University Press Inc., New York

British Library Cataloguing in Publication Data
Data available

Library of Congress Cataloging in Publication Data
Data available

Typeset by SPI Publisher Services, Pondicherry, India
Printed in Great Britain
on acid-free paper by
the MPG Books Group, Bodmin and King's Lynn

ISBN 978–0–19–928056–8

1 3 5 7 9 10 8 6 4 2

To Hugh Patrick
and to my Mom and Dad

Preface

More than a decade has passed since US–Japan trade relations was one of the most important, and most controversial, of US foreign policy issues. In the post-9/11 world, with American attention preoccupied with issues of war and terror, it may be hard for younger readers to imagine a time when issues involving international trade openness and access to the Japanese market were deemed to be prime foreign policy problems. Also, given the very positive US–Japan relationship today, marked as it is by security cooperation and the near disappearance of bilateral trade frictions, it may be hard to imagine a time when such frictions were the source of so much anger and resentment.

However, the passage of time cannot erase the intensity of the anger and resentment that characterized the relationship just a decade ago, especially for those who were involved in those events. During the 1980s and 1990s there was an incredible amount of tension in the relationship, with talk of a growing Japanese economic threat, views that Japan was America's new international rival, concerns over a 'Japanese invasion,' and the like. In Japan, a growing sense of resentment over American trade complaints and a rising dislike of Americans led many to seek to place the blame on American incompetence or dishonesty. Some scholars who studied Japan and who happened to agree with the Japanese side of the story were dismissed as 'Japanapologists' or 'agents of influence.' Conversely, critics of Japan—notably the so-called 'revisionists' who are at the core of this book—were at times accused of hating the Japanese or, worse, being motivated by racism. (Both sets of charges, I firmly believe, were without merit—that is, their differences were mostly academically and intellectually honest ones.) In this context, I vividly recall one senior scholar warning me that doing a book on the revisionists was too risky for an (then) untenured professor. I decided to ignore this advice. In any case, today, for better or for worse, the topic is no longer as controversial as it once was (better, perhaps, for US–Japan relations, but probably worse regarding interest in the topic).

I got the idea for my first book when one of my professors did not have a satisfactory answer to one of my questions. The idea for this book came when I could not come up with an adequate answer to one of my own student's questions. That question came during a discussion of the different views of the Japanese economy, pitting traditionalists who conceived of the market there as essentially capitalist in nature and Japan as an important ally, versus the revisionists who portrayed that economy as different, inherently closed, and Japan as a growing economic threat to the US. The student asked something along the lines of, 'Traditionalists and revisionists are both talking about the same Japanese economy, but come to polar opposite conclusions. They can't both be right. They all seem to be smart people, so how can one side (or the other) be so totally off?' I don't remember my answer then, but my answer now would start with, 'it all depends on one's initial assumptions ....'

In this case these two schools of thought started with entirely different *assumptions* about how the Japanese economy really worked, and what that implied for the US. Because their analysis and interpretation of the issues was based on these incompatible initial conceptions, quite naturally their diagnoses and prescriptions differed wildly. This book is about how these new, revisionist assumptions about the Japanese economy rose, coalesced, and were adopted by the US government in the 1990s, and then subsequently had a visible impact on American trade policy toward Japan.

Much of the material for this book was obtained through more than 100 in-depth interviews of the relevant policy makers on both sides of the Pacific. In conducting these interviews I was reminded very much of the Kurosawa samurai-era movie *Rashōmon*, in which the story of a crime is told four separate times, from the point of view of an accused criminal, his two victims, and a hidden bystander. Each protagonist, however, paints a completely different picture of the same events, and in doing so manages to portray themselves and their behavior in the best possible light. Some were being deceitful, but seemed to have convinced themselves of their versions of events; even the bystander telling a version that seems closest to the 'truth' managed to interpret events through self-serving lenses. In the end, one is not sure whom to believe; we simply have to filter each version according to who is telling the story.

So, too, with those involved in US–Japan trade relations. In speaking with officials from both governments, I often had the feeling that I was in the middle of my own version of the movie, with each person talking about the same events, but voicing diametrically opposite interpretations.

It struck me that this enormous gap in assumptions was real and often not reconcilable. And this gap definitely affected how policies were constructed and implemented, and how the two countries conducted their negotiations.

This impression became even more vivid during 1996–7, when I served as a Director of Asian Affairs in the National Security Council (NSC). Although I do not (and cannot) discuss the policy issues I dealt with during my service in the Clinton White House, that opportunity gave me an insider's view of how Clinton administration officials made policy. I was also able to meet many of the officials who made Clinton's Japan trade policy and had the privilege of working directly with some of them. Most importantly, I was able to put myself in their shoes, and thus I think am better able to understand how American officials conceived of the issues. I have tried to impart some of the character and color of how decisions were being made in the Clinton White House.

One thing that I discovered during my time in the Clinton White House was how competent and knowledgeable about Japan most top US government officials were, and how much direct experience with Japan actually existed in government circles. It is common to hear professors of all orientations criticize policies that they disagree with by arguing that US policy makers 'don't understand Japan,' lack experience, or are simply incompetent. What I found was that officials on all sides of the debate in fact *did* understand Japan—it was just that each side understood Japan differently.

Another thing that struck me during my interviews was how open and forthcoming all of the American officials were; all were very eager to tell their story, of course from their own point of view. I was even more impressed with how open and forthcoming the Japanese government officials were. In my previous research, on industrial policy toward troubled industries, I found that it was often very difficult to get Japanese officials to divulge any 'inside' information. This time, however, these officials were not only eager to tell their side of the story, but they were quite forthcoming in providing even more information that I had asked for. Quite early it dawned on me that the reason for this was simple—in the Framework talks, Japan was successful in beating back US trade demands, perhaps permanently. As a result, many of these officials were proud of what they had accomplished, and almost bursting to tell their version of events.

I am especially grateful to the many individuals who agreed to sit for interviews. I made it a blanket policy to not quote *any* of these individuals by name, in an effort to get at the 'inside story.' I should also note that I made it absolutely clear to each interviewee that the interviews were strictly for academic purposes, and had nothing to do with my duties at the NSC. On this note I should also stress that none of the information discussed in this book was derived from restricted sources or documents—I was not a participant in the policy deliberations described in this book, and I pointedly did not access any related classified materials. Furthermore, all of the events that I discuss in detail occurred before I entered the NSC. The views expressed in this book are completely my own, and do not reflect the views of the NSC or the Clinton administration.[1]

The research for this book was carried out under two main grants. One was an International Affairs Fellowship from the Council on Foreign Relations, which allowed me the opportunity to enter the NSC. The second was a Fulbright Fellowship for research in Japan, where I conducted the interviews for the second half of the book. I also received smaller grants from the Social Science Research Council and from my current institution, the University of California, Irvine.

In the course of researching and writing this book—a process that took far too long a time, I realize—I have accumulated many intellectual and personal debts. All or parts of the manuscript have been read by Hugh Patrick, Gerry Curtis, Ellis Krauss, T. J. Pempel, and other unnamed readers from Oxford University Press. I have received comments from these scholars and many others, including Merit Janow, S. Linn Williams, Kenji Hayao, Patti MacLachlan, Taka Suzuki, Jennifer Holt Dwyer, Michael Green, Kojo Yoshiko, Hiwatari Nobuhiro, Saori Katada, John Odell, Richard Katz, and I am sure others who I failed to record. I also thank my family—my wife Noriho and my sons Masato and Kazuto—for being so patient with me. It has become my standard New Year's resolution over the past few years to 'finish the book,' so now I can finally think of a new resolution.

I dedicate this book to three individuals who have had the biggest impact on my development. First is Hugh Patrick, my main mentor during the time I spent as a student and assistant professor at Columbia University. For my first book and for this one Hugh provided me with

---

[1] Despite these disclaimers, the NSC legal staff has objected to some of the material in this book, notably the discussion of the deliberations inside the Clinton White House, on the grounds that my status as a former NSC official *implies* direct knowledge of or participation in the secret deliberations, hence 'release of such information would compromise the deliberative process.' This discussion, of course, lies at the very heart of this book. These objections were finally resolved only in January 2007.

more than 25 pages of single-spaced comments, all of which were pointed and helpful. He is the kind of mentor that every student hopes to get; he is also the scholar and mentor who I have tried—but failed—to emulate.

I also dedicate this book to my parents, Kay and Alice, who have never stopped nurturing me. I was lucky to grow up in a stable and supportive household where doing your best was always the highest value. Truly, I would not be the person I am today without their love and guidance. I will always be grateful. On a sad note, my father passed away in mid-2008. Although he knew that I have been working on this book, I am saddened that he never had the chance to see the finished product.

Robert M. Uriu
Irvine, California

Contents

Contents

List of Interviews (selected)

National Security Council / National Economic Council

Bowman Cutter
Michael Froman
Sandra Kristoff
Robert Kyle
Stanley Roth
Nancy Soderberg
Bob Suettinger

Department of State

William Clark
Rust Deming
Jim Foster
Ellen Frost
Lawrence Greenwood
Ed Lincoln
Robert Manning
Jonathan McHale
William Rapp
Bob Reis
Joan Spero
Laura Stone

Department of Defense

Paul Giarra
Michael Green
Robin Sak Sakoda

Department of the Treasury

Roger Altman
Timothy Geithner

Department of Commerce

Phil Agress
Kevin Kearns
Marjory Searing

Office of the US Trade Representative

Wendy Cutler
Glen Fukushima
Merit Janow
Charles Lake
James Southwick
S. Linn Williams
Ira Wolf

Other Clinton Administration Officials

Raymond Ahearn
Barry Carter
Robert Fauver
Ira Magaziner
Ezra Vogel

Ministry of International Trade and Industry

Fujiki Toshimitsu
Hirai Hirohide
Hirose Naoshi
Oi Atsushi
Okamatsu Sozaburo
Sakamoto Yoshihiro
Shibota Atsuo
Takatori Akinori
Terasawa Tatsuya
Toyoda Masakazu

Ministry of Foreign Affairs

Horinouchi Hidehisa
Ito Naoki
Ono Keiichi
Oshima Shotaro
Shikata Noriyuki
Sasae Kenichiro
Takeuchi Yukio
Tanigawa Hiromichi
Ueda Naoko
Watanabe Akio
Yamanouchi Kanji

Business, Politics, Academia, and Journalism

Arthur Alexander
Daniel Bob
Steve Clemons
Kenneth Courtis
Richard Cronin
Peter Ennis
Ishihara Nobuo
Iwatake Toshihiro
Kashiyama Yukio
Karube Kensuke
Kimura Tadakazu
Komori Yoshihisa
Miki Tatsu
Michael Mochizuki
Don Oberdorfer
Robert Orr
Elizabeth Terry
Nathaniel Thayer

List of Tables and Figures

Tables

Figures

List of Abbreviations

AAMA	American Automobile Manufacturers Association
AAPA	Automobile Parts and Accessories Association
ACCJ	American Chamber of Commerce in Japan
ACTPN	Advisory Committee for Trade Policy and Negotiations
BRIE	The Berkeley Roundtable on the International Economy
CEA	Council of Economic Advisors
CIA	Central Intelligence Agency
DARPA	Defense Advanced Research Projects Agency
DC	Deputies Committee
DITI	Department of International Trade and Industry
ESI	Economic Strategy Institute
G-7	Group of Seven
GATT	General Agreement on Tariffs and Trade
IMF	International Monetary Fund
IR	International Relations
ITC	International Trade Commission
JAMA	Japan Automobile Manufacturers Association
JEI	Japan Economic Institute
JFY	Japan Fiscal Year
LDP	Liberal Democratic Party
MITI	Ministry of International Trade and Industry
MOF	Ministry of Finance
MOFA	Ministry of Foreign Affairs
MOSS	Market-Oriented, Sector-Specific
NAFTA	North American Free Trade Agreement
NEC	National Economic Council
NPT	Non-Proliferation Treaty

List of Abbreviations

NSC	National Security Council
NTT	Nippon Telegraph and Telephone
OECD	Organisation for Economic Co-operation and Development
SCA	Semiconductor Agreement
SIA	Semiconductor Industry Association
SII	Structural Impediments Initiative
STR	Special Trade Representative
UAW	United Auto Workers
USTR	United States Trade Representative
VER	Voluntary Export Restraint
VIE	Voluntary Import Expansion
WTO	World Trade Organization

PART I

Setting the Stage

The Rise of Revisionism

1

Explaining the Framework Negotiations

The US–Japan Framework negotiations of 1993–5 represent perhaps the nastiest and most confrontational of bilateral trade disputes ever. In retrospect, it is also clear that these negotiations marked a turning point in postwar US–Japan relations. First, the Framework led to a sea change in terms of the tone and substance of the relationship. A growing level of confrontation and distrust between the two countries marked the two decades that preceded the Framework. In the US, the perception in the late 1980s was that Japan's economic juggernaut represented a real threat—first to jobs, then to the survival of many industries, and finally even to the high-tech future of America. With the Japanese economy booming, and America's in seemingly inexorable decline, some predicted that the Japanese economy would outstrip the US in a few short decades; some pessimists predicted the premature 'end of the American Century.' With Japan's bilateral trade surplus reaching historic highs year after year, a growing chorus of voices blamed the Japanese for not playing by the rules, and called for drastic measures to end unfair Japanese trade practices, or to otherwise respond to 'The Japan Problem.' On the security side of the relationship, a basically cordial tie was also becoming beset by growing tension, as America's military community worried that Japan might soon overrun its high-tech domestic manufacturing base, thus making the US dangerously dependent on a foreign country.

In Japan, meanwhile, government and business leaders were becoming resentful over what was seen as constant badgering by US trade officials. To many Japanese, the problem in the trade relationship lay squarely with the US, either because of its own economic policies or because its firms were 'not trying hard enough.' Tired of being blamed for America's short-comings, the mood in Japan was becoming surly: at some point, Japan had to stand up and reject American trade demands. In terms of the security relationship, many were becoming resentful about having to host American bases on their soil, and these resentments were magnified by the horrendous Okinawa rape of September 1995, which occurred only weeks after the Framework talks formally concluded.

The first years of the Clinton administration saw these tensions reach a boiling point. In 1993 the new administration ratcheted up America's trade demands to a new level. The focal point of these demands became the negotiations over increasing American access to Japan's auto and auto parts market, and here the two sides came closer to a 'trade war' than anytime before. Up to then, cooler heads in both governments could always be counted on to forge some last-second compromise, lest trade frictions spilled over to the overall relationship. Now, in the summer of 1995, both governments allowed extreme voices to dominate the negotiations, and both held to a stubborn hard-line position all the way through the end of the Framework. This period featured the first and only failure of a postwar US–Japan Summit meeting and a marked decrease in amity between the two governments. The blowup over autos, coupled with the fallout from the Okinawa rape, led many to worry that even the *spirit* of compromise, the desire to cooperatively diffuse trade tensions for the sake of the overall relationship, seemed to be dissipating. One could hear expressions of concern over the very future of the bilateral relationship, on both sides of the Pacific.

Since this period, however, the bilateral relationship has steadily improved, in all facets. Since 1996 the US has essentially refrained from raising contentious market-opening demands. Although there is always tension when US and Japanese negotiators get together, the level of confrontation has been miniscule compared to the Framework period. Also, on the security side, the US and Japan have reaffirmed the importance of the relationship. The two sides have cooperated on crises such as dealing with North Korea, and both sides have recognized the mutual benefit of maintaining some US military presence in Japan. In more recent years, Japan's support of America's 'Global War on Terror,' and then its invasion of Iraq, prompted the George W. Bush administration to label the relationship 'the best ever.' It is as if the tensions and economic rivalry that marked the previous two decades had never even happened.

The Framework was also a turning point in that the substance of American trade demands has changed dramatically and perhaps permanently. Prior to the Framework, American demands had focused on liberalizing the market *process* in Japan by identifying and removing barriers that protected the economy—first by lowering trade barriers and then by reforming structural features of the economy that were blamed for impeding imports. In 1993, however, the US sought to negotiate a concrete 'results-oriented' or 'managed trade' agreement that would require the Japanese government to somehow set aside or guarantee a share of the domestic market for foreign imports. This implied an agreement that would include some form of quantitative indicators, and that these numbers would be used to measure, verify, and enforce Japan's compliance with the agreement. Although the US stopped short of publicly demanding explicit market share targets, it hinted privately that this was exactly what it wanted. This new emphasis on results and market *outcomes* represented a major policy change. America was now interested in 'specific reciprocity' in terms of assuring a favorable outcome, rather than 'diffuse reciprocity' in terms of gaining a fairer opportunity.[1] Furthermore, the US was calling for this distinctive trade policy to be applied only to a single country: Japan. 'The Japan Problem' was considered to be a unique one and had to be dealt with as such.

In retrospect, the Framework demands were the high water mark in terms of American trade pressures on Japan. In part, this was due to Japan's utter refusal to compromise with what it saw as unacceptable demands. At every phase of the Framework negotiation, Japan was able to force the US to retreat to its fall back position, first seeking concrete numerical targets, then to a basket of quantitative indicators to measure increased import penetration, and then to even neutral indicators that could be used to monitor the agreement. By the end, the US was hoping for the inclusion of 'numbers, any numbers' and something that would at least have a 'directional feel.' It failed even in this. US negotiators subsequently have had to live with the consequences of Japan's victory over 'managed trade'; since then, the few trade discussions that have occurred have not gone near this now 'taboo phrase.'

The Framework thus marked a new era in that, for the first time, the Japanese stood up squarely to US trade demands, said 'no,' and made it stick. Up until the Framework, the Japanese government could always be counted on to make a last-minute concession to avoid a breakdown of talks, even if these concessions turned out to be cosmetic ones.[2] But now, even with the US threatening stiff punitive tariffs on automobiles in the summer of 1995, Tokyo held firm. Now, for the first time, it was the United States that was forced to give up on nearly all of its demands.

---

[1] Krasner makes this distinction in Krasner (1987).

[2] In Michael Blaker's (1997) apt phrase, 'probe, push, and panic,' Japan could almost always be counted on to concede at the final moment, often in the face of American pressures.

In the immediate aftermath of the Framework talks, one senior Japanese government official presciently declared that the 'era of bilateralism is over'—meaning that Japan henceforth would deal with American trade complaints only in a multilateral setting.[3] Since then, the US has been forced to scrap its five-decade-old approach of applying bilateral or unilateral pressures to force open the Japanese economy. Japan's victory in the Framework thus set the tone of bilateral trade relations ever since: the US and Japan might still talk about some bilateral trade issues, but now only if *Japan* is willing to talk.

* * *

How can we best explain these momentous developments? Specifically, how can we understand why the Clinton administration chose to initiate a new results-oriented trade approach to Japan? Numerous factors were involved, ranging from the end of the Cold War to important changes in domestic politics in both countries. But while these factors played some role, I focus my analysis on an important and necessary ideational feature of the story, in that it was the American *understanding* of the Japanese economy that underwent a profound shift in this period.

This new paradigm, known loosely as 'revisionism,' conceived of the Japanese economy as inherently different, structurally closed to foreign imports, and a threat to US interests. The revisionist paradigm called for new policy thinking about dealing with Japan. The bottom line policy prescription of this new paradigm was that US exports to Japan would increase only if the Japanese government were forced to set aside a portion of its market for foreign imports. Throughout the 1980s revisionist ideas had been growing in resonance in the US in government circles, in the business community, among academics, and in the popular media. By the beginning of the Clinton administration these assumptions had clearly replaced traditional thinking. The institutionalization of these assumptions led to a fundamentally different conception of the Japanese economy, and ushered in a profound change in approach. My essential argument is that we cannot explain this shift in policy without an understanding of how American assumptions about Japan and its economy had shifted over time. The institutionalization of revisionist ideas led to a change in assumptions on which policy makers based their deliberations, and ultimately had a visible and important impact on trade policy.

[3] *Inside US Trade* 3/22/96: 3.

The Importance of Policy Assumptions

Orthodox political science theories can partially explain these developments, but only down to a certain level of content. Standard theories of International Relations (IR), which focus on the distribution of power in the international system, would point first to major changes in the external context of the US–Japan relationship. With the Cold War ending and the Soviet threat no longer dominant, IR specialists at the time predicted that previously suppressed tensions and conflicts would be unleashed.[4] In the case of the US and Japan, the military value of the security relationship naturally declined, and America now felt less constrained in pushing its longstanding economic complaints for fear that doing so would damage the overall relationship. Another fundamental change was the rising economic power of Japan at the same time that American power seemed to be inexorably declining. Now Japan, as the world's second largest economy and one with tremendous growth prospects, represented a new structural threat. The US, enjoying its 'unipolar moment,' still had to worry about future shifts in power in the international system. When IR specialists in the early 1990s warned that any such shifts would come about as the result of change in economic power, quite often it was Japan that they had in mind. Given these structural changes, some degree of rising conflict seemed inevitable.[5]

Numerous theories that stress domestic-level determinants of foreign policy also provide some insight, but again only to a limited extent.[6] In this case domestic analysts would point to the growing discontent and anger directed at Japan that was simmering throughout the 1980s, and that reached a boiling point in the early 1990s. These feelings were especially strong in the Democratic-controlled Congress. Demands that the US fix 'The Japan Problem' were intense and widespread, and with the election of a Democratic president in 1992, the way seemed open for a radical new approach. Furthermore, specific industries that were the most damaged by Japanese competition had long been active in pushing the US government to solve their competitive problems.

While standard theories would predict a stronger US response to Japan in the 1990s, they are not able to explain the specific content of the policy choices that were made. That is, America could have responded in any

---

[4] Mastanduno 1991; Huntington 1993; and Waltz 1993.
[5] Mastanduno 1991 and 1998; Layne 1993; and Huntington 1993.
[6] See Moravcsik (1997) for a useful summary.

number of ways that would have been consistent with these various theories. The US could have tried to counter Japan's expanding economic
power by trying to protect its strategic industries, building up its economy
through an industrial policy of its own, threatening to punish Japan if it did
not open its markets, and so on. Similarly, there were a variety of policy
options that could have diffused the growing anger in the US, or that could
have placated seriously affected industries. For instance, many assumed
that Clinton would appeal to labor by calling for straightforward trade
protection, while others assumed that he would seek further liberalization
of the Japanese market through a stronger policy of unilateral pressure. But
the Clinton administration decided to take a very different route, and
standard theories have a hard time explaining exactly why the US chose
its results-oriented approach.[7]

Each of these orthodox explanations has some explanatory power—and
perhaps just enough supporting evidence so that proponents of these
theories may not feel compelled to question their approach. Furthermore,
supporters of these approaches, especially the IR specialists, argue that their
theories are designed more to explain broad trends rather than specific
policy choices. This may be, but is it enough to simply understand 'broad
trends'? In other words, did the *details* of policy choice matter?

In this case, I argue that policy details did indeed matter: it was the
specific choice of a results-oriented approach that itself proved to be the
catalyst that touched off the unprecedented level of conflict in the bilateral
relationship, leading eventually to the temporary breakdown in relations
and widespread fears that worse was to come. Given the wide range of
policy options available, different choices at different points would have
led this crucial bilateral relationship in very different directions; and, given

---

[7] Furthermore, a closer look at the policy debate inside both governments shows that the
causal mechanisms espoused by standard theories also were not operating as predicted. Structural power changes may have relaxed important constraints on policy, but were not always
reflected in the shifting debate inside the US government. Even at the height of the Cold War
under the Reagan administration, revisionist ideas had already taken root inside the US government and were at least partially reflected in the US trade policy approach. And during the
Clinton administration, with the Cold War long over, traditionalist, Cold War thinking
remained strong and had a partial impact on policy. Furthermore, the balance between positions was precarious and shifting throughout—again, these shifts did not always track well with
shifts in the international system. The imperatives of the international system—so clear and
unambiguous to rationalist IR scholars—were by no means clear or unambiguous to the policy
makers who had difficult choices to make. Schoppa makes a similar argument in Schoppa
(1999: 318–20). Similarly, a wide variety of domestic groups attempted to influence the Clinton
team's policy choices, but none was able to capture the policy process. While domestic interest
groups may have opened up a 'space' for new policy initiatives, they did not directly determine
them.

the importance of these policy choices—and their lasting impact on the US–Japan relationship—we should demand that our theories be able to explain them.

* * *

So, what is the best way to explain the choices that were made? In this book I delve into the policymaking process itself, and pay particular attention to the interactions between contending policy positions that shape final decisions. I focus on the role of new policy ideas, and their impact on the policy assumptions that policy makers came to hold.

Over the past few decades a number of IR scholars have focused on the impact that non-material factors, including new policy ideas, may have. These scholars question the assertion that interests can be taken as given or that they are completely reducible to material factors. Rather, the ideas approach argues that interests are also influenced by non-material factors that help to shape how an actor understands his or her situation and interests. Furthermore, these scholars take seriously the question of how interests change—not simply because material factors change, but rather because actors are also motivated by non-material factors such as norms and values that can shape and reshape their definitions of interests.[8] Finally, these scholars argue that ideas are not always simply tools that actors use to justify actions they desire to take for other reasons. Rather, since ideas can affect how actors define their interests, they can provide a tangible motivation for behavior.[9] Other scholars have explored the process through which free-floating ideas come to have an impact on policy, most notably through new ideas being institutionalized or adopted by policymaking organizations. This process is more likely when new ideas are championed by actors who are committed to these ideas. That is, the

[8] As Goldstein and Keohane (1993: 13), put it, the rationalist approach is beset by 'empirical anomalies that can be resolved only when ideas are taken into account,' and so 'policy outcomes can be explained only when interests and power are combined with a rich understanding of human beliefs.'

[9] The literature on ideas straddles the rationalist-constructivist divide. Goldstein and Keohane (1993) have taken a step beyond rationalist assumptions, but have not gone far enough for some constructivist critics. In particular, the authors in their volume have been criticized for remaining too faithful to their rationalist roots, and for spending too much time analyzing the role of 'principled beliefs,' which specify what is considered right or wrong, and 'causal beliefs,' which pertain to more specific beliefs about cause and effect relationships. Constructivists argue that these authors need to spend more time considering the impact of 'world views'—broader concepts such as 'Christianity' or 'sovereignty,' that 'define the universe of possibilities for action'; this would allow the authors to take more seriously the role that ideas can play in shaping the *identity* of actors (see Blyth 1997; and Ruggie 1998. Other useful reviews include Woods 1995; Yee 1996; and Jacobsen 1995).

institutionalization of ideas is more likely if they are pushed by 'epistemic communities,' 'expert communities,' or 'norms entrepreneurs.'[10]

The book adopts this general orientation, but with a twist: I assert that ideas will have their clearest impact on policymaking when they reach the point of defining the *policy assumptions* held by decision makers. The dictionary defines assumptions as 'prior accepted beliefs that are taken for granted.' I thus define policy assumptions as *prior accepted beliefs about the nature of a policy issue and the interests involved* in that issue.

Policy assumptions are thus a more concrete, tangible, and visible manifestation of ideas or beliefs. The concept should be familiar to actual policy makers, since the first task of any decision making group is to figure out just what the issue is all about and how to define its scope and parameters. Furthermore, policy makers must determine what is at stake in the issue, and more particularly, how to prioritize the different stakes involved. Indeed, prevailing assumptions are usually spelled out quite clearly. In writing policy memos, the most crucial paragraphs are often the opening ones, in which one's assumptions about the nature of the issue and the interests and trade-offs involved, are all clearly defined. Prevailing policy assumptions are often readily discernible even just by listening as policy makers define the issue and interests that are involved.[11]

The struggle over policy assumptions plays a huge role in the policy-making process. First, much of the policy process involves a struggle between contending policy assumptions. At times, long debates are not needed, since policy makers may already share the same set of assumptions. But, at other times policy makers fight viciously over which competing set of assumptions is going to be recognized as the basis for policy discussions. Thus policy assumptions are not only contestable, but they are most definitely contested. In my experience in the US government, I was struck

---

[10] These terms are from, respectively, Haas (1992); Mendelson (1998); and Finnemore and Sikkink (1998).

[11] In some ways this conception of policy assumptions is another way to formulate the definition of 'national interests', but I believe brings this term to a more concrete and tangible level.

The concept of policy assumptions is not quite the same as 'ideas,' even if they are often intertwined. It is at a more specific level than what Goldstein and Keohane (1993) labeled 'world views'—broad conceptions of the world that define 'the universe of possibilities for action'—although world views certainly help determine policy assumptions. At the same time, because policy assumptions encompass definitions of interests and objectives, it is a broader concept than Goldstein's and Keohane 'principled beliefs,' which specify what is considered right or wrong, or 'causal beliefs,' which pertain to more specific beliefs about cause and effect relationships. Again, causal and principled beliefs certainly can be one aspect of the formation of assumptions, but are not the same thing.

by how crucial actual policy makers recognized policy assumptions to be, and how strongly they were willing to fight for their own favored versions.[12]

Second, once assumptions are agreed upon, they set the parameters of the subsequent debate, and can sharply narrow the range of possible strategies and tactics that are considered. That is, given a particular understanding of an issue and what is involved, the choice of which strategy or tactic to pursue at times follows logically. Debate may continue about the specific tactics to choose, but rarely about the general direction of policy. Once assumptions are agreed upon, a great deal of the subsequent policy process becomes almost automatic.

Third, once policy assumptions are agreed upon and adopted, they can become entrenched and very difficult to change; that is, they can 'take on a life of their own.' Once a decision making group has determined its assumptions, there is often a reluctance to go back to square one. As in the concept of bounded rationality, decision makers do not constantly reexamine every shared prior belief, either because they are too busy or more often because it is no longer necessary to do so. Furthermore, at some point assumptions can become so fixed and ingrained that they are no longer even recognized by policy makers themselves—that is, they are 'taken for granted.' At this point it becomes very difficult to challenge or even to question the basic premises underlying policy.[13] Many analysts have noted that policymaking often seems static and determined by inertia; a significant cause of this is entrenched assumptions.

---

[12] Policy assumptions are also not a simple matter of determining 'where you sit,' the notion that one's policy position will reflect the interests of one's bureaucratic agency Allison (1971). There is no simple formula that determines an agency's position, even if these positions are often sterotyped. For instance, the Department of Defense is of course concerned with military matters, but is also concerned with economic, trade, and industrial issues, as these have an impact on the military's underlying strength and autonomy. Defense and all other agencies must thus determine the priority attached to an issue, and the trade-offs involved—again, something that is not reducible to simple axioms. Finally, the political appointees at the top of each agency will always be torn between the bureaucracy they represent and the president who has appointed them. Often political loyalties are the more compelling, particularly at the start of an administration, when the new political appointees are not yet well-versed on their agency's policy positions.

[13] It is often the case that people in US decision making positions get there precisely because they share some common assumptions about US national interests and its place in the world. That is, those who hold radically different ideological conceptions are not 'on the same page' and thus less likely to be promoted to powerful positions—or may actively avoid entering such a career track in the first place. Policy makers often believe that there is a rich array of perspectives represented, when in fact most *are* on basically the same page. Indeed, assumptions often play their most powerful roles precisely when they are not recognized. See Jervis (1970) on the 'stickiness' of perceptions.

At this point, a few concrete examples might clarify how this concept works in practice. When the North Korean economy began to collapse in the mid-1990s, the US government might have defined the issue as a humanitarian one, since estimates were that millions of North Korean civilians would die as the result. Or, policy makers might have conceived of the situation as an opportunity to end the Kim regime and solve nuclear proliferation concerns once and for all. Instead, officials ended up focusing mostly on the incredible costs of what was seen as imminent conflict. This assumption was based on the view that Kim Jong Il would never give up power quietly, but rather would lash out in desperation if his regime were seriously threatened. The impending implosion of the economy—the so-called hard landing scenario—was thus seen as something that had to be prevented at all costs. Given these assumptions about the issue, policy makers defined the immediate objective as one of warding off the imminent collapse scenario, and the subsequent choice of providing food and other economic aid naturally followed.

At nearly the same time, in the case of relations with China, by 1996 the administration's assumptions had shifted to the view that China's economic growth and development was a stabilizing trend that should be welcomed and encouraged. That is, the administration adopted a 'neo-liberal' assumption that the more stakes China developed in the global system, the more constrained and peaceful it would be.[14] Furthermore, an operating assumption of the administration was that the opportunities of more trade with China far outweighed the possible costs. Once these assumptions were agreed upon, the policy of engagement and encouraging China's integration into the world economy became the logical choice.

In both cases, a different set of initial assumptions would have led to very different policy choices. But once initial assumptions were in place, viable options narrowed considerably. And once these assumptions were adopted, and policy based upon them, it became very difficult to convincingly argue for, or perhaps even to conceive of, a radically different course of action.

And yet, when significant policy change does occur, it is often only after prevailing assumptions are contested, challenged, and overthrown.

---

[14] In my experience in Washington, I was amazed at how relevant IR theories actually were, at least at an implicit level. That is, policy makers would often think and reason as a neo-realist would—even if this theoretical label was never mentioned, or perhaps even know. Similarly, others might base their analysis on neo-liberal assumptions; none of these policy makers had ever been trained in IR theory and would have stared blankly if told that they were a 'neo-liberal institutionalist.'

Put another way, those seeking to change policy must first go to the root of policy assumptions and seek to redefine them. It is often only after existing policy assumptions have been discredited and replaced that significant policy change even becomes possible.[15]

It is often the case that policy change is most notable when governments change, as a new policymaking team often brings with it a different set of policy assumptions (or at times *restores* old assumptions). Indeed, policy reversals toward both North Korea and China occurred once the Bush administration came into power in 2001. Again, I would call attention to the shift in assumptions that occurred at the time. In the case of North Korea, the new administration began with the assumption that Kim Jong Il only understood the language of power and deterrence, and that any sort of engagement policy would be taken advantage of and would only encourage worse behavior. The administration also placed a higher priority on non-proliferation concerns, especially after 9/11. Given these different assumptions, a policy of engagement made little sense, and even the idea of seriously negotiating with Kim was discarded. Similarly, with China, the new administration adopted a more 'realist' view of the world, and thus assumed that China's economic growth would be a source of concern, since an economically more powerful China would be a militarily more threatening China. The desire to seek engagement with the Chinese, and to further encourage it to integrate into the world economy, all but disappeared.

This focus on policy assumptions raises many of the problems of any ideational analysis. First, it is often difficult to separate 'material' factors from ideational ones. Indeed, my conception of policy assumptions is that they can also be based on, or derive from, rationalist and materialist sources. For instance, policy makers often employ rationalist concepts of materially defined interests, cost-benefit analyses, and the like, in debating assumptions. But the formation of policy assumptions is almost never reducible to some simple, rationalistic formula. Rather, each policy issue affects multiple interests in complex ways. Policy makers must not only decide which vital interests are at stake, but also have the more difficult task

---

[15] As one example, once the Clinton administration adopted the assumption that America's strategic and economic interests in China were positive and important, human rights advocates faced a tough task in shifting policy back in their direction. Human rights advocates tried to redefine US assumptions about its security and economic interests to include a concern for human rights—for instance by arguing that a lax human rights record in China implied a low level of democracy that might make it *more* unstable or aggressive, or that failure to uphold human rights standards was having a negative impact on the image of corporations that invest there. These arguments never carried the day.

of deciding which of these interests are the most vital and therefore deserve the highest priority.[16] That is, policy issues always involve trade-offs between specific interests; seeking to protect one set of interests might come at the price of compromising, or even sacrificing, other interests. Because the choice of policy assumptions encompass these complex trade-offs, it is difficult to explain using simplistic rationalist formulas. Rather, the values, perceptions, experiences, biases, and judgments of policy makers are also heavily involved.

Second, it is not always easy to determine the direction of causality. At times, new goals and new policy assumptions are announced simultaneously, so it can be unclear which is driving which. The analyst must have at least some access to those making policy, and even then causality is not always clear. Furthermore, one can think of cases where an end goal is defined first, and then policy assumptions are cynically manipulated to justify that goal. (A good case in point is the Bush administration's decision to invade Iraq in 2003, and the evidence that intelligence was cherry picked to magnify the threat, and the various rationales for invading that were put forward, modified, and subsequently dropped.) Clearly, at times, policy makers try to use assumptions strategically or instrumentally to hide ulterior motives. Furthermore, it can be difficult to tell when a set of policy assumptions is sincerely believed in. That is, policy makers very often, or perhaps always, 'spin' their analyses in self-serving ways.

These are problems that all ideational analyses must deal with. My view is that these weaknesses are not fatal in that careful analysts can often discern when policy assumptions are truly operating, even if this can never be done with mathematical precision or complete certainty. The fact that policy assumptions are tangible and defined makes the task a bit easier. That is, since they are a concrete element of the policymaking process, one can more easily trace the contest over their adoption, and can thus more easily discern when they have a causal impact on policy change. Conversely, we

---

[16] Even in cases where a nation's policy assumptions are focused, as they were for the US during much of the Cold War, or perhaps after the 9/11 terrorist attacks, the policy process remains a complex one with multiple courses of action available. IR theorists may seek to reduce interests and assumptions to single-factor analysis, but policy makers cannot.

Clinton's championing China's entry into the WTO is one example that touched on the whole range of US foreign policy interests—strategic, political, economic, humanitarian, environmental, and others. Policy makers had to decide whether these or other issues were actually relevant to China policy, and the value and priority attached to each. Would more international trade with China make it an interdependent, status quo oriented nation, or does it only increase its potential military power? Could the US maximize its business interests in China without sacrificing its concern for human rights?

can question whether policy assumptions are important in cases where assumptions are not internally logical, or if policy goals do not follow from stated assumptions, or if stated assumptions constantly change while the end goal remains the same (again, think Bush and Iraq). Similarly, analysts can often tell when policy makers are not being honest or sincere—an ever-present problem. Analysts must be careful to read between the lines, and not automatically accept stated assumptions at face value. However, those experienced in policy making and interpreting diplomatic double-speak can most often tell the difference. Here, triangulation, or contrasting one official's version with another, can be an effective methodology.

In spite of these problems, I believe that the concept of policy assumptions is still a useful one. Most cases of policy making do not reflect such strong motivational biases. This is particularly true of decisions that are not highly politicized or extremely controversial—i.e., the vast majority of decisions. But even when there is a degree of motivational bias present, a focus on policy assumptions can still be useful, as they are still the focal point of the debate over policy change. Furthermore, they may be 'sticky' in that once in place—regardless of how they got there—they can constrain subsequent policy change. Finally, the alternative—dismissing ideational factors entirely and limiting one's explanation solely to 'objective' factors— seems to me to preclude a potentially important explanation of policy change.

A focus on policy assumptions begs the question of why some are adopted over others. Here the large literature on the role of ideas and norms is helpful. As I conceive things, policy assumptions are often the concrete manifestation of prevailing ideas. That is, when ideas are persuasive and compelling, and resonate well in a society, they can end up being adopted as policy assumptions. That is, persuasive ideas can help define and re-define the issue itself, the stakes and goals involved, and can sway policy makers to change the relative priority and trade-offs between the different interests involved in the issue. In a sense, then, the contest over policy assumptions is an important access point for ideas, the nexus in which free-floating ideas can become concretely accepted and institutionalized.

From Ideas to Policy Assumptions: Revisionism Defined

This book describes one such process of policy change in which a new set of ideas rose to challenge and ultimately overthrow existing orthodoxy, eventually becoming adopted as core policy assumptions of the US government, and then exerting a concrete impact on a key international relationship.

I focus in Part I on the changing assumptions in the US government, tracing the development of this new conception as an alternative to traditional assumptions about the Japanese economy. In Chapter 2, I first discuss in detail the origins and institutional basis of 'traditionalist' assumptions about Japan.[17] This orthodox view was based on the overriding assumption that Japan was an important military and political ally, and that close relations needed to be maintained. Given its importance as an ally, trade and economic tensions thus needed to be managed or diffused, lest they spill over to harm the overall relationship. In terms of economic assumptions, traditionalists understood the Japanese market to be a protected one, but assumed that if its trade barriers could be identified and removed, then market forces would operate and exports would increase. That is, the market there may have more 'imperfections' than others, but at its core Japanese capitalism was not fundamentally different than elsewhere. Although the US should encourage further market opening, it could do so using the same approach adopted for every other country, that is, through multilateral negotiations. Over time, US market-opening demands became increasingly stringent and unilateral, in part reflecting America's growing anger at Japan, and the growing recognition that the Japanese government would only make concessions when it was pressured or threatened. I still characterize this more punitive approach as 'traditionalist' in the sense that it was based on the assumption that liberalization of the Japanese economy would naturally result in higher exports. Through the 1980s these policy assumptions were most strongly institutionalized in the 'pol-mil community' (the diplomatic corps and the military services), but were also not challenged by the economic agencies.

Revisionist thinkers disagreed strongly with all of these core assumptions. As summarized in Table 1.1, I define this alternative school of thought in terms of three basic assumptions:

- that Japan's economy was so inherently *closed* that efforts to merely remove protectionist barriers were doomed to fail;
- that the Japanese system was so fundamentally *different* that it represented its own unique brand of capitalism, in which market forces operated differently than in all other capitalist systems; and

[17] Richard Katz (1998b) also uses 'traditionalism' to describe the older, orthodox view of the Japanese economy.

Table 1.1 Revisionist views of Japan and the US–Japan relationship

A. Revisionist assumptions

– Japan's economy is inherently closed
  • Japan's market is protected by more than tariff barriers: state regulations and economic practices are designed to impede access

– Japan's economy represents a unique form of capitalism
  • Japan's economic structures are unique
  • Neo-classical rules and signals operate differently in Japan than elsewhere
  • Orthodox policy is failing because Japan is not an orthodox economy; simply liberalizing market rules and processes will not lead to increased imports

– Japan's economic system is adversarial and a threat
  • Japan's economic system is designed to gain industrial dominance by undermining its foreign competitors
  • Economics trumps security: economic power is a fundamental source of power and needs to be maximized

B. Revisionist policy prescriptions

– The US needs to adopt a new understanding of Japan, recognizing Japan as different, closed, and a threat
– The US needs to make a concerted effort to meet Japanese economic challenge, on an industry-specific basis, by emulating Japanese institutions and practices
– The US needs to pursue numerical market share targets in order to gain access to the Japanese market

– that Japan's 'adversarial' economic system represented a genuine *threat* to the American economy and even to its national security interests.[18]

The first tenet of revisionism was that the Japanese economy was not merely protected, but that it was utterly and inherently closed. That is, protection in that economy was not only due to tariff barriers that could be identified and removed, but rather that closed markets was central to

---

[18] The term 'revisionism' has been used by a great number of analysts, and is often defined to include different elements. I limit my definition to the core components of revisionism. I argue that 'getting tough on Japan' to open its markets was not an element that set the revisionists apart—everyone at the time, even many traditionalists, wanted to get tough with Japan. My definition is thus quite different than that of S. Javed Maswood (1997: 1 and 6), who argues that 'revisionist logic is premised on the utility of foreign pressure,' and is equal to using 'unilateral pressure in order to produce verifiable and real trade liberalization in Japan.' It is also not the case that all revisionists argued that the Japanese system was necessarily *better* than the American system, although by building up Japan as a dominant competitive threat many revisionists gave this impression. Some did argue that the US should adopt a Japanese-style industrial policy, but most recognized this as not politically feasible. Prestowitz later argued that 'we revisionists have never claimed that Japan's system is superior or that America should adopt it' (*International Herald Tribune* Nikkei Needs Database <http://www.nikkeieu.com/needs/>, April 18, 1995).

Japan's industrial development strategy, and inherent in the very nature of the economy. Revisionists pointed first to a long list of regulations that the government used to shield favored or strategic industries from imports. For a century, the Japanese government had 'nurtured' industries of the future, not only through industrial promotion policies, but also by helping to shield the industries from foreign competition. In addition, there were numerous 'non-tariff barriers' that provided a degree of 'natural' protection against imports.[19] A favorite metaphor of the revisionists was to compare the Japanese market to an onion: even after removing one layer of trade protection and then another, there would always be another layer underneath.

The second tenet of revisionism was that the core characteristics of Japan's economy were so different that it should be thought of as a unique form of capitalism. Revisionists pointed first to the dominant role played by the state in pursuing its unique developmental strategy, which was aimed at increasing Japan's national economic power. In this system the state bureaucrats were largely autonomous from political control or influence from societal actors, free to devise and implement industrial policies that channeled resources to strategic industries. The result was that the system was strongly tilted in favor of the producer, rather than the consumer. In addition, revisionists pointed to a series of unique economic structures that set Japan apart from all others—the industrial conglomerates (*keiretsu*) and the extensive cross-holding of stocks among them, the importance of the industry associations (*gyōkai*) in helping domestic businesses to collude, the distribution system, the unique form of enterprise unions, and the like. The revisionist argument was that these differences, taken together, were so great that the Japanese system represented an entirely different form of capitalism, in which market signals did not operate in the same way as they did in all other capitalist systems. That is, Japanese economic actors faced entirely different incentives compared to actors everywhere else. Put another way, these economic actors perceived market signals differently than their counterparts elsewhere, and as a result responded differently.

Revisionists further argued that the Japanese system was highly resistant to change, not only because its structures were a part of its society and culture, but also because they had proven themselves to be extraordinarily successful during the rapid growth period. Japan had very little incentive to change its economic structure, so efforts to make the Japanese 'more like us'

[19] Dore 1986.

were a waste of time.[20] Thus, efforts to 'liberalize' or free up the market mechanism were inherently futile: orthodox approaches were doomed to fail precisely because Japan was an unorthodox economy that operated on other-than-neoclassical principles. To return to the onion metaphor, even if one were able to remove all possible layers of protection, the core of the 'Japanese onion' would not look anything like capitalist 'onions' anywhere else.

Third, the revisionist school of thought warned that the Japanese economic system was not only different, it was also dangerous in that it represented a threat to American economic interests. Revisionists argued that the closed economy meant more than just that US firms were denied sales opportunities. Rather, the insulated market gave Japanese firms a safe haven in which they could earn excess profits that they then used to launch export offenses against overseas competitors. Further, the skewed incentives of the system led to excessive investment in targeted industries, with the resulting surplus capacity often leading to export deluges and dumping. In sum, the Japanese system was seen as one that was consciously designed to achieve international industrial dominance by undermining its competitors abroad. America's fundamental incompatibility with Japan's 'adversarial trade' system thus made it unwise to deal with Japan using the same rules as everyone else. Trying to compete with Japan using the same rules would only put US economic actors at an unfair disadvantage. Revisionists argued that this was the main reason that the US was losing the economic battle. Not only were mature industries being undermined, so too were the more competitive industries that embodied future-oriented technologies. And in some cases, the US military was growing dangerously dependent on Japan in critical defense technologies.

More fundamentally, the revisionist position called for a rethinking of what Japan meant to the United States. Rather than seeing it as a necessary and dependable political ally, the revisionists conceived of Japan as an increasingly powerful economic adversary whose unique system threatened to undermine America's position of power in the world. During the late 1980s, then, alarm over Japan's economic prowess was also transforming American perceptions of Japan itself. The debate over 'how the Japanese economy works' had sparked a deeper debate over how America should define its interests in the bilateral relationship. Now the debate was no

---

[20] Fallows 1989b. Yamamura (1990: 28) makes this point in his analysis of 'J efficiency,' which he describes as the competitive advantage that 'large Japanese manufacturing firms gained or strengthened by various structural characteristics of the Japanese economy.'

longer merely one of how to address trade frictions, but a deeper debate over whether Japan should be conceived of as a dependable political ally or a potential economic threat—in other words, a debate over the very meaning of the bilateral relationship.

In terms of policy prescriptions, the revisionists pleaded with the US government to come to grips with the reality that the traditional approach was failing precisely because it was based on incorrect traditional assumptions about the Japanese political economy. America had to recognize Japan as first and foremost an economic threat, and this called for elevating the economic problem above the traditional focus on the military relationship. America needed to make a concerted effort to close the gap, lest it find its position of power in the world undermined. At home, the US urgently needed to get its act together by dealing with its budget deficit problem and by making its own industries more competitive, including the emulation of Japan's industrial policy of identifying strategic industries for nurturing, promotion, and protection.

In terms of trade policy, the logic of revisionism led to a very different trade policy prescription. Efforts to liberalize the market process or manipulate price signals were doomed to fail because Japan had a distinctive form of capitalism. Rather, the only way to deal with the trade problem was to focus on managed trade *outcomes* in which the Japanese government would be forced to set aside a share of the market for foreign producers. In short, the revisionist position argued that because market liberalization would not lead to increased imports anyway, Japan's unique system called for a unique focus on government-guaranteed results.[21]

During the 1980s the revisionist position was rising just as traditional assumptions were increasingly called into question. Peter Hall has argued that successful new ideas must first be compelling in terms of their 'economic viability,' defined as the 'apparent capacity to resolve a relevant set of economic problems.'[22] This condition is likely to be met when orthodox ideas are perceived to have failed, and when new policy ideas offer novel solutions that promise to alleviate the policy crisis. This was exactly the situation during the crisis atmosphere of the mid-1980s. As I outline in Chapters 2 and 3, the repeated failure of orthodox policy prescriptions led to a crisis for traditionalist views. In this atmosphere, revisionist ideas

---

[21] Clyde Prestowitz (1988: 62) put it quite clearly when he argued that 'the Japanese market did not respond along Western line (so) we needed a comprehensive agreement including affirmative action by Japan to achieve some specific market share or sales target.' Prestowitz was referring to the US position leading up to the 1986 Semiconductor Agreement.

[22] Hall 1989: 371.

presented a new and simple solution to a seemingly intractable problem, and held out the promise of remedying the 'policy failure' of the traditional approach.

Hall further argues that ideas must attain both 'political' and 'administrative viability' if they are to be adopted—that is, an idea is 'more likely to become policy if it also had some appeal in the broader political arena', and when it is consistent with the 'long-standing administrative biases of the officials responsible for approving [policy change].'[23] Revisionist ideas were certainly appealing in the broader political arena, as most of the US Congress had adopted the revisionist position by the mid-1980s. In this period, the revisionist position also became increasingly adopted in the US government, and particularly among career officials who dealt with the Japan trade issue in Commerce and the USTR. Nevertheless, traditionalist thinking remained strong at the top levels of both the Reagan and Bush administrations, thus constraining the full adoption of a revisionist agenda. The continuing split between revisionist and traditionalist assumptions helps to explain the two-track approach in the late 1980s, which included both efforts to liberalize the Japanese market process as well as a growing interest in achieving concrete results. Despite the broad appeal of revisionist ideas and their achievement of political and administrative viability, they were still not yet accepted as policy assumptions.

It was during the first Clinton administration that revisionist assumptions reached the height of their influence. In a very short period of time, as described in Part II, the new administration rejected traditional thinking in favor of a new approach based on revisionist assumptions. In Chapter 4, I argue that the key change came at the level of the top political appointees who were involved in the making of Japan policy, all of who shared a strong revisionist orientation. Their deliberations, described in detail in Chapter 5, led the US to adopt a new policy approach that was centered on numerical indicators and results; this approach became the focus of the new Framework talks that began in 1993. After more than a decade of struggle, revisionists now saw their assumptions finally entrenched, leading to the adoption of the policy approach they had long advocated.

The story, however, did not end there. Rather, the Clinton team discovered during the Framework negotiations that new policy assumptions must be 'internationally viable' as well—that is, powerful actors that are the most affected must also give their consent if they are to form the basis of international relations. I describe in Part III how the new trade approach,

---

[23] Hall 1989: 373–4.

and the assumptions on which they were based, fared in bilateral negotiations—in a word, badly. That is, just as the US was finally making up its
mind to go fully in the revisionist direction, Japan was making up its mind
to oppose it.

While my narrative through the first five chapters is entirely from the
American perspective, I take a step back in Chapter 6, and relate the
Japanese response to America's adoption of the new set of policy assumption. I adopt this structure purposely, as the debate in the two countries
occurred in isolation and with little effective communication, as in the apt
phrase, 'same bed, different dreams.'[24] I first sketch the evolution of Japanese attitudes toward the US–Japan trade relationship and the growing
resentment at what were seen as increasingly unreasonable American demands. By the 1990s, the Japanese government had also become divided
between 'cooperationists' who favored the continued accommodation of
US demands, and a growing group of 'rejectionists' who argued that Japan
had to say no to the US, and especially calls for specific reciprocity.

In Chapter 6, I also introduce a different ideational lens to the analysis: a
focus on contested international norms. In essence, the Japanese government perceived America's revisionist-based agenda as an attempt to create a
new international standard for the treatment of Japan—a new 'international norm'—based on its conceptions of the Japanese economy as
closed, different, and an economic threat. The Japanese government feared
that accepting US demands for managed trade would be taken as a tacit
admission that the revisionist assumptions that underlay those demands
were indeed correct. If these assumptions went unchallenged, Japan would
be admitting that its economy was an 'outlier' that so deviated from normal
economic practices that it could not be dealt with using normal trade
policies. The US and all of its trading partners would then be justified in
demanding harsh and exceptional trade demands, including numerical
market share targets, in any market where trade complaints arose.

This was something that Tokyo refused to accept. Instead, it embarked
on a concerted campaign to refute and undermine the new American
approach. Japan's counterattack came in the form of a very effective public
relations campaign aimed squarely at discrediting revisionist arguments and
assumptions, and in some cases tried to attack the integrity of some of the
revisionist scholars themselves. Rejectionists in the Japanese government
also launched a successful lobbying campaign within their own bureaucracy
to undermine cooperationists who still favored compromising with the US.

[24] Romberg 1990.

The Japanese government response, and the subsequent negotiations with the US, boiled down to a battle over assumptions, a contest to see which set of assumptions would be accepted and legitimized. I explain in Chapter 7 how this battle led to the unprecedented breakdown in US–Japan diplomacy in 1994–5. So long as both sides stuck to their fundamentally different assumptions, the room for common ground and compromise was simply never there.

Japan's counterattack ultimately proved to be effective in undermining America's new revisionist assumptions, as described in Chapters 8 and 9. By 1996 the Clinton administration was already backing off from its initial desire for quantitative indicators and results. In part this was due to the effectiveness of Japan's attack on revisionist arguments, and the surprisingly strong negotiating position it maintained through the end of the Framework talks. There were other factors that also helped to shift the balance inside the US government back towards traditionalist views. The traditionalist position was first strengthened by the rising threat posed by North Korea, which was at that time seeking to develop a nuclear capability. Traditionalists also were worried that the negativity resulting from the Framework talks was damaging the overall US–Japan relationship. The pol-mil community thus made a concerted effort to return to traditionalist assumptions about the importance of the security alliance, and by 1996 had largely succeeded. Furthermore, policy makers were influenced by the growing evidence that Japan's economic downturn was more serious than earlier believed. Now, many began to doubt just how much of an economic threat Japan really was.

The period in which revisionist assumptions about Japan were the unchallenged core of official US policy was thus relatively brief, limited to the first Clinton administration. Yet in this short time, these new assumptions had an important impact on the relationship: they were crucial in determining the radical departure from traditional policy taken by the Clinton team in 1993; their advent led directly to the most contentious US–Japan negotiation in the postwar period; and the subsequent rejection of these assumptions helped to shape a radically different US–Japan relationship.

2

Traditionalist Views and the Emergence of Revisionism

The emergence of revisionist conceptions about Japan's economy occurred against a backdrop of rising tensions between the US and Japan that reached an emotional peak in the late 1980s. Before continuing, I need to stress that I have tried to strip away the venom and name-calling that characterized much of the debate in the US at the time. By the late 1980s this debate had become hopelessly polarized. Not only did traditionalist and revisionist scholars hold incompatible assumptions about the Japanese economy, but at a deeper level some proponents of both schools of thought began to question the very motivations of those holding different assumptions. That is, each school criticized the other not only for being uninformed or wrong, but also for being willfully naïve or even dishonorable.

On the one hand, revisionists were often charged with having a special animus against Japan, that they were motivated by fear, anger, or hatred—or worse, by racial animosity. Many were branded as 'Japan bashers' (or the more racially charged 'Jap bashers'), implying that their arguments were motivated by something other than reason.[1] On the other extreme, those who held to traditionalist ideas, or who understood Japan's position and dared to articulate or defend that position, were charged with being overly sympathetic to the Japanese. These analysts were often labeled as 'Japanapologists' or members of the 'Chrysanthemum Club,' with the implication that their loyalties lay with the Japanese. Another popular term was 'agents of influence,' taken from a book of the same name that charged that the

---

[1] As I discuss in Chapters 6 and 7, some of these insinuations were made by Japanese government officials, at times as part of an effort to discredit revisionist ideas by discrediting the revisionists themselves.

Japanese government had used donations to essentially bribe American opinion leaders.[2]

The natural effect of these personal attacks was to kill all rational debate; once aspersions about an opponent's sympathies and motivations became the focal point, rational discourse became impossible. That is, if the revisionists were racially motivated, then all of their criticisms of Japan—even where those criticisms were correct and legitimate—were to be rejected and ignored. Similarly, if the arguments of the 'bought-and-sold Japanapologists' were just as tainted and inherently biased, they therefore should be dismissed—again, even where these perspectives had some legitimacy.

I have always taken strong exception to both of these types of personal attacks. I have met most of the figures mentioned in this book, on both sides of the debate, and have come to know many of them well. Almost without exception I perceive these people in a less suspicious light—that is, as individuals who defined an issue and a problem in two very distinctive ways. In the following sections I try to portray them in this light, and try to give each person the benefit of the doubt.

I should also note that my purpose is not to judge the relative 'correctness' of either the revisionist or traditionalist schools of thought; there have been enough writings on both sides of this contentious debate over the past decades, and proponents of both schools still believe that they are in the right. Rather, my task is to analyze from what sources revisionist assumptions originated, and then to trace the extent to which this alternative paradigm coalesced and then influenced US policy. Regardless of whether one agrees with revisionist assumptions or not, the issue that concerns me is whether they had an important and concrete impact on policy assumptions and choices.

In the first section of this chapter, I discuss the assumptions of the traditionalist view and their institutional basis. This review will be familiar to some readers, but is important in that these assumptions were the foundation of America's postwar Japan policy. I then go back to trace the emergence and growing institutionalization of the revisionist paradigm, paying special attention to the role played by certain individuals from the business community, the US government, media, and academia. These actors came from very different backgrounds, but were similar in that they all had had intimate experience with the Japanese economy, and all

---

[2] Choate 1990. To be sure, some individuals—the paid lobbyists—were agents of influence, in a formal and legal sense. This was not the case with the traditionalists discussed in this book.

shared the deep-rooted conviction that traditionalist assumptions about Japan were wrong.[3]

Traditionalist Assumptions Defined

As summarized in the left column in Table 2.1, the traditionalist view was based first on the assumption that Japan in the postwar period had been a crucial military and political ally that shared America's interest in fighting and winning the Cold War. Japan was described as a 'bulwark against Communist expansion' and the key to Washington's entire Asian policy. In particular, Japan's willingness to allow the US to maintain bases on its soil was crucial not only to the strategic balance in the region, but also to America's global military strategy. Japan's ardently anti-Communist government shared America's interest in capitalism and democracy, and thus could be counted on to support American foreign initiatives, even when it was reluctant to do so. Not without good reason was it described as 'America's most important bilateral relationship, bar none'.

A related assumption was that these military and political ties were far more important than the economic side of the relationship. Reflecting Cold War policy in general, US policy was dominated by the 'high politics' of security relations, with 'security' being defined largely in military terms; trade and other issues were relegated to a separate, and subordinate, track. Thus, while traditionalists were of course aware of growing trade complaints, they preferred to prevent tensions stemming from 'peripheral' issues from harming the underlying security relationship. Rather, the two governments made 'managing the alliance' the key goal.[4]

---

[3] In this sense, the revisionists can be thought of as an epistemic community or expert community (Haas 1992; and Mendelson 1998).

[4] Destler et al. 1976. Prestowitz recalls an incident in which revisionists and traditionalists were in a debate over some trade policy issue when Gaston Sigur, the NSC official in charge of Asian Affairs, pounded his chair, saying 'We must have those bases. Now that's the bottom line.' Even though access to the bases was not the issue, this assertion ended the debate (Prestowitz 1988: 295; and Dryden 1995: 298).

Even in the case of the Textile Wrangle of 1969–71—the major exception to the containment of trade tensions—negotiations took place within the context of a mutual interest in preserving the security relationship. This dispute was especially serious because it involved some very evident animosity toward Japan on the part of US President Nixon, which contributed to the subsequent Nixon Shocks, including America's surprise rapprochement with China and the decision to end the fixed exchange rate regime. In addition, the US sought to 'hold hostage' the return of control over Okinawa. Still, the two sides were able to avoid a permanent negative impact on the security relationship (Destler 1976 and 1979).

Table 2.1 Contending views of Japan and the US–Japan relationship

I. Traditionalist views of Japan

A. Traditionalist assumptions

- Security: Japan is a crucial political and military ally
  - Japan is an important source of alliance support, including access to bases in Japan; preserving security relations is more important than resolving economic frictions
- Japanese capitalism is essentially the same as elsewhere
  - Japan's economy is protected, but not inherently closed
  - If the market process is liberalized, economic actors there will respond to market signals, and imports will rise
- Causes of the trade imbalance
  - The bilateral deficit is not a serious problem; trade imbalances are caused by macro-economic factors; multilateral negotiations can be effective
  - Trade-hawk traditionalists: attention to sectoral protection in Japan is also needed; existing multilateral trading rules are not strong enough; the Japanese government will only make concessions when threatened with retaliation

B. Traditionalist Policy Prescriptions

- The political relationship should be insulated from economic frictions; Japan should be encouraged to contribute more to the alliance relationship (burden sharing)
- Manipulating macroeconomic factors is the best way to resolve the trade imbalance
- It is not worth the diplomatic costs to negotiate away trade barriers; opening the Japanese market should be done multilaterally
- Trade-hawk traditionalists: Bilateral trade negotiations are needed where specific barriers exist; Japan will open its markets only if it is pressured and threatened

II. Revisionist views of Japan

A. Revisionist assumptions

- Japan's economy is inherently closed
  - Japan's market is protected by more than tariff barriers: state regulations and economic practices are designed to impede access
- Japan's economy represents a different form of capitalism
  - Japan's economic structures are unique
  - Neo-classical rules and signals operate differently in Japan than elsewhere
  - Orthodox policy is failing because Japan is not an orthodox economy; simply liberalizing market rules and processes will not lead to increased imports
- Japan's economic system is adversarial and a threat
  - Japan's economic system is designed to gain industrial dominance by undermining its foreign competitors
  - Economics trumps security: economic power is a fundamental source of power and needs to be maximized

B. Revisionist Policy Prescriptions

- The US needs to adopt a new understanding of Japan, recognizing Japan as different, closed, and a threat
- The US needs to make a concerted effort to meet Japanese economic challenge, on an industry-specific basis, by emulating Japanese institutions and practices
- The US needs to pursue a managed trade approach, including numerical market share targets, in order to gain access to the Japanese market

For the most part, these core assumptions about the political side of the relationship were so deeply held that they were sometimes not even recognized as assumptions. This position was most entrenched in the agencies in charge of political and military affairs—the 'pol-mil' community consisting of the Departments of State and Defense, and the National Security Council—but was also unchallenged even by agencies more concerned with trade and economic policy. State Department officials were solidly in support of strengthening the bilateral relationship. Basic Department policy emphasized the importance of Japan as a political ally, not only because of its cooperation on defense but also because of its consistent support for overall US foreign policy. Similarly, the Defense Department through the end of the 1970s was unified in its view that it was in America's interest to preserve and strengthen the bilateral relationship. Although some Defense officials were beginning to worry about becoming dependent on Japan for military-related technology, a concern that would deepen over the course of the 1980s, this issue was still on the back burner. If anything, Japan was thought of as a potentially valuable source of new technology.

Traditionalists, however, were also aware that Japan's expanding wealth put it in the position to bear more of the costs of maintaining the alliance. Traditionalists saw these contributions as one way to silence the growing number of critics in the US who charged that Japan was 'free riding,' accepting military protection while limiting its own defense efforts. The debate in the early 1980s thus centered on 'burden sharing,' or ways in which Japan could be encouraged to, in the catch phrase of the day, 'play a political role commensurate with its economic power.' Japan responded by raising its military spending, including its host-nation support for the US bases. Tokyo was also persuaded to expand its roles and missions, to increase the transfer of dual-use technologies to the US, and to increase its total spending on 'comprehensive security,' which included non-military contributions such as foreign aid.[5]

In contrast to the comfortable and unquestioned assumptions about the security relationship, traditionalist views about the Japanese economy became more controversial and contested as trade frictions went from bad to worse during the 1970s and 1980s. As seen in Figure 2.1, Japan's bilateral trade surplus rose from the then 'politically unsustainable' level of US$4.1

[5] Prime Minister Suzuki Zenko in 1980, for instance, pledged to defend the sea lanes out to 1,000 nautical miles. Japan also relaxed its prohibitions on the export of military-related technology. Japan also began to extend aid not only for economic development but also in support of US strategic goals. Orr (1990) makes an important point that US played a role in Japanese aid policy, but underemphasizes the extent to which Japan was able to define and pursue its own interests (see also Miyashita and Sato 2001).

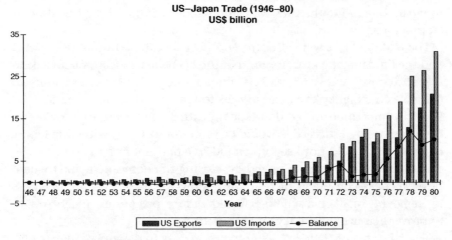

Figure 2.1 US–Japan Trade (1946–80)

billion in 1972 to an even more unsustainable level of US$12.0 billion in 1978. Numerous industries found themselves losing out in head-to-head competition. Trade dislocations were strongest in politically powerful industries such as textiles, steel, and automobiles, but many other industries joined the chorus calling for protection. Anger at Japan's trade surpluses was especially strong in the US Congress, leading to rising protectionist pressures, particularly during periods of economic downturns.

The traditionalist understanding of the economic problem rested on the core assumption that Japanese capitalism was essentially the same as capitalism anywhere else. Traditionalists of course recognized that market imperfections and barriers to trade in Japan existed, but did not see Japan as unique in this regard. Reflecting neoclassical thinking, the traditionalist position argued that any such deviations that caused economic actors there to perceive inappropriate market signals needed to be corrected.[6] Once these distortions were removed, and market competition made more 'perfect', then the market mechanism would function more normally, American firms would be able to compete effectively, and imports would naturally rise. Essentially, the best way to deal with the chronic trade deficit was to change market signals and then leave it to economic actors

---

[6] For instance, government regulations favoring Japanese producers made Japanese goods cheaper relative to imports; similarly, government policy that encouraged overinvestment also contributed to the tendency of Japanese industries to engage in export deluges (see Komiya et al. 1988; and Yamamura 1982).

in Japan to respond; the trick was simply to ensure that these signals were 'appropriate.'

The traditionalists were also strong believers in the power of the market and the fundamental assumption that the US benefited from freer trade in overall terms.[7] Access to markets abroad forced American exporters to compete on a higher level, and to thus to remain world-class competitors. Import competition forced domestic industries to increase their own efficiency: those that succeeded would be more competitive, while the failure of those who could not keep up would free up resources to be shifted to other firms or industries. Conversely, closing the domestic market would hurt American consumers by restricting access to less expensive goods and, by removing market discipline, would reduce businesses' incentives to improve their own efficiency and competitiveness.

The faith in free trade led some traditionalists to downplay the seriousness of the bilateral trade deficit itself. Some viewed bilateral trade imbalances as not only tolerable, but also almost a good thing in that imports increased competition. Furthermore, the US should not overreact to the bilateral trade deficit since an imbalance with any one trading partner would be offset by surpluses with others. If protectionist pressures were so high that some political response became necessary, traditionalists felt that relief should be temporary and kept to the absolute minimum necessary to deflect pressures for significant market closure.

Traditionalists further believed that the bilateral trade imbalance with Japan was *not* due primarily to barriers in the Japanese economy, but rather to other structural factors, most notably the exploding US government budget deficit and the disparity in savings rates. As a key bilateral commission, the Wiseman's Group, put it in 1981, the trade imbalance 'would exist even if there were perfect access to the Japanese market... [The trade imbalance] reflects an efficient allocation of resources for the two countries.'[8] Thus, while traditionalists were of course aware of trade

---

[7] As Goldstein (1993) has demonstrated, these beliefs were deeply rooted in the US, and imbued in institutions of the US government.

[8] Wiseman's Group 1981a: v–vi. The clearest and most influential statement of the traditionalist view of the Japanese economy is the report of the Japan–United States Economic Relations Group, more commonly known as the 'Wiseman's Group,' which was established in 1979 by the two governments. The group was chaired by two diplomats, former Deputy Secretary of State Robert S. Ingersoll and former State Minister for External Economic Affairs, Nobuhiko Ushiba. The other members of this small group included businessmen Akio Morita of Sony, Isamu Yamashita of Mitsui Engineering and Shipbuilding, and Edson Spencer of Honeywell; bankers A W. Clausen of Bank of America and Shuzo Muramoto of Dai-Ichi Kangyo Bank; and two academics, Kiichi Saeki from the Nomura Research Institute and Hugh Patrick of Yale University (Wiseman's Group 1981b). The group issued two reports, in January and then October of 1981.

protectionism in Japan, proponents did not believe that this was the main reason that US firms were not cracking the Japanese market.[9] Traditionalists thus did not favor making market opening the core of trade policy toward Japan, as this would not put a big enough dent in the overall imbalance; further, many believed that the diplomatic costs of pressuring the Japanese government to remove these barriers would not be worth the economic payback.[10]

Yet traditionalists did support efforts to liberalize the Japanese economy—just as they advocated freer trade everywhere. Efforts to remove barriers to trade were important because the principles of free trade held that the market should be allowed to operate unfettered. The traditionalists, however, did not believe that trade negotiations should be carried out on a sector-by-sector basis, but rather called for across-the-board liberalization efforts. Furthermore negotiations should not be bilateral in nature, but rather *multilateral*. Many argued that America's campaign to liberalize global trade had already succeeded in partially opening Japan, which in the 1960s had reduced its tariffs so far that it could boast that its nominal tariffs were the lowest of any OECD nation, and was gradually removing government restrictions on foreign investment.[11]

The basic assumptions that Japanese capitalism was like capitalism everywhere and that the trade imbalance was due largely to macroeconomic factors, remained the core consensus of the US government through the 1980s. Most of the economic agencies were unified behind this position, from career officials to top political appointees. Traditionalist assumptions were strongest in the Council of Economic Advisors (CEA), which had long been dominated by neoclassical economists, and also in the Treasury Department, which had jurisdiction over general macroeconomic policy. Officials in these agencies certainly recognized the existence of barriers in the Japanese market, but argued that macroeconomic solutions would be enough to solve the problem.

[9] Even at the end of the Reagan administration many top officials were still not sympathetic to business complaints, in some cases criticizing US firms for not trying hard enough, and then turning to the government for a handout.

[10] Traditionalists did recognize that market opening was important politically, since it would diffuse the growing American discontent over the rising costs of free trade and in particular the popular perception that the Japanese market was closed and unfair. Removing these barriers might diffuse these resentments and thus insure domestic political support for free trade.

[11] These efforts were largely undertaken in the multilateral tariff negotiations (MTN), beginning with the Kennedy Round in 1964, and followed by a succession of similar rounds. Japan took an important step in December 1980 with the repeal of the Foreign Investment Law of 1950 (Wiseman's Group 1981a) See Dryden (1995) for a detailed discussion of the role of the USTR in these efforts.

The core of the traditionalist approach to the trade imbalance thus stressed macroeconomic solutions, and in particular by pressuring the Japanese government to use fiscal stimulus to increase domestic growth rates.[12] The assumption was that if Japan were to expand aggregate domestic demand, then imports would naturally rise. US government pressure on the Japanese government to inflate its economy was thus a constant theme of bilateral interactions through this entire period. Traditionalists also held that the relative prices of goods were out of whack due to the dollar being overvalued, which made the price of Japanese goods in the US market (in dollar terms) artificially low, while US goods in Japan were overly expensive in terms of yen. America thus engaged in various efforts to manipulate the yen–dollar exchange rate, first as part of the 'Nixon Shocks' of 1973 and then more cooperatively in 1978. Reagan officials showed great faith in this approach in their efforts to devalue the dollar in the 1985 Plaza Accord.[13] Finally, the traditionalists argued that a huge part of the solution involved America: that is, it was the US that needed to get its own house in order, particularly by reducing its chronic government budget deficit and improving the competitiveness of its own industries and firms.

Over the course of the 1970s and 1980s, however, as the bilateral deficit continued to grow, a subset of traditionalists, which might be called the 'trade hawk traditionalists,' began to advocate bilateral negotiations to opening specific Japanese markets and increasingly called for the use of threats of trade retaliation. The trade-hawk traditionalists were naturally strongest in the trade-related agencies, the Department of Commerce and the Office of the US Trade Representative (USTR), which were the most directly involved in the frustrating task of increasing access to the Japanese market.

The trade-hawk traditionalists argued that the US needed to pay attention to protection in specific Japanese markets, and that doing so would be the best way to increase American exports. Furthermore, they believed that the multilateral and across-the-board approach to reducing trade barriers would not be enough to address the trade imbalance. Given Japan's long list of remaining quotas, government rules and regulations, and other non-tariff barriers that worked to impede imports, their

---

[12] These pressures formed the core of US policy in 1978, as the Carter administration pressed Japan to stimulate its economy in the hopes that a rapidly growing Japan would absorb much of the world's excess production, and thus operate as a 'locomotive' pulling the world behind it (see Suzuki 2000).

[13] Odell 1982; and Funabashi 1989.

argument was that existing multilateral trade rules were too weak or too general to be able to identify and remove the pervasive protectionist barriers that shielded certain Japanese markets. Rather, the assumption that many officials began to adopt was that market-opening negotiations would only succeed if they were done on a *sectoral* and *bilateral* basis, with the US government identifying specific barriers to trade and then negotiating directly with the Japanese government for their removal.

In addition, the trade-hawk traditionalists argued that the Japanese government would only agree to remove barriers to trade under threat of retaliation. Many understood that powerful vested interests in Japan, along with their political and bureaucratic allies, were often able to veto trade liberalization efforts. And because leadership at the top of the Japanese system was usually weak, the Japanese government often could not take any steps absent foreign pressures, and at times even found it useful to blame the US for making trade concessions unavoidable. Over time, the trade hawks advocated stronger and stronger threats of retaliation, initially bilateral in nature but then increasingly including unilateral threats as well.

Most analyses of US–Japan trade relations treat the traditionalists and the trade-hawk traditionalists as the main warring factions in US trade policy thinking at the time, and analyze the policy process accordingly.[14] I classify the trade hawks as a subset of traditionalism in that they shared some important underlying assumptions. The trade hawks did not dispute the assumptions that the security relationship with Japan was crucial, that freer trade was a good thing, and that the basis of the trade problem was macroeconomic in nature. More importantly, the trade hawks still believed that Japanese capitalism was essentially similar to capitalism everywhere, and that economic actors there would respond to changing market signals in the same way as in any other capitalist system. Thus, even if some sectors were highly protected in Japan, the market was not inherently closed. If barriers in the Japanese market were removed, then Japanese consumers would have freer access to more price-competitive imports, and imports would rise. To return to the onion metaphor, both sub-schools believed that the inner workings of the Japanese economy were similar to other market economies, and that once enough of the outer layers had been peeled away, the access problem would be solved.

---

[14] These two sub-schools have been given a variety of labels by other scholars and policy-makers, from free traders, soft liners, white hats for the former, and hard liners, black hats, and even Japan bashers for the latter.

Furthermore, most scholars treat the revisionists as merely an offshoot of the trade hawk traditionalists, in that both called for elevating the trade issue, and argued for the need for retaliation against Japan.[15] But it is important to remember that the revisionists were *not* simply those who wanted to get tougher with Japan. What set them apart was their belief in a fundamentally different set of assumptions about the Japanese economy—namely that the market in Japan was so closed and that the system there was so different, that it operated on other-than-capitalist principles. The logical conclusion of the revisionists was that trying to manipulate market signals was futile; rather, getting the Japanese government to guarantee some sort of market share was the only solution.

The Early Roots of Revisionism: The 1960s and 1970s

Traditionalist assumptions about Japan never completely disappeared from inside the US government, and in recent years have reasserted themselves in the policy debate. Through the 1980s, however, new, revisionist ideas about Japan and its economy were being developed by a handful of US government officials, academics, and within the business community. As summarized in Table 2.1, revisionist assumptions rested on three core assumptions: that Japan's economy was so inherently *closed* that efforts to merely liberalize the market process were doomed to fail; that it was so *different* that it represented a unique form of capitalism; and that it represented a genuine *threat* to America's overall economy and even its national security interests.

The remainder of this chapter emphasizes the earliest development of this revisionist paradigm, analyzing its origins, institutionalization, and impact. I thus do not attempt to chronicle every aspect of US trade policy

[15] John Kunkel, for instance, portrays revisionism as an outgrowth of the learning process undertaken by the trade hawks. I have drawn the dividing line between the schools of thought somewhat differently, stressing the difference in underlying assumptions rather than differences in policy prescriptions. By adopting a narrower and more specific definition of revisionism, I realize that I am making my task of showing its impact more difficult. But the narrower definition makes more analytical sense to me.

I agree with Kunkel (2003), however, that the US policy story can in large part be understood as an ideational one. In this sense, trade hawk traditionalists played an important role in helping to undermine what they saw as the more naïve of the original traditionalist arguments—namely that trade imbalances don't matter, and that the problem could be resolved entirely via macroeconomic policy. In this sense, they helped to pave the way for revisionist assumptions to take hold. But while trade-hawk traditionalists and revisionists thus agreed that the original traditionalist approach was not working, they disagreed on what needed to be done about it.

toward Japan.[16] This focus on revisionism may exaggerate the degree to which revisionist ideas had entered the mainstream; readers should keep in mind that at least until the Clinton administration, revisionism was only beginning to challenge traditionalist assumptions, but had not yet overturned them.

The ideas that eventually made up the revisionist paradigm stemmed from a variety of sources and in some cases have had very long traditions, at times traceable to America's earliest impressions of Japan. Until the 1980s the American debate centered on whether Japan's economy was different and closed; the concern for Japan as an economic threat was to come later. At a trivial level, few Americans needed to be convinced that Japan was different; many had long thought of it as an exotic, even inscrutable, 'other.' As Japan entered into the era of its postwar 'economic miracle,' however, it went from exotic to important, as a stunning example of industrial development that needed to be explained. And from 1965 on, when Japan began to run consistent trade surpluses with the US, it became the focal point of America's rising discontent with trade Japan's 'miraculously' rapid industrialization and persistent bilateral trade-surpluses thus raised the first anomalies for traditionalist assumptions: was Japan's industrialization explainable by orthodox market economics, or were there other 'secrets' to its success?[17]

Americans also needed little convincing that Japan was a highly protected economy. Indeed, it was the case that Japan in the early postwar period *was* highly closed, sheltered by relatively high tariffs.[18] True, as a condition for joining multilateral institutions such as the GATT, IMF, and OECD, Japan had agreed to lower these tariffs and remove most of its import quotas and restrictions on foreign capital flows; but it was also becoming clear to many that even though Japan had significantly lowered its formal barriers to trade, import levels were not rising as fast as predicted. Clearly, the market was protected by more than just tariff barriers. This anomaly—Japan being one of the most open of the industrialized economies

---

[16] There have been numerous summaries of the development of America's overall trade policy toward Japan. Notable accounts include Destler et al. 1976; Yamamura 1982; Bhagwati and Patrick 1990; Destler 1992; Janow 1994; Katz 1997; Schoppa 1997 and 1999; Lincoln 1999; and Kunkel 2003.

[17] In this search scholars mostly debated about the importance of the Japanese state and its industrial policy (see, for example, Patrick and Rosovsky 1976).

[18] Many have noted that in the immediate postwar period the US had agreed to allow Japan to maintain relatively high tariffs, mostly because of the desire to make Japan a stable and dependable Cold War ally.

(on paper) while imports seemed to be blocked—gave growing credence to the view that protectionism in Japan was somehow unique.

American trade complaints in this period also began to emphasize the protectionist practices of the Japanese government, which seemed to many to be a reflection of Japan's overall industrialization strategy. It was widely recognized that Japan was reluctant to fulfill its multilateral obligations, for instance resorting to 'residual quotas' to a greater degree than the rest of the world.[19] But even when it did liberalize, the government often used new regulations to shield these sectors in an effort to negate the effects of market liberalization. In particular, it was slow to fully liberalize restrictions on capital flows, and instead followed what Dennis Encarnation later termed a 'strategic investment policy' to discourage foreign investment.[20] T. J. Pempel described the Japanese government as playing a 'gatekeeper' role, in that it was able to limit or control goods, capital, and investment flowing into (and out of) the country.[21]

Complaints about the Japanese market in this period stemmed first from the small subset of American firms that had been trying to enter the market there. In some celebrated cases, competitive US firms such as IBM and Texas Instruments had spent years fighting the Japanese government before successfully establishing a market presence; others, such as Motorola, still faced difficult obstacles. As Encarnation puts it, 'only a very few American multinationals in Japan have achieved success through investments in majority subsidiaries,' and then only after 'years of very difficult and often bitter negotiations.'[22] Other industries also complained of Japanese government actions that served to seal off its market, ranging from regulations such as quality and health standards that discriminated against foreign goods, to the extensive formation of cartels officially approved by the Japanese government.[23] These firms certainly shared these complaints with the US government, both individually and through

---

[19] Encarnation 1992: 58. For instance, Japan in 1963 retained some 192 quantitative restrictions; in 1969 Japan still maintained import quotas on 120 items, including 43 GATT-illegal import restrictions (Dryden 1995: 138).

[20] Encarnation 1992: 37; see also Mason 1992. This policy combined formal restrictions on trade and capital flows with 'private restrictions on interfirm relations', i.e., the *keiretsu*, which made entry through mergers and acquisitions more difficult.

[21] Pempel 1978. In particular, the Japanese government was seen as very effective in terms of de-linking foreign technology from foreign ownership. That is, the government was effective in forcing or encouraging foreign firms to transfer technology to Japanese competitors while keeping foreign direct investment, and ownership, to a minimum.

[22] Encarnation 1992: 41.   [23] Tilton 1996; and Uriu 1996.

business organizations such as the American Chamber of Commerce in Japan (ACCJ).[24]

American government officials who worked on Japan trade-related issues were already well aware of the problems of Japanese government restrictions on goods and investments for strategic industries. The development of these views was not just a case of government officials being receptive to private sector pressures. Rather, in many cases they brought with them their own personal experiences—mostly bad ones—trying to operate in the Japanese market, and thus were already intimately aware of how the government was reluctant to allow a truly open market. While industry pressures may have reinforced these views, these officials were coming to the same conclusions simultaneously and independently.

One concrete example of Commerce's early thinking is a 1972 document entitled *Japan: The Government–Business Relationship*. This booklet, drafted by a Commerce staff member, Eugene Kaplan, foreshadowed some important elements of the revisionist view:

> the American business community has come to view Japan with decidedly mixed feelings compounded of admiration and growing uneasiness...The uneasiness stems...from the feeling that Japan may be playing the economic game under a different set of rules than obtain in this country...The essence of this difference resides in the relationship of business and government.[25]

Kaplan went on to spell out the crucial role that the Japanese government, and especially its economic bureaucracy, had played in the country's

---

[24] The ACCJ was founded in 1948 by 40 US firms, and has played an active role in trade issues ever since. Encarnation notes the ACCJ's active participation in the controversy over Japanese restrictions on investments in the 1960s (Encarnation 1992: 65–6).

On the other hand, American firms that had already gained entry into the Japanese market had mixed incentives regarding US government pressures on Japan. To a large extent their success depended on good relations with local producers as well as Japanese government regulators. So in periods of excessive US–Japan trade frictions, American businesses in Japan at times called for cooler relations. Dryden notes, for instance, that in the early 1970s, 'business executives stationed in Japan were unhappy with the administration's manner of confronting Japan over trade.' W. H. Kyle, the ACCJ president, for instance, sent a letter to the US government complaining about the US style of negotiations (Dryden 1995: 169). Furthermore, these firms also realized that they enjoyed an advantage over their American competitors that were still shut out of Japan. These firms thus had less of an incentive to push the US government to insist on the removal of barriers to entry into Japan. As others have noted, once these firms established themselves in Japan they often began to behave more like an insider Japanese firm—that is, after becoming an insider, they also became more interested in cooperating with the rest of the Japanese industry, and gave little support to US government efforts to remove barriers to entry.

[25] Kaplan 1972: iv. Kaplan was then Director of the Far East Division of the Bureau of International Commerce. The booklet was written at the request of the Commerce Secretary, Maurice Stans.

industrial development, analyzing in detail its role in targeting key industries for special treatment and support, including computers, autos, and
steel.[26] To a remarkable degree, this document captured the essence of
much of later revisionist ideas about the power of the government, its
strategy for Japan's industrial development, and the close and collusive
nature of business–government relations.

One important early experience was the US–Japan negotiation over government procurement of telecommunications equipment during the
1970s. John Kunkel outlines in some detail the intellectual impact these
negotiations had on US trade officials.[27] In particular, US officials came to
understand just how closely tied the government-owned telecommunications firm, Nippon Telegraph and Telephone (NTT) was to the Japanese
private firms—the so-called NTT family. Over the course of the negotiations, US officials came to realize that the government's deep role in
terms of industrial targeting, protectionist regulations to restrict access to
the market, and the proclivity of Japanese firms to take advantage of a
protected home base to launch export offenses abroad, were all part of an
overall picture of Japan's political economy that did not look at all traditionalist. As Maureen Smith, a Commerce official involved in the issue put
it in an interview with Kunkel:

(the negotiations were) an excellent roadmap and learning experience to get into
the broad, naked, blood-bleeding heart of Japanese industrial policy . . . It was just an
incredible experience to walk through this dialogue with NTT and that started
telling us an awful lot about what was really going on in Japan.[28]

Over the course of the 1970s a small group of trade-related officials in the
US government began to advocate a more activist and aggressive approach
to opening the Japanese market. There is today little evidence of the
positions these officials took in policy discussions, but later memoirs and
interviews paint a picture of a small cadre of junior officials who were
gradually coming to a common understanding that Japan's economy was

---

[26] These industry case studies were carried out by the Boston Consulting Group. Kaplan's
booklet today is probably best remember for putting a quasi-official stamp on the popular
term 'Japan, Incorporated,' which envisioned a smoothly working system of interactions
between business and government, coordinated from the top, down. Indeed, much of the
booklet stresses the bureaucracy's role in guiding and directing industrialization. But it
should also be remembered that the booklet also stressed the deep interactions between
government and business, the consensual nature of developmental policy, and the role of
cultural differences.

[27] Kunkel 2003. The NTT issue is also covered in Curran 1982; and Okimoto 1989.

[28] Kunkel 2003: 59.

unique and needed to be dealt with differently.[29] These officials were highly critical of Japan's trade and industrial polices, and now came to believe that America's trade policy needed to be much more aggressive. Although these officials had not yet developed specific policy alternatives, they agreed that something different needed to be done.

These critics of the traditionalist position, however, were still in the minority, and were constantly frustrated by opposition from the traditionalist camp. As one example, analyst Steve Dryden reports that as early as 1969 the Special Trade Representative (STR), Carl Gilbert, wanted to retaliate against Japan's remaining trade barriers by empowering 'the president to withhold most favored nation (MFN) status from countries that failed to make reciprocal concessions during trade negotiations.'[30] The Departments of State and Defense, however, opposed this idea because they were worried about the 'political consequences' of putting too much pressure on Japan, while the Council of Economic Advisors, let by Herbert Stein, feared that this action would 'unravel the international trade system.'[31] Dryden reports that the traditionalists drafted a memo in which they argued that the deficit 'would correct itself without external intervention.' The STR tried unsuccessfully to amend this draft. As one official put it, the desire was 'to seize control and stop this crap about the invisible hand solving things.'[32]

In the US Congress, however, Japan was becoming the clear target of American anger and discontent over the costs that its rising exports were causing to domestic constituents, most notably labor. Indeed, Japanese exports had been a source of economic dislocation ever since the 1950s, when the US and Japan entered into their first voluntary restraint agreement, on cotton textiles.[33] As Japanese exports continued to rise, a growing number of US industries pressed for some form of import relief. Not surprisingly, the central focus of Congress was how to slow the flood of Japanese exports in order to alleviate the domestic pain of trade adjustment.

Anger and even an element of fear were also evident at the top levels of the US government, and particularly during the Nixon administration. In

---

[29] The sectoral approach has always been pushed most strongly at the staff level (*Inside US Trade* 11/25/83: 1–2; Prestowitz 1988).

[30] Dryden 1995: 139.   [31] Ibid.: 139.

[32] Ibid.: 163. The official was James McNamara, the STR's specialist on Japan.

[33] At the end of the 1960s, Congressional anger at Japanese exports was still focused on the textile industry, and particularly their devastating impact on textile mills in the South. Nixon and Southern strategy, leading to Textile Wrangle and Nixon shocks (see Destler 1979). The VER on cotton blouses morphed into the STA and LTA.

1971, for instance, *Time* magazine quoted a Nixon cabinet member arguing that the Japanese 'are still fighting the war,' only now using economic means; furthermore, their 'immediate intention is to try to dominate the Pacific and then perhaps the world.'[34] American anger over trade frictions occasionally boiled over, as in the Textile Wrangle of 1969–71, a nasty confrontation that resulted from US pressure on Japan to extend the Voluntary Export Restraint (VER) on cotton textiles to synthetic fibers.[35] This episode was soon followed by the 'Nixon Shocks' of 1972, during which the US unilaterally ended the convertibility of the dollar to gold, imposed a 15 per cent import surcharge on Japanese products, and limited American exports of soybeans.[36]

Top officials in the Ford and Carter administrations tended to hold less harsh attitudes toward Japan, but also faced enormous pressures to deal with the rapid rise of Japanese exports, which by the late 1970s were undermining a growing number of industries such as steel, consumer electronics, and automobiles. The dislocations caused by rising imports were magnified by the economic problems of stagflation, energy dependence, and unemployment that America faced during the 1970s.

* * *

In sum, revisionism's roots are long and deep; and, like a paleontologist, the more one digs, the more one finds bits and pieces of revisionist thinking from early on, especially the view of Japan as closed and different. I place the origins of revisionism in the early 1970s, as growing anomalies for the traditionalist view were becoming more apparent, and some early revisionist perspectives were being put forward. In particular, industry complaints about the uniquely protectionist nature of Japanese bureaucrats coincided with the views being simultaneously developed inside the US trade agencies, leading to rising calls for a more aggressive, sector-specific approach to market opening.

However, while traditionalist assumptions about the Japanese economy were increasingly being questioned, they were by no means in danger of being overthrown. Through the end of the 1970s even the most critical views of Japan were only the precursors to the full revisionist paradigm, as I define it: that is, few argued that the economy was so closed that exporting

[34] Quoted in Dryden 1995: 161. Dryden speculates that the official was Commerce Secretary Maurice Stans. This issue of *Time* was also the origin of the term 'Japan, Inc.,' which was used in the cover story, 'How to Cope with Japan's Business Invasion.'

[35] Destler 1979.

[36] These shocks were evidently linked to the Textile Wrangle, the result of Nixon's anger at Japan for being so uncooperative. Another 'Nixon Shock' was the decision to open relations with the PRC without even consulting with the Japanese (Destler, et al. 1976).

there was impossible, or so different that it constituted a unique form of capitalism. In any case, the 'proto-revisionist' arguments that were then being developed were limited to a small cadre inside the trade agencies that was still clearly the minority. Even if some top officials had adopted the view of Japan as different and closed, the vast majority of career officials and political appointees in the rest of the government were still strongly traditionalist in their fundamental commitment to free-trade principles. Japan's market may be a tough nut to crack, but it did not yet merit a unique approach.[37]

America's overall policy toward Japan through the 1970s was also squarely based on traditionalist assumptions about the importance of the political relationship. The consensus within the US government was still that the bilateral security relationship was of paramount importance to US national security interests, a view best symbolized by Ambassador Mansfield's oft-repeated 'bar none' quote. The defense establishment held this assumption most strongly, but even the trade agencies did not challenge them; neither Commerce nor USTR wanted to push economic issues so far as to damage the overall relationship. Similarly, most Congress members felt that the security relationship had to come first. Although trade frictions needed to be addressed, this should not be at the cost of the political and security relationship. Furthermore, many in the pol-mil establishment could not have cared less about economic issues; in their view the benefits of continuing cooperation with Japan on the military side completely outweighed any possible economic costs. Officials in these organizations were adamantly opposed to allowing economic pressures to spill over to harm the security side of the relationship. Also, because these organizations represented the core of American foreign policy making, they were in a position to ensure that security clearly trumped economics.

The result was that traditionalist assumptions constrained the range of policy options available through the end of the 1970s. First, trade frictions were clearly subordinated to the pol-mil relationship—that is, the two governments were intent on preventing trade frictions from complicating

---

[37] Curtis (2000: 5) disagrees, arguing that revisionist roots can be traced back to the first Nixon administration, where top officials such as Henry Kissinger and Treasury Secretary John Connelly were already adopting the view that 'Japan is somehow unique, that its economic institutions and basic cultural characteristics make it an outlier among trading nations, and that this uniqueness requires and justifies tailor-made approaches and policies.' These officials, however, were clearly more motivated by the traditionalist assumption that the security relationship was more crucial than trade frictions—which Curtis (2000: 4) refers to as the 'fire wall' between trade and security.

their efforts to 'manage the alliance.' Second, America's trade policy toward market access remained firmly traditionalist. Although the US government had identified three Japanese markets that were protected by excessive government regulations (beef, citrus, and telecommunications), and had entered into negotiations to remove these barriers, the bulk of market-opening efforts were made in the context of the multilateral fora. Finally, and almost by default, the US government focused on how to slow Japanese exports, using a series of measures that at least partially shielded the US market. The policy tool of choice in this era was the VER, in which the Japanese government was persuaded to somehow control the outflow of Japanese goods.[38] While economists tended to view the VERs as a violation of liberal trade principles, political economists tended to portray them as temporary and ad hoc, and thus as an acceptable attempt to alleviate the domestic pain of trade adjustment in order to avoid further protectionism.[39] In any case, the US in the 1970s maintained a solid commitment to free trade principles, as well as a substantially open market.

Revisionism in the Early 1980s: Japan's High-tech Threat

The rapid rise of Japan's economy in the 1980s, combined with its ever-expanding trade surplus, continued to defy traditionalist expectations. But it was the rising threat to America's high technology industries that represented the most fundamental anomaly for the traditionalist paradigm. Now it was the most advanced industries, embodying technologies deemed crucial for the economic future, that seemed unable to meet the competitive challenge. It was one thing to see Japan conquer mature industries such as textiles or steel, but here were industries being undermined and overtaken at the height of their competitiveness. To many, the

[38] During the Carter administration the US and Japan negotiated a long series of bilateral agreements that sought to at least temporarily slow Japanese exports, using not only the VERs, but also orderly marketing arrangements, the trigger price mechanism, and the like, in such industries as TVs, footwear, steel, and autos. It should be noted that the resort to the VER reflected the (revisionist) belief that the Japanese government bureaucracy was powerful enough to control the behavior of its industries. In this sense, the US was already demanding a form of 'managed trade,' in which the government was asked to step in to control the market behavior of the private sector, although this was on the flow of goods out of Japan.

[39] Ruggie (1998), for instance, argues that temporary protection was fully justified as a core element of the postwar compromise of 'embedded liberalism,' in which nations could shield themselves from the negative impact of international trade. Thus, the use of the VER, though extensive, was still done on an ad hoc basis, and in response to political pressures, rather than as a part of a US strategy to deal with Japan.

gut feeling was that this simply should not be happening; the conclusion was that 'something was wrong.'[40]

Another anomaly that the traditionalist school had a hard time reconciling was that the Japanese economic challenge now implied a direct and negative impact on American national security. That is, Japanese competitiveness in this period seemed most formidable in the 'dual-use' technologies that were not only economically important but were also deemed crucial for America's military capabilities. Although Japan was not yet seen as an overall economic threat, the pol-mil community was beginning to worry about American dependence on Japan for specific technologies—most notably semiconductors, but also other industries 'at risk.' The crisis in these dual-use technologies thus served to blur the traditionalist 'firewall' that had previously protected the security relationship from trade frictions.[41]

These anomalies that emerged in the 1980s provided an important impetus for the fuller development of the revisionist paradigm. As before, revisionist thinking was pushed hardest by American high-technology industries and Japan-related officials in the Department of Commerce and USTR; what was different now was that a number of officials in the defense establishment were also beginning to modify their assumptions. Revisionists in all of these groups still emphasized the consequences of industrial policies that advantaged Japanese industry, but were now also looking at distinctive 'business practices' and structural features such as the *keiretsu* relationships, that allowed Japanese firms to systematically undermine their overseas competitors. The growing consensus was that the Japanese system was organized for industrial dominance. Furthermore, many now began to see a growing threat that stemmed from Japan's conscious *strategy* of seeking industrial preeminence; clearly, the US needed to do something to respond.

Although many American high-technology industries provided input that helped to develop the revisionist paradigm, none was more central than the semiconductor industry. This industry epitomized all of the concerns about high-technology competition with Japan—it was a crucial future industry, with linkages to all parts of the industrial economy; it was an industry that was being undermined by a Japan that had targeted it for conquest; and most importantly, it was a core defense-related technology.

---

[40] Senator Pete Wilson echoed these views when he argued that the semiconductor industry 'has no smokestacks,' but rather represented an industry that was 'state of the art' (US Congress 1985: 1–2).

[41] Curtis 2000.

The industry was also a highly organized one, represented by the influential Semiconductor Industry Association (SIA), which aggressively discussed its complaints with US officials.[42] In this context the role played by attorney Alan Wolff must be mentioned. Wolff had previously been one of Robert Strauss' top deputies at the office of the STR, from 1974 to 1979, where he had developed a reputation as a hard-liner on Japan. In 1980 Wolff had joined the SIA and became the chief advocate of what Kenneth Flamm labels the SIA's 'theory of Japanese industrial practices,' which contained the main elements of my definition of revisionism.[43] As described below, Wolff was to play an important insider's role in the formation of US trade policy toward semiconductors, and in the development of revisionist thought.

The industry painted a vivid picture of a Japanese system that 'tilted the playing field' to its advantage. First were industrial targeting policies that channeled extra resources to the domestic industry, including direct subsidies, tax breaks, and the like. These policies meant that the Japanese industry benefited from a lower cost of capital, which was especially crucial for industries in which technology changed so dramatically and at such a fast pace.[44] The industry's characteristics made it a highly volatile and capital-intensive one, where firms with deep pockets—either their own or through the help of the government—had an enormous advantage. Second, the Japanese government actively protected its semiconductor industry against all forms of foreign participation in the market—that is, not only against imports but also against foreign investment. This conferred a crucial

---

[42] The SIA was founded in 1977, by the 'pioneers of the industry,' including Robert Noyce and Andy Grove, both of Intel, Robert Gavin of Motorola, and others. According to Prestowitz, an additional fact that magnified the psychological shock of the industry's troubles was that these industry leaders represented the best qualities of the successful American entrepreneur. Many of these businessmen had started their firms from scratch, and had risen to world leadership. The prevailing image was thus the lone American entrepreneur, having succeeded in world markets through their brilliance and hard work, being taken down by a Japanese system in which government funneled massive support to gigantic industrial conglomerates. Even so, the SIA evidently received less than a warm welcome in Washington in this early period; Flamm reports that in the late 1970s SIA executives briefed STR Robert Strauss on the Japanese threat, only to receive a reaction of 'so what?' (Flamm 1996: 138).

[43] Ibid.: 140.

[44] There were few industries that had a shorter product cycle than semiconductors. In addition, the nature of demand for semiconductors was that once a new generation of chips was commercialized, demand for the older one virtually disappeared. This meant that a firm that invested in the facilities to produce the newest generation of chip could easily find that these investments were nearly worthless just a few years down the road. Firms that were caught on the wrong side of a generational change could be very quickly forced out of the market. The only solution was to keep investing in more than one generation of technology at the same time, an expensive proposition.

advantage on an industry where producers needed synergistic contacts with their high-volume consumers. Third, the industry charged that certain structures of the economy also prevented foreign participation. The *keiretsu* came under special attack, not only for the propensity of member firms to buy from each other, but also because extensive cross-shareholding acted as a barrier to foreign investment.

The industry's basic argument was that Japan's closed market was the key source of its competitive edge. Because American firms were not able to participate there, Japanese firms enjoyed a 'captive market' in which they could take advantage of economies of scale and learning that were crucial for rapidly changing strategic industries. Furthermore, the SIA argued that this 'secure demand base...contributed to the phenomenon of "capacity expansion races"—intensive expansion of capacity with little reference to market conditions,' which led to the problem of dumping.[45] And because of the government's promotion policies, and the deep pockets provided by the *keiretsu*, Japanese firms did not have to worry about short-term profits the way that American firms did. Thus, Japanese firms continued to invest even when worldwide demand did not exist and other firms were cutting back; once demand picked up, they were in an even stronger position. The industry also argued that Japan's closed market gave its industries a 'safe haven' in which it could earn extra profits, which it in turn used to mount export offenses. This ability to subsidize exports meant that the Japanese industry could sell its chips abroad at cutthroat prices. Even if it stopped short of outright 'dumping' it still allowed Japan to undermine its competitors, and especially the smaller, less financially strong firms in the US industry. Once US firms were driven from the field, Japan would be in a position to monopolize future world production.

In other words, the industry was advancing the argument that not only was the Japanese economy closed, but that this closure made a huge difference in a crucial industry. The SIA was thus very careful to point out that it was not asking for protection, a demand that the Reagan administration was opposed to on philosophical grounds, but rather that it needed to crack the Japanese market if it hoped to survive.[46]

It is tempting to think of the semiconductor and other high-tech industries as no more than lobbying groups out to maximize their own interests. In the mid-1980s a number of other high-tech industries were advancing a similar set of arguments about Japan, although in a less public or vocal

---

[45] Wolff 1985: i.   [46] *Inside US Trade* 6/7/85: 1–2.

manner. These industries included high-end electronics, telecommunications, medical equipment and pharmaceuticals, aerospace, and the supercomputer industry.[47] All served to reinforce the basic arguments being championed by the semiconductor industry: that the Japanese government's strategy of promoting their industries gave them enormous advantages; that Japan was uniquely closed, which allowed a safe haven from which Japan could mount export offensives; and that the US industry as a result was in danger of being driven from the market.

There was undeniably a large element of self-interest in what these industries were attempting to accomplish.[48] However, the deeper significance of their role was not simply their lobbying efforts, but rather their articulation of a new understanding of the peculiar nature of the Japanese economy. That is, by highlighting the coordinated and closed nature of the system, these industries helped to shift basic assumptions about how the economy operated. It was at the level of ideas that these industries had their most fundamental and long-lasting impact.

* * *

It is also important to remember that policy makers did not merely adopt the positions advocated by the high-tech industries. Rather, industry lobbying efforts were effective precisely because the perspectives they put forward dovetailed with the revisionist-oriented assumptions about Japan that were already held by a growing number of US government officials. Revisionist ideas thus further developed out of the interactions between the industry and these like-minded officials.

As mentioned, some mid-ranking officials in the Commerce Department had long been championing the position that the closed nature of the Japanese economy had to be countered by more aggressive market-opening efforts. In the early 1980s, these officials applied these arguments to the high-tech industries, and in particular pushed the national security implications of allowing Japan to dominate world production. A key figure in this regard was Clyde Prestowitz, later a leading revisionist who first joined the Department as counselor to the Secretary in the fall of 1981. In his best-selling book, *Trading Places*, Prestowitz provides an inside glimpse of the

---

[47] Tyson 1992.

[48] Irwin (1994), for instance, describes in some detail the efforts that the SIA and individual industry leaders expended in order to get their policy demands heard (see also Yoffie 1988 and Kunkel 2003: 83–102). O'Shea (1995: 24) describes the strong political backing the industry received in the form of the Semiconductor Congressional Support Group, which consisted of some 20 legislators mostly from California and Texas.

debates going on within the US government.[49] By this time, many career officials and political appointees in Commerce were espousing revisionist arguments. Most notable in this regard were a handful of officials who, in addition to Prestowitz, had had business experience in Japan. One example was Maureen Smith, the career official quoted earlier who served as the Director of the Department's new Office of Japan, who had had some experience with the Japan market during her time working for General Electric.[50] Similarly, Under Secretary Lionel Olmer had developed many of his ideas about Japan while representing the Motorola Corporation in its efforts to enter the Japanese market in the 1970s, and was now convinced that America's security was being undermined by the Japanese system. Secretary Malcolm Baldridge had also had some Japan-related experience in his position with Scovil, a maker of tire valves.[51] The USTR also shared Commerce's desire for a more aggressive market opening policy. Prestowitz describes the two agencies as 'realists' in that they recognized the national security consequences of losing the high-tech competition.[52]

These officials now argued that the US needed to use all of its available tools to open the Japanese market. Furthermore, the US needed to think more in terms of a market-opening *strategy*: rather than waiting for industries to raise complaints, the government needed to decide which industries were the most crucial and worth fighting for. To these officials, this meant the high-tech industries, and most of all, semiconductors.

The task of convincing the rest the rest of the government of the wisdom of revisionist assumptions was, however, to prove more difficult.

[49] Prestowitz 1988. The word 'revisionism' does not appear in Prestowitz's book, as the term was not even coined until the year after its publication.

[50] Prestowitz (1988: xv and 260) compliments Smith as an important source of institutional memory, without going into any detail. Some later described Smith's attitudes as bordering on antipathy; according to one former colleague, 'she hated the Japanese' (interview with Commerce official, 7/26/98). The Office of Japan was created in 1981 'as a separate entity to give greater prominence to trade relations with Japan' (Whalen 1990: 56).

[51] Dryden (1995: 281) offers a Baldridge quote that is harsh, if not necessarily revisionist: at one point he is reported to have told an aide, 'When are you going to learn? . . . All the Japanese are trying to do is fuck us, and they will keep on trying to fuck us until we stop them.' Prestowitz mentions two other officials, William Finan and Frank Vargo, both Department economists. Other line officials in the Department played roles in developing and pushing revisionist ideas, although their roles have been much less publicized than Prestowitz's (in part because he and not they wrote the bestselling book). Dryden (1995) presents a similar description of attitudes inside the office of the Special Trade Representative, later the USTR. Dryden also focuses his attention on the top officials of the agency. Another official who deserves mention is Glen Fukushima, an official in the USTR.

[52] Prestowitz (1988) notes that the key 'realists' were USTR William Brock and Commerce Secretary Malcolm Baldridge. Prestowitz also notes that the Departments of Agriculture and Labor also often sided with the realists, although for different reasons: whereas Labor was interested more in protection, Agriculture was more aggressive in demanding access to the Japanese market. I thank Hugh Patrick for this point.

Prestowitz describes extremely strong traditionalist views in the agencies of the US government that dealt with economic and financial issues. This group of agencies, which included the Office of Management and Budget, Treasury, and the President's Council of Economic Advisors, evidently dubbed themselves the 'White Hats' because of their strong philosophical defense of 'good' free trade ideas. Prestowitz reports that these agencies could be counted on to oppose any proposals that deviated even slightly from free trade principles, and in particular anything that smacked of 'managed trade.' Rather, these agencies were the most adamant in their faith that liberalizing the market process in Japan would solve the trade problem.[53]

Prestowitz also describes the pol-mil community, led by the Departments of State and Defense and the National Security Council, as another obstacle to a more aggressive trade approach. According to Prestowitz, these agencies automatically 'opposed anything that might disturb political and military relations with Japan,' and thus preferred to avoid applying too much trade pressure.[54]

Beneath the surface, however, the high technology crisis was spurring a questioning of assumptions inside the Department of Defense. In contrast to officials who worked on bilateral relations, a subset of officials who dealt with technology issues were becoming more alarmed about the consequences of Japanese domination of crucial technologies. Defense concerns about dependence on foreign sources of technology was not entirely new, but seemed to reach a crisis level in the 1980s. These concerns were directed mostly at Japan. One symbol of this rising concern was the warning issued by the President's Defense Science Board in October of 1984 that the US was rapidly losing some crucial advanced technologies to the Japanese.[55] Similar conclusions were, evidently being drawn by some in the intelligence community as well. As Dryden reports,

analysts at the CIA had long been attentive to Japan's rising economic power, and there was a school of thought within the intelligence community which held that

---

[53] Prestowitz (1988: 224) singles out David Stockman of the OMB, Treasury Secretary Donald Regan, and CEA head William Niskanen for special criticism. The Department of Justice also often took this position. Dryden (1995: 291) reports that the White Hats often referred to the realists as 'Jap bashers.'

[54] Prestowitz 1988: 224. Prestowitz (1988: 56) claims that Defense maintained this position even though it was growing concerned about losing technology; even as late as 1985 it was not prepared to take a hard line on the semiconductor issue.

[55] These included 'artificial intelligence, optoelectronics, and systems engineering and control' (Prestowitz 1988: 11). A later report, by the National Academy of Engineering, concluded that the US trailed Japan in 25 of the 34 technologies then deemed crucial.

the maintenance of America's high technology preeminence (and not losing it to Japan) was more important to the US–Soviet conflict than the levels of arms.[56]

One early focal point of these concerns was over Japan's inroads into the advanced machine tool industry, a relatively unknown technology that was in fact a crucial one in the production of nearly all industrial machinery, and so was seen as a core building block of the defense industry. The Japanese industry had grown dramatically in the 1970s, and by 1986 had passed the US as the world's largest machine tool producer.[57] In May 1982 an American firm, Houdaille Industries, had filed a 1,000-page unfair trade petition with the USTR that provided details of the Japanese industry's cartel behavior as well as the pervasive industrial policy support provided by the Japanese government. Prestowitz later described this petition as 'the most comprehensive vivisection of Japanese industrial policy and trade practices to date.'[58] Although traditionalists in the Reagan White House were at the time able to persuade the President not to take action on this petition, by the fall of 1985, the Pentagon had become so worried about 'the defense consequences of nearly complete dependence on foreign machine tool suppliers,' that it joined Commerce in successfully urging the President to provide the industry with some relief.[59] The machine tool problem surfaced again in 1987 when it was revealed that the Soviet Union had been able to acquire machine tools that allowed them to mill quieter propellers for their submarines. It turned out that it was a Japanese firm, the Toshiba Machine Company, who had secretly sold this equipment to the Soviets, in violation of export control rules. Ironically, this sale had occurred right at the time that the President was rejecting the initial Houdaille petition.[60]

It was the semiconductor crisis of 1984 that stirred new thinking in the defense establishment about the relationship between economics and military security. Here was an industry that was not just important commercially, but one on which the entire US defense industry depended. Defense policy makers realized that nearly all of their key weapons systems relied on semiconductor technology, from the most mundane to the most advanced. In addition, the military's entire command and control capabilities were dependent on supercomputers and advanced

---

[56] Dryden 1995: 289.

[57] Japan's lead was even greater in numerically controlled machine tools (Prestowitz 1988: 222; see also Friedman 1988).

[58] Prestowitz 1988: 223. Dryden (1995: 292), in contrast, describes this report as a 'less than airtight critique of Japanese industrial policy.'

[59] Prestowitz 1988: 6, 218, 224–229, and 244.

[60] Ibid.: 6 and 218. Another firm, the Kongsberg Corporation of Norway, was also involved in this sale.

telecommunications equipment, and thus ultimately on semiconductors.[61] Furthermore, in an era when military officials were enamored with the potential of 'smart weapons,' military acquisition planners worried that allowing the domestic base to decline would make the US overly dependent on foreign sources of supply. The fact that the main supplier was a current ally eased some of these concerns, but officials in the defense establishment felt strongly that this was one high tech industry that the US could not afford to lose.[62] Unlike economic orthodoxy, then, the idea of more trade being better was not shared by the military.

By the mid-1980s defense concerns had risen far enough to spur a shift in positions. The defense establishment thus lent its considerable weight in support of a full range of policies to protect and nurture this key defense-related industry. In October 1986, for instance, Secretary of Defense Caspar Weinberger teamed up with Secretary of Commerce Baldridge to persuade the Fujitsu Corporation to withdraw its bid to buy the Fairchild Semiconductor Company, 'on the grounds that the United States was becoming too dependent on Japan for critical technology.'[63] Defense was also a key backer of a more active industrial policy to ensure America's future technological competitiveness. As described below, the defense establishment was also a critical actor in the push for greater access to the Japanese semiconductor market, a push that culminated in the Semiconductor Agreement of 1986.

* * *

Other prominent individuals in the US played a role in clarifying and consolidating revisionist ideas. In the early 1980s, for instance, some noted academics highlighted the central role of Japan's economic bureaucrats. The view of the bureaucrat as elite and powerful has had a long tradition in academic studies of policy making, but these academics now helped to bring these ideas to the public in general and the foreign policy elite in particular. One example is Ezra Vogel, who argued in his popular book, *Japan as Number One*, that the bureaucrats had been instrumental in overseeing Japan's industrialization process.[64] Even though Vogel wrote

---

[61] In 1984–5, for instance, Defense became worried over the future of the US supercomputer industry. The US at that time had only one producer, the Cray Corporation, but Cray depended on Japan for its advanced semiconductors. Defense now worried that Japan would withhold key components from Cray, thus giving its own fledgling supercomputer industry a key advantage (Prestowitz 1988: 20).

[62] In this period Defense officials were more concerned that shipments from Japan would be interrupted in the event of war; it was only later that concerns over the trustworthiness of Japan was called into doubt.

[63] Prestowitz 1988: 5.   [64] Vogel 1979.

more in admiration than alarm, he underscored the view that the Japanese system operated differently.

But it was Chalmers Johnson, later labeled the 'godfather of Revisionism,' who did the most to cement the view that Japan's economic success was not due to the free play of the market, but rather to the pervasive industrial policy role of the state. First in a series of articles in the 1970s, and then in his seminal 1982 book, *MITI and the Japanese Miracle,* Johnson set out a clear and compelling case that the state was a mercantilist one, pursuing industrial targeting policies designed to build up national power through the nurturing of key, strategic industries. His term for the Japanese model, 'the capitalist developmental state,' painted a picture of a different form of economy that needed to be understood on its own terms. Johnson's MITI book was and is still today the clearest and most influential statement of the economic role played by the state, and was to have a definite impact on all later revisionist thinkers.[65]

A small subset of American economists were also beginning to challenge standard neo-classical ideas. In 1983 economist Paul Krugman led the way by publishing his first work on 'strategic trade theory,' the argument that governments could effectively intervene to capture scale and learning advantages in certain strategic industries, thus producing spillover benefits for the domestic economy. Other economists were similarly analyzing the negative consequences of declining industrial competitiveness. One important group in this regard was the Berkeley Roundtable on the International Economy (BRIE), founded in 1982. One of this group's main arguments was that what mattered was not so much the size of America's trade deficit, but rather its composition; of greatest concern was that the US seemed to be losing in the high technology industries of the future. As this group argued in their most widely read book, 'manufacturing matters.'[66]

---

[65] It should be noted that Johnson's early academic publications were not highly critical of Japan; on the contrary, Johnson's MITI book exhorted America to pay more attention to the 'lessons from Japan.' The Japanese had done things differently from the neoclassical model, but in many ways had done them better. Johnson was also not making the argument that the Japanese economy represented a threat to the US; in his 1982 book, Johnson spoke more in admiration than alarm. Finally, despite his focus on the state's intervention and protection of key industries, I do not believe that Johnson in 1982 was making the argument that this made Japan inherently closed: that is, protection was a government policy that, presumably, could be ended or removed without the need for drastic trade remedies. It is also worth noting that the 1972 Commerce document appeared a full decade before Johnson's book.

[66] Cohen and Zysman 1987. BRIE was founded by academics John Zysman, Laura Tyson, Stephen Cohen, and Michael Borrus, on the premise that 'there can be no long-term low-tech prosperity for the American economy. Continued leadership in the development, production, and use of new technologies here in the United States is the key to America's economic health' (BRIE website, <http://www.brie.berkeley.edu>).

Similarly, the Congress also helped to push revisionist ideas forward in the policy process, even if it did not play a central role in the *development* of those ideas. First, Congress was already one of the most vocal critics of the traditionalist approach for its failure to put a dent in Japan's ever-expanding trade surplus, and was especially exasperated with the failure of past market liberalization efforts. The debate in Congress in the 1980s centered on 'unfair trade,' the view that the Japanese government provided advantages to its industries which 'tilted the playing field' in its favor. With evidence of closure in the Japanese economy continuing to accumulate, Congress now adopted the argument that American industries needed greater market access in order to remain competitive worldwide. Many in Congress thus began to shift away from the previous goal of protecting the American market, to become strong advocates of using the power of the institution to pry open Japan. These members were also angry at what they saw as the Reagan administration's reluctance to utilize its executive powers to enforce American trade law. Thus as early as 1982 politicians such as Senator John Danforth (R-Missouri) were discussing the concept of reciprocity, or the idea of retaliating against countries that did not provide the same level of openness to US exporters. Later, in the spring of 1985, Congress debated a bill that would have required retaliation against Japan in the form of a 25 per cent tariff if it did not achieve greater market access.[67]

Another key role played by Congress was to put teeth into US efforts to open the Japanese market. In particular, changes to the 1984 Trade Act allowed the administration to identify and remove trade barriers in specific foreign markets, and required the administration to present an annual report on the impact of trade barriers on US trade.

In this period Congress contributed to the formulation of trade policy by turning up the heat on the issue, thus putting pressure on the Reagan administration to 'do something.' Looking at transcripts of the frequent and furious debates in this era gives a sense of the outrage and antipathy directed at Japan. Still, it is my sense that while revisionist ideas certainly resonated with many members, Congress was more of a receptacle for

---

[67] Dryden 1995: 309. This legislation, which also named Brazil, India, and South Korea, was co-sponsored by Representatives Dan Rostenkowski (D-Illinois) and Richard Gephardt (D-Missouri), and Senator Lloyd Bentsen (D-Texas). This was the precursor to the so-called Super 301 amendment in the 1988 Trade Act. Other bills were put forward by Bob Packwood and John Dingell (*Inside US Trade* 4/5/85: 1, 6, 5/3/85: 3). Still, it was not the politicians who took the lead in developing the rationale for prying open the Japanese market; indeed, the politicians were probably the last group to advocate a strategy of market opening—but once adopted it was pursued with a vengeance.

thinking and ideas developed elsewhere. Thus, when Senator Lloyd Bentsen argued for 'a trade policy based on results,' he was, in Dryden's words, 'sounding like Commerce Department maverick Clyde Prestowitz.'[68] Rather, the intellectual environment and level of the debate was perhaps better captured by an anonymous staff aide who opined that, in Congress, it was simply that 'everyone hates the Japanese.'[69]

Revisionism's Early Impact: The Semiconductor Agreement

Revisionist ideas never became the dominant mode of thinking in the Reagan administration, but did have an impact on two policy departures: the consideration of some form of market share target for semiconductors, and efforts to create a domestic industrial policy for strategic, high technology industries. It should be noted that both of these were driven by the administration's concern over the Japanese threat to future *military* technologies, most notably semiconductors.

The idea of pressing the Japanese government to intervene to correct the overall trade imbalance had been considered by previous administrations, but had been rejected on the traditionalist grounds of not poisoning the overall relationship, and because such efforts would violate free-trade principles. As early as 1978, for instance, a policy group chaired by then USTR deputy Alan Wolff recommended that the Japanese government be pressured to 'publicly set a timetable for balancing its trade account.'[70] In the ensuing Strauss–Ushiba agreement of 1978, however, the Japanese agreed only to make 'all reasonable efforts' toward reaching equilibrium. In response, the Fukuda government agreed to further market-opening measures and to use fiscal stimulus to increase the domestic growth rate to the 7 per cent level.[71] Then in the fall of 1981, Prestowitz reports that a Reagan White House strategy meeting considered as one of two approaches the negotiation of 'an overall target for imports of manufactured goods.'[72] Again in the Fall of 1984, the USTR and Commerce included in a position

---

[68] Dryden 1995: 310.　　[69] *Inside US Trade* 8/9/85: 7.　　[70] Dryden 1995: 224.

[71] Ibid.: 228–9. This was the so-called 'locomotive strategy.' Dryden (1995: 225) reports that the US did not press harder because of Carter's 'worries that US–Japan relations would be seriously damaged.'

[72] Prestowitz 1988: 273. Actually, this approach had been suggested by Etienne Davignon, the Commissioner for Trade of the European Economic Community. Davignon argued that all other industrialized countries tended to import and export the full range of industrialized goods; but where Japan was a strong exporter, its imports were almost nonexistent. Dauvignon's suggested solution was an import target.

paper the idea of having the Japanese government set an overall target for the increase of imports. As described by Prestowitz, however, these proposals were always vehemently opposed by traditionalists in the administration, and were quickly dropped.[73]

It was in semiconductors, however, that the idea of negotiating a sectoral import *target* was first considered, and ultimately adopted in the 1986 Semiconductor Agreement (SCA). In this agreement, for the first time, a market share number was included: the now-famous 'secret' side letter in which the Japanese government recognized the 'expectation' that sales of foreign chips would reach the level of 20 per cent of the Japanese market within five years.[74]

The origins of the market share proposal is open to some debate, with at least three groups—the industry, and government officials from both the US and Japan—involved to some degree. The idea was certainly shared among a small group of like-minded individuals in the SIA and the US government. An early suggestion of seeking a concrete market share came in June 1985, when Alan Wolff, the SIA's main lobbyist advocated 'a negotiated pledge by the Japanese government that foreign companies should enjoy a specific market share.'[75] Wolff remained intimately involved in the negotiating process, and had a clear influence on his former boss, chief negotiator Michael Smith. The SIA was even given a room in the USTR's Winder Building, where the bulk of the negotiations took place; one participant recalls that on at least one occasion Wolff was able to put a halt to a proposed American concession, telling the US negotiators that 'if you agree to that, we're dead.'[76]

---

[73] Prestowitz 1988: 279–80 and 296. As mentioned below, the compromise solution in 1984 was the initiation of the MOSS talks.

[74] The administration had actually engaged the Japanese in discussions beginning in 1981, with the initiation of working-level talks between Commerce and MITI to expand American access to the Japanese market. In November 1983 the two sides concluded an agreement to which the Japanese government attached a confidential note in which it agreed to 'encourage' Japanese firms to expand their purchases of imported chips and to seek to establish long-term relationships with foreign firms. This was the second Semiconductor Agreement; the first, signed in November 1982, simply initiated a new system of collecting statistics on bilateral semiconductor trade. Kunkel (2003: 83–102) covers this episode in some detail.

With the 301 clock about to expire, the two countries concluded the Semiconductor Agreement on July 31, 1986. In addition to the side letter, the Japanese government agreed to provide assistance to increase sales, further encourage long-term relationships, and to monitor chip prices.

[75] Dryden 1995: 313. Dryden (p. 314) quotes Wolff as later recalling 'I was fearful, as a lawyer coming out of Washington, talking of a market share. It's a very foreign concept.'

[76] Interview with veteran State Department official, 4/8/97, and veteran Commerce Department official, 7/26/98.

Administration officials later argued that the push for the market share target came from inside the government. Kunkel quotes former USTR Clayton Yeutter as saying that 'the industry demands weren't all that relevant at that time. We were clearly getting input from the industry, but the 20 per cent number was essentially a USTR-developed number.'[77] Indeed, some negotiators such as Prestowitz had from before been hinting at the need for some form of 'affirmative action' for semiconductors, and by 1985 used clearly revisionist reasoning in his insistence that 'the Japanese market did not respond along Western lines, and we needed a comprehensive agreement including affirmative action by Japan to achieve some specific market share or sales target.'[78] In any case, both Yeutter and Smith favored the market share target, and pushed this concept in their talks with their MITI counterpart, Kuroda Makoto.

Finally, Japanese negotiators had long been amenable to the idea of a market share target in general, and may have been the first to raise the suggestion during the semiconductor talks.[79] Smith later commented that the 20 per cent target 'was a Japanese idea. Now SIA say it was their idea—nonsense.'[80] It should be noted that Kuroda later explicitly denied Japanese government involvement, but it should also be remembered that the idea of 'numerical targets' was not then as taboo as it was later to become.[81]

The problem for Wolff, Prestowitz, and Smith, however, was that support inside the US government for a market share target was limited to

---

[77] Kunkel 2003: 97.

[78] Prestowitz 1988: 51–2 and 62. Prestowitz (1988: 53) also argued that 'experience told us that larger sales in Japan were unlikely as a result of agreements to remove trade barriers.'
The origins of the 20–30 per cent figure, according to Prestowitz, came from an analysis done by a department economist, William Finan. But the semiconductor industry had been repeatedly mentioning this number for at least three years, based on their comparison of the industry's market shares in neutral third markets, where the two industries engaged in head-to-head competition.

[79] Although most later accounts stress Japan's and MITI's reluctance to agree to a market share, Japan seems to have been the government that first openly broached the possibility: sometime between early October and mid-November 1985, *Inside US Trade* (11/19/85: 5) reports that Japanese government officials had informally suggested a 25 per cent market share as a reasonable level of foreign imports. Further, in the midst of the semiconductor negotiations, the head of Japan's Keidanren proposed that the Japanese government should set targets for the expansion of imports in general. Others reacted more negatively, and nothing came of this suggestion. Prestowitz (1988: 60) mentions only that Japan in October 1985 had offered to arrange for a 25 per cent increase in US semiconductor sales.

[80] Kunkel 2003: 98. Smith later told Kunkel that the number was originally meant to be 30 per cent, which was felt to be unrealistic politically, and that the 20 per cent figure 'came up at the last moment.'

[81] Kunkel 2003: 98–9.

revisionist-oriented officials, mostly in Commerce and the USTR. Prestowltz reports that traditionalists were still reluctant to violate free trade principles, while others were afraid that accepting the market share would create an international cartel.[82] Thus, as Dryden puts it:

Smith knew other senior officials within the Reagan administration would balk. So he set up a very small negotiating team, composed of himself, Bruce Smart, and Douglas McMinn, a former USTR aide to Smith who was then an assistant secretary of state . . . The setup allowed Smith to pursue the market-share goal confidentially. 'This was so difficult for us that we never told the other agencies,' (Smith) says today.[83]

The revisionist position eventually prevailed, and the Reagan administration finally agreed to allow Smith 'to suggest to the Japanese that a reasonable market share for the US producers might be 20 per cent to 30 per cent,' but did not authorize him to negotiate a specific amount. As Prestowitz put it, 'our task was to get measurable increases in sales without asking for them.'[84]

That America took this unprecedented step was due in part to the severity of the crisis that the industry was experiencing. Revisionists in the industry and in government warned that the continuing semiconductor crisis threatened the industry's very survival—if the US was to avoid the demise of this crucial technology, some quick and decisive action was needed *now*. The immediate cause of the crisis was the massive price cuts that Japanese semiconductor firms were offering in an effort to maintain their pre-recession export levels.[85] But the industry and US officials were also concerned that America's penetration of the Japanese market remained below the 10 per cent level, the same level as prior to the initial liberalization efforts that had begun in 1970.[86]

Equally important were the national security implications of these negotiations. In particular, the defense establishment had become concerned over the prospect of losing a domestic semiconductor capability, and now agreed that something drastic had to be tried to save this

---

[82] Prestowitz 1988.

[83] Dryden (1995: 319) notes that 'it is unclear if officials at the State Department above McMinn knew about the market-share idea.'

[84] Prestowitz 1988: 64.

[85] It was in this context that a 'smoking gun' was uncovered—the infamous Hitachi memo which encouraged its sales force to keep cutting prices, going as low as necessary in order to secure new deals, ending with the exhortation: 'Don't quit until you win!' (quoted in Fallows 1993: 100).

[86] Prestowitz 1988: 63. The US share was 10 per cent in 1973, and had actually fallen to the 9 per cent level by 1986.

militarily crucial industry. These arguments seemed to have a clear impact on US government thinking. Smith later described showing intelligence reports to USTR Clayton Yeutter that painted a bleak future for the US industry, with the comment that these reports 'were corroborating a lot of what Alan Wolff and SIA were telling us.' Yeutter later recalled that these reports became the 'primary consideration' in his view that 'the semiconductor question needed special government action.'[87] Finally, there is evidence that this thinking went right to the top: officials involved in the process report that Reagan himself was most concerned about the importance of the industry to national security, and thus tilted the outcome in favor of including a market share target.

The importance of the semiconductor industry to national security also helps explain the administration's support for a more active industrial policy to boost American competitiveness. The crucial step in this regard was the administration's support in 1987 for the creation of Sematech, which described itself as 'a consortium of chip manufacturers dedicated to improving manufacturing technology.'[88]

* * *

By the mid-1980s the outline of a revisionist alternative was becoming visible, and was having a growing impact on how American officials understood Japan. However, it is crucial to remember that through the 1980s these ideas were still in the minority, and that their visible impact in this period was limited to a particular issue that had clear national security implications.[89] That is, policies adopted for the semiconductor industry in part reflected early revisionist ideas, but were also due to the industry's

[87] Dryden 1995: 317; see also Kunkel 2003.

[88] SIA web page <http://www.sia-online.org>. Pressures for an American industrial policy to counter Japan's targeting practices had been present since the 1970s. But it was in the context of the high-tech crisis in the early 1980s that this debate picked up steam. In particular, in the early 1980s a handful of Congressional Democrats proposed the creation of a Department of International Trade and Industry (DITI), modeled and named after Japan's MITI, that would design and implement an American version of industrial policy that would convene 'a panel of government, business and labor leaders that would draft plans to help ailing industries or spur growth industries' (*Inside US Trade* 11/4/1983: 5).

The debate over this institution reflected the continuing strength of traditionalist ideas inside the Reagan administration, where top economic advisors opposed the plan as running counter to free market principles, likely to be inefficient and ineffective, and to become hopelessly politicized. The Reagan administration was eventually able to defeat the DITI plan, and in the process demonstrated its underlying commitment to liberal trade principles (*Inside US Trade* 10/14/83: 1, 5, 11/4/1983: 11).

[89] The pol-mil community thus reacted only when economic problems crossed into military issues, as in semiconductors and machine tools, where the neat dividing lines between traditionalism and revisionism had been blurred.

extraordinary position, and especially its importance to American national security—without this dimension, many doubt whether the US would have pursued or even accepted a numbers-oriented agreement. Furthermore, it is important to point out that the departure represented by the SCA did *not* signal the beginning of a new approach to Japan trade policy: the US government at that time was not considering market share targets for any other industry.[90] As Michael Smith later put it, 'the semiconductor agreement was a special, one-time, never-to-be-repeated negotiation.'[91]

Rather, the bulk of Reagan's trade policies remained aimed at liberalizing the market process in Japan. The administration's main efforts to open the market, most notably the Market-Oriented, Sector-Specific, or MOSS talks, were based squarely on the traditionalist assumptions about the Japanese economy in that they were designed to identify and remove specific barriers that impeded the workings of the market—'unfettering' the market mechanism so that consumers would receive the correct price signals.[92] Not only were the MOSS talks not a managed trade solution, they were mostly designed to deflate pressures for the US to move in the managed trade direction.

The administration also stressed the manipulation of macroeconomic variables as the best way to correct the trade imbalance, in part because of the recognition that the bilateral talks were generating too many frictions with Japan. The US thus initiated talks on changing the value of the yen relative to the dollar, culminating in the Plaza Accord of 1985.[93] The US also engaged in continuing pressures on the Japanese government to do more to stimulate domestic demand through fiscal spending to stimulate internal growth. The Reagan administration thus strongly endorsed the 1986 Report of the Maekawa Commission, which had advocated a shift in the Japanese economy to a more domestic-oriented, less export-dependent model.[94] With the exception of policy for the semiconductor industry,

[90] Interview with veteran Commerce Department official, 7/26/98; Kunkel (2003: 101–2) also makes this argument.

[91] Ibid.: 102.

[92] The original four MOSS sectors were medical equipment and pharmaceuticals, telecommunications equipment, electronics, and forest products (including lumber, plywood and paper). The auto parts industry was added in 1986, after the medical equipment and pharmaceuticals issue was 'resolved.' The US also pursued another traditionalist policy: protectionism. In particular, in 1981 the US and Japan negotiated a major VER on automobiles (see Schoppa 1997: 65–6).

[93] Economist and US Treasury official C. Fred Bergsten gave testimony that year that optimistically predicted that this action would resolve the bulk of the trade deficit problem.

[94] The report was acknowledged that Japan's economy had been too externally focused. Now the idea of channeling the Japanese economy into a domestically oriented direction would further ease the trade imbalance, and this gave some cause for optimism to the traditionalist proponents of the broader, macroeconomic approach.

then, the Reagan approach to trade essentially followed along orthodox, traditionalist lines.

Traditionalist assumptions about the political relationship also remained strong in the US as a whole. Even in Congress, most members still placed primary importance on the security alliance, even if they no longer believed that the two parts of the relationship must be kept completely insulated.[95] Inside the administration, traditionalists continued to argue that the security alliance was of overriding importance and that it should be protected from economic frictions. In this they were mostly successful, as symbolized by the Ron–Yasu relationship—the close, personal tie between Ronald Reagan and Prime Minister Nakasone Yasuhiro—and their agreement on strengthening already close military and political ties. Even with concerns rising over the loss of technological leadership, and in spite of the reductions of Cold War tensions due to the coming to power of Mikhail Gorbachev in the Soviet Union, the pol-mil crowd was still largely convinced of the value of the security arrangement. To the end, the Reagan administration remained first and foremost concerned with national security issues, and thus the insulation of the bilateral security arrangement from trade frictions remained the number one priority.

---

[95] In addition, many Republicans did not favor an overly harsh approach, both because of their commitment to free trade and their desire to support, or at least not contradict, the Reagan administration's chosen approach.

3

'The Japan Problem': The Coalescence of the Revisionist Paradigm

By the mid-1980s the outline of revisionist thought had been established, but it was in the latter half of the decade that this alternative paradigm was consolidated, popularized, and deepened throughout the US foreign policy establishment. The resonance of revisionist ideas came in the context of a mounting American economic crisis. In this period, fears that the economy was in a permanent downward spiral were inextricably linked to the view of Japan's economy as an unstoppable juggernaut, destined to dominate world markets. In this period of crisis, traditionalist assumptions about the Japanese economy came under increasingly harsh attack for failing to deal with 'The Japan Problem.' At the same time, the revisionist alternative offered a simple and compelling message: the traditional approach was not working precisely because Japan was not a traditional economy.

America's Economic Crisis

In retrospect, fears of the inevitable decline of the US economy were unfounded, but in the late 1980s these concerns were real and were deeply held by many. America's economic problems were best symbolized by its 'twin deficits': the enormous and intractable government budget deficit and an equally intractable trade deficit. Between 1982 and 1987, America's annual trade deficit had increased almost six-fold, from US$27 billion to US$152 billion.[1] As seen in Figure 3.1, the bulk of this deficit was with Japan, reaching a peak of US$56.3 billion in 1987.[2] In addition, America

---

[1] Whalen 1990: 1.
[2] Note that the scale of the y-axis differs from Chart One by a factor of three.

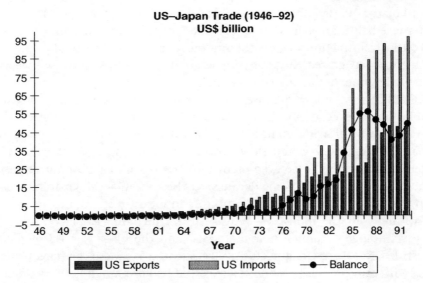

US–Japan Trade (1946–92)
US$ billion

Legend: US Exports — US Imports — Balance

Figure 3.1 US–Japan Trade (1946–92)

had by 1986 become the world's largest debtor nation. As Prestowitz noted, 'by 1987, the proud US Treasury was totally dependent on Japan,' in the sense that only Japan had the willingness and ability to continue to purchase government-issued debt.[3]

The spreading feeling of economic malaise in this period is perhaps best captured by the term 'declinism'—the view that the once hegemonic American economy had matured past the point of recovery, and was now entering an inevitable downward spiral. This mood was strongly captured by the argument that the country was suffering from 'imperial overstretch', as popularized in historian Paul Kennedy's 1987 book, *Rise and Fall of Great Powers*. Kennedy's argument was that all past global hegemonies had made international commitments at the peak of their power that later proved to be a drain on resources and eventually power. In all cases past hegemons had found that their domestic economic strength had been weakened by these burdens, and found that reversing these trends was impossible.[4]

---

[3] Prestowitz 1988: 6 and 20.
[4] Kennedy 1987. Robert Gilpin (1981) had earlier provided a more theoretical explanation for imperial overstretch that may or may not have influenced Kennedy. But it was Kennedy's popularization of this thesis, which was widely read not only in the US but also in Japan, that brought these arguments to the public debate.

To many, this described exactly what seemed to be happening. The crash of the stock market in October of 1987 only served to confirm this. Prestowitz at the time made this point quite dramatically when he opined that 'few recognized the event for what it was—the end, twelve years before its time, of the American century.'[5]

Fears of inevitable decline were also connected to the seemingly invincible Japanese economy. In the late 1980s Japan's economic strength seemed to be growing in an ever-upward direction; there were no signs that this trajectory would slow down. Extrapolating from the growth trends of the time, some even predicted that Japan's GNP would surpass America's within the coming decades. At the sectoral level, Japan seemed on the verge of taking the leadership role in industry after industry, most alarmingly in the industries of the future, including supercomputers, biotechnology, ceramics, new materials, and the like.[6] The US seemed destined to lose its manufacturing base to the Japanese, perhaps being left with only a service economy, a fear that had prompted then presidential candidate Walter Mondale to remark that the only jobs left to Americans in the future would be sweeping up around Japanese computers.

Mondale's nightmare scenario seemed even scarier as Japan seemed poised to dominate even in key service sectors. By 1986, for instance, seven of the world's largest banks were Japanese.[7] Japan was becoming more competitive in other service sectors as well, ranging from financial services such as the securities industry to even large-scale construction. In overall terms, it had become the world's largest creditor nation—that is, more money now flowed out of Japan, in the form of investment, loans, and aid, than any other country. Now, with the US as the world's largest debtor nation, the two indeed seemed to have 'traded places.'

Perhaps nowhere was the power of Japanese money more evident than in the rapid increase in direct investment in the US. With the buying power of the yen nearly doubled as the result of the 1985 Plaza Accord, a wider range of Japanese firms had begun to invest heavily in the US. Direct investment usually implies the creation of new manufacturing facilities that provide rising employment and incomes, as well as the transfer of skills to the local labor force, and so is usually welcomed and even sought

[5] Prestowitz 1988: 5

[6] As mentioned, the National Academy of Engineering in 1987 reported that Japan had taken the lead in 25 of 34 crucial technologies (Prestowitz 1988: 11).

[7] Prestowitz 1988: 12; in contrast, in 1980, just six years earlier, only one of the top ten were Japanese. Again, in retrospect, the growth of Japan's banks reflect the bubble economy as well as the exchange rate changes of the mid-1980s; few then predicted the dire crisis Japanese banks would face in the subsequent decade.

after by local officials. Indeed, US state and local governments often went to great lengths to attract Japanese investment.[8] Publicly, though, Japanese investments at the time seemed to attract only criticism, ranging from the lack of hiring of minority workers to the Japanese reluctance to transfer technology and skills to the American work force.[9]

The rapid rise of Japanese investment had an even deeper impact on American attitudes as a symbol of the two countries' reversal of fortunes. In many ways, American alarm was reminiscent of attitudes in the 1970s, when the success of OPEC led to a rapid increase in Arab purchases of real estate; Americans reacted with considerable alarm to the 'Arab invasion.' Now, many feared a 'Japanese invasion,' even if, as some pointed out, Japan as a whole was still only the third largest foreign investor in the US (after Britain and, not known to most, the Netherlands). Still, American concern was focused on Japan, in part because of the sheer speed at which these investments had risen in the 1980s: Japanese investment in the US through the 1970s was essentially zero, then grew to around US$5 billion by 1980, to US$20 billion by 1985, and then to US$70 billion by 1989.[10] Americans worried that because the Japanese economy seemed destined to keep on expanding, so too would this 'flood' of Japanese investments.

Perhaps most shocking was the rise of Japanese purchases of so-called 'trophy investments,' or social icons and landmarks that carried deep symbolic value. In the late 1980s, for instance, Japanese companies purchased landmarks such as Rockefeller Center, Saks Fifth Avenue, as well as sports-related investments such as Pebble Beach and baseball's Seattle Mariners. Japanese investments in American media, including Sony and Matsushita's purchase of major Hollywood movie companies, led to alarm over excessive Japanese influence over American thought and culture.

Some commentators later were to dismiss such fears and concerns as hysteria, even racism. Economist Jagdish Bhagwati, for instance, later derisively attributed these feelings of angst to a 'diminished hegemon

---

[8] A growing number of American states had established investment offices in Japan by this time. Others, such as the new governor of Arkansas, Bill Clinton, made numerous trips to Japan in this period, for the explicit goal of wooing Japanese investors.

[9] A number of studies argued that Japanese firms were merely setting up screwdriver assembly plants, but that the higher value added jobs and R&D and design work was being done in Japan, or by Japanese workers transferred to the US. Growing complaints were also heard that the spillover effects on local areas was limited because the Japanese firms were either continuing to rely on their traditional Japanese suppliers, or else that these supplier firms were following the manufacturers into the American market. Either way, local American suppliers were being shut out by the importation of the vertical *keiretsu* (see, for instance, Smitka 1991; and Encarnation 1992).

[10] Ibid.: 101.

syndrome,' with the clear argument that Americans had no excuse to feel so insecure. At the time, however, it must be remembered that these fears were real and deeply felt by many Americans and among policy makers. Indeed, it is difficult to fully convey the depth of these feelings to someone who did not witness this era.

The Coalescence of Revisionist Thinking

It was in this context of economic crisis that the revisionist paradigm coalesced as a full-fledged alternative to traditionalist views, and then found a deepening resonance within the foreign policy community and the country at large. As one analyst put it later, revisionism 'fell on fertile ground,' in large part due to the 'policy crisis' that the traditionalist approach was facing by the end of the 1980s.[11] Critics of these views now argued forcefully that more than two decades of attempts to liberalize the Japanese market—the lowering of overall tariff barriers, efforts to negotiate away barriers in specific sectors, attempts to liberalize financial and investment flows, and the like—had done almost nothing to put a dent in the overall trade imbalance or to increase market access. Similarly, efforts to manipulate macroeconomic growth rates, for instance pressures on the Japanese government to use fiscal policy to increase domestic demand, had also not led to an easing of the trade imbalance. Critics were especially scornful of efforts to manipulate exchange rates, where, despite the enormous appreciation of the yen between 1986 and 1987, there seemed to be no major impact on the trade deficit.[12] To many Americans, these developments reinforced the deepening view that 'something was wrong' with traditionalist explanations; despite repeated optimistic predictions and reassurances that the normal workings of the market would lead to a natural correction of the trade imbalance, things only seemed to be getting worse.

As Chalmers Johnson put it, by 1989, 'major questions arose about why policies that worked with other advanced industrial democracies and that were based on the best wisdom of America's official oracles, its professional economists, did not work when it came to Japan.'[13] Into this breach

[11] Alexander 1997: 9.
[12] Some economists argued that it would take some time before the trade balance would be affected, which they attributed to the 'J-curve effect.' Although the Japanese surplus did decline over the subsequent years, it was soon growing again.
[13] Johnson 1989a: 5.

stepped revisionism, which offered a clear and compelling answer to the policy failures of the traditionalist approach—simply put, that Japan was winning because Japan was different.

The year 1989 turned out to be a key year in the coalescence of revisionist thought. For one thing, it was at the end of that year that this alternative paradigm was officially given the name 'revisionism', a term coined by Robert C. Neff in a *Business Week* article. Neff wrote that 'no less than a fundamental rethinking of Japan is now under way at the highest levels of US government, business, and academia. The standard rules of the free market, according to the new school, simply don't work with Japan.'[14]

Four individuals were soon recognized as the leading revisionist thinkers: Johnson, Prestowitz, and two journalists, James Fallows and Karel van Wolferen. These four, dubbed the 'Gang of Four,' certainly played the most visible role in solidifying and crystallizing revisionist thought, and thus deserve some credit for deepening revisionism's resonance in the general public and among policy makers. Of the four, it was Chalmers Johnson, whom Neff referred to as 'revisionism's intellectual godfather,' who had the biggest overall impact.[15] Although it is difficult to judge the influence of any single scholar, all of the policy makers to whom I have spoken were at least familiar with Johnson and his arguments, even if many had never actually read his entire 1982 book on MITI. Johnson subsequently published numerous academic and policy-oriented pieces that hammered on the theme that Japan was structurally different, and these appear to have been more widely read among policy makers. In addition, his writings took on an increasingly alarmist tone that had been largely missing from his earlier work. Johnson's arguments also formed the basis of much of the arguments of the other three, and especially the two journalists, and gave their writings greater intellectual credibility.[16]

The most influential in terms of the direct impact on policy was certainly Prestowitz, who was able to use his position inside the government to disseminate revisionist ideas and to put them into practice, as he had done with the semiconductor industry in the mid-1980s. In his 1988 bestseller, *Trading Places*, Prestowitz's insider status gave him considerable credibility with government officials; whereas Johnson's writers were considered by one official as 'too erudite', Prestowitz spoke the

[14] Neff 1989: 44.   [15] Ibid.: 49.
[16] See, for instance, van Wolferen 1986/7: 292–4. Prestowitz also cites Johnson (along with Ezra Vogel) as the inspiration for his 1988 book.

language of policy making.[17] He was also very active in subsequent policy discussions about Japan and trade policy. Beginning in 1990, Prestowitz's voice on trade matters was magnified by his Economic Strategy Institute (ESI), an organization he had created after he had 'convinced a number of manufacturers and trade unions to fund an alternative voice in the capital to the conventional wisdom on international trade questions.'[18]

The revisionists in journalism contributed by helping to disseminate these ideas to a broader population, but had less to do with the development of revisionist thought. Van Wolferen, a Dutch journalist, published the *Enigma of Japanese Power* in 1989, in which he chronicled in a very readable manner the various aspects of Japan that made that country unique. He also wrote a widely read article in *Foreign Affairs*, in which he coined the term, 'The Japan Problem.'[19] James Fallows, in 1989, also published an influential article in the *Atlantic*, entitled 'Containing Japan,' in which he invoked the imagery of the Cold War in warning of the dire consequences if America did not take the Japanese challenge seriously.[20] Although Fallows was basically giving a popular voice to ideas developed elsewhere, this and his later articles received a great deal of publicity.

Although many today still associate 'revisionism' with these four individuals, the story presented here paints a more complicated picture. As I argued in the last chapter, many revisionist arguments had much longer histories and stemmed from a wide variety of other sources, particularly from the business community and inside the government. As Neff put it, 'the new thinkers come from a wide spectrum including journalists, academics, Bush Cabinet members, and CEOs.'[21] Even if the Gang of Four became the most visible and widely quoted standard bearers for revisionism, there were many others who contributed in less visible ways to advancing revisionist thought.[22] In the following sections I quote

[17] Interview with senior USTR official, 9/12/04.
[18] Dryden 1995: 366. Even before this, Neff (1989: 49) described Prestowitz as 'practically a one-man industry in Washington...He churns out op-ed pieces, lobbies Administration officials, and cultivates journalists.'
[19] Van Wolferen 1986/87.   [20] Fallows 1989a.   [21] Neff 1989: 46.
[22] The Neff article mentions many others notably Commerce officials such as secretary Robert A. Mosbacher, undersecretary Michael J. Farren, and assistant secretary Maureen Smith; USTR officials including Michael B. Smith and Deputy USTR S. Linn Williams; State Department undersecretary Richard T. McCormack; and private business officials including William T. Archey of the US Chamber of Commerce, James D. Robinson III of American Express, and James R. Houghton of Corning. Johnson also identifies four others: former USTR official Glenn Fukushima, author Pat Choate, academic Marie Anchordoguy, and novelist Michael Crichton (Johnson 1995a: 102).

extensively from the Gang of Four's writings, but in part this is because many of the other contributors to revisionism never put their thoughts into writing.

What is crucial here is that revisionists as a whole were able to fundamentally shift the intellectual background of policy making, and thus shaped the parameters of the policy debate. Specifically, the revisionists helped to undermine traditionalist assumptions and policy prescriptions, and then were able to cement the view that the Japanese economic system was so different that it represented a unique form of capitalism, that it posed a threat to American interests, and finally that the US needed to respond aggressively, including, among others things, with a results-oriented trade policy.

* * *

Revisionists first were largely successful in discrediting the traditionalist assumption that Japan's economy operated according to universal capitalist rules. As van Wolferen put it, the basic 'fiction that hampers the formation of an effective policy toward Japan is the premise...that Japan belongs in that loose category known as capitalist free-market economies.'[23] Prestowitz similarly argued that 'the Japanese society, market, government, and companies do not operate according to the rules and assumptions of Western logic.' Prestowitz, however, noted that 'US policy [incorrectly] assumes that the Japanese economy responds more or less in the same way and to the same stimuli as the US economy. We assume also that Japan's economic policy has the same consumer-oriented objectives.'[24] Prestowitz also argued that 'the US develops negotiating demands based on the assumptions that Japan works like the US. Since the negotiating goals are based on false assumptions, they are usually not achieved or, if achieved, do not fulfill expectations.'[25] Economist Alan Blinder articulated this position in his brief article, 'There are Capitalists, Then there are the Japanese,' in which he contended that 'market capitalism, Japanese-style, departs so much from conventional Western economic thought that it deserves to be considered a different system.'[26] Johnson

[23] Van Wolferen 1986/7: 291–2. He also argued elsewhere that 'the United States does not understand the nature of the Japanese political economy.' That is, to 'Western academic economists, including current presidential advisers...the idea that there can be a successful economy which is not based on the free play of market forces is tantamount to heresy.' It was therefore time, van Wolferen (pp. 288, 292, and 302) believed, for US policy makers to 'jettison the fiction that Japan has a free-market economy similar to those of the West.'
[24] Prestowitz 1988: 70 and 23.   [25] Prestowitz 1987b: 12.
[26] Blinder 1990: 21. Blinder served as Laura Tyson's top lieutenant in the CEA in the early stages of the Clinton administration.

perhaps put it most pointedly when he opined that 'revisionism vis-à-vis Japan is merely the intellectual recognition that Japan's alleged fundamental similarity to the Western capitalist democracies was always based on ignorance of Japan itself.'[27]

Revisionists focused their analysis on the various institutions, economic structures, and practices that made Japan so inherently closed. As before, the bulk of the analysis emphasized the different nature of the state, and now centered on Johnson's view of Japan as a 'capitalist developmental state.' Revisionists gave a great deal of credit to the economic bureaucracy for its successful pursuit of a nationalistic, mercantilist industrial development strategy, in which industrial policy was used to protect and nurture strategic industries, and thus to increase national strength. Johnson was more specific in his analysis of Japan's domestic 'institutions' that, taken together, added up to a truly unique form of economy. In a 1987 article, for instance, Johnson listed nine such differences, including its use of patent law to restrict foreign investments; *dango*, or collusion among domestic firms; predatory pricing; limits on mergers and acquisitions; and the role of the *keiretsu* in limiting free competition.[28] It was probably the *keiretsu* that received the most attention as the one institution that set Japan apart from all others. As Johnson put it, 'the *keiretsu* form of industrial organization . . . makes a mockery of much of the economic theory that is predicated on the workings of "market forces." '[29]

Revisionist thinkers were also instrumental in clarifying the view of Japan as a growing *threat*, at various levels. A new phrase, 'adversarial trade,' seemed to best capture this sense of Japan's economic threat. According to its originator, economist Peter Drucker, 'adversarial trade aims at dominating an industry . . . [the goal] is to drive the competitor out of the market altogether rather than let it survive.'[30] Thus, the growing view was that Japan's closed, mercantilist economic system and strategy were in fact designed to overwhelm its foreign competitors. That is, the

---

[27] Johnson 1990: 107. As he put it later, revisionism's 'antonym would appear to be 'ignorance' (p. 136). Part of the problem, according to Johnson was that Americans could only understand Japan through their own ideological blinders, and in particular those of the hegemonic neo-classical economic thought. As he (1990: 107) put it, 'the influence of a set of theological principles—the doctrine of free trade—serviced by an entrenched priesthood—the professional economists—that is much more interested in defending its articles of faith than in understanding what is going on in international economic relations.' Johnson later extended these criticisms to political science in his attack on rational choice.

[28] Johnson 1990.

[29] Johnson 1989b: 23–4. Other American academics also focused on this unique form of economic organization (see, for instance, Gerlach 1992).

[30] Drucker 1989, quoted in Fallows 1993: 90.

revisionist consensus was that Japan's bureaucrats had carefully and consciously crafted an economic strategy that was uniquely suited to economic warfare in the twenty-first century. Now not only was the Japanese economy portrayed as a threat, it was understood as an *intentioned* threat, a much more alarming matter.

Revisionists thus raised the crucial issue of trust. As mentioned earlier, the fact that the US had long been dependent on Japan for capital and technologies had always been tempered by the view of Japan as a dependable current ally. Now, however, revisionists insinuated that if their system had been designed to dominate international markets, what did this imply about Japan's deeper intentions?

The revisionists' clear message was that the US urgently needed a new approach to deal with the Japanese economy. If the US tried to deal with Japan using the same rules and policies that it used with other capitalist economies, this would put American firms at a fatal disadvantage. Clearly, if Japan was so different, normal trading rules did not apply. As Johnson put it,

[if] Japan's foreign economic policy reflects genuine mercantilism—protecting its domestic market, overcharging domestic consumers, using the overcharges to subsidize exports, and predatory pricing abroad to destroy competitors—then GATT rules are irrelevant and policies tailor-made for Japan will be required.[31]

Fallows further argued that 'Japan and its acolytes, such as Taiwan and Korea, have demonstrated that in head-on industrial competition between free-trading societies and "capitalist developmental states," the free traders will eventually lose.'[32]

Failure to respond effectively would have dire consequences. Johnson warned that 'the United States must either begin to compete with Japan or go the way of the USSR.'[33] In justifying his call for 'containment,' Fallows argued that 'we do have the right to defend our interests and our values, and they are not identical to Japan's.'[34] Prestowitz was the most alarmist of all, arguing that 'as a result of policies based on false assumptions and ignorance, the power of the United States and the quality of American life is diminishing rapidly in every respect.' Furthermore, Prestowitz issued the melodramatic warning that the Japanese challenge even threatened 'our ability not only to lead the free world but also to play our historic role as haven for the world's weary and huddled masses yearning to breathe free.'[35]

[31] Johnson 1990: 129.   [32] Fallows 1989b: 54.   [33] Johnson 1990: 135.
[34] Fallows 1989a: 54.   [35] Prestowitz 1988: 24–5.

Given these assumptions, it is not surprising that the revisionist school also drew very different policy conclusions than the traditionalist view. First, because Japan was such an economic threat, it needed to be elevated in terms of its policy importance. No longer should the political and military relationship be allowed to overshadow important issues involving economics. Second, the US needed to respond by strengthening its own economic competitiveness, including an industrial policy of its own that targeted strategic, high technology sectors. Third, the revisionists argued that American industries not only needed greater access to the Japanese market, but that this access could not come about using the traditionalist approach. As van Wolferen put it, 'international trade legislation of the most general kind is unlikely to have enough effect on Japan. Only action that specifically singles out Japan will be effective.'[36]

More specifically, revisionists called for a results-oriented approach, including pressure on the Japanese government to set aside a specified portion of some markets for foreign imports. As Prestowitz argued, 'our negotiations should always be for results. To negotiate over the procedures of a foreign culture in hopes of obtaining an undefined "open" market is to court failure and frustration.'[37] Johnson was even more specific, arguing that, 'in my opinion Japan requires narrowly focused, tailor-made, closely monitored, and minutely verified policies—i.e. those based on specific reciprocity rather than the unconditional most-favored-nation status.'[38] Johnson later argued that 'we must adopt results-oriented trade. This is the logical conclusion from our recognition of the differences we have vis-à-vis Japan and from our record of failures to negotiate acceptable trade rules with Japan.'[39]

* * *

The revisionist message that Japan was different and dangerous, and that it needed to be dealt with in novel ways, resonated deeply in all parts of American society, from popular culture to academia, the business community, Congress, and eventually the executive branch.[40]

The view of a growing Japanese threat had long been simmering in journalistic circles, as described in the last chapter. A 1985 piece by the

---

[36] Van Wolferen 1986/7: 302.

[37] Prestowitz 1988, p. 332. In addition, van Wolferen (1986/7: 303) alluded to this when he advocated the negotiation of 'direct fixed commitments between Western and Japanese economic institutions for an international division of labor.'

[38] Johnson 1990: 133   [39] Johnson 1995a: 112.

[40] It is important to remember, however, that it is difficult to draw simple, one-way causal arrows, in that ideas and debates in each of these levels also contributed to the development of revisionist thought.

respected journalist Theodore White in the *New York Times Magazine*, 'The Danger From Japan,' was an important milestone. White argued that 40 years after the end of World War II, 'the Japanese are on the move again in one of history's most brilliant commercial offenses, as they go about dismantling American industry... [only ten years from now] will we know who finally won the war 50 years before.'[41]

These sentiments and the constant echoing of revisionist alarmism had certainly affected the American public mood toward Japan. In 1989, for instance, *Business Week* reported that some 68 per cent of respondents considered the Japanese to be a greater threat than the Soviet Union. Numerous other polls seemed to back up this statement.[42]

The growing view of Japan as a potential threat was also reflected in popular culture. Michael Crichton's 1992 *Rising Sun*, for instance was based explicitly on revisionist thought, as evidenced by his bibliography that cited all of the key revisionist scholars. As Crichton put it in an Afterword to the book:

Sooner or later, the United States must come to grips with the fact that Japan has become the leading industrial nation in the world... But they haven't succeeded by doing things our way. Japan is not a Western industrial state; it is organized quite differently. And the Japanese have invented a new kind of trade—adversarial trade, trade like war, trade intended to wipe out the competition—which America has failed to understand for several decades.[43]

A more egregiously alarmist novel appeared two years later in Tom Clancy's *Debt of Honor*, which posited a near war between the two countries stemming from economic frictions.[44]

The theme of inevitable conflict with Japan was also reflected in academic works at the time. One such alarmist publication was the 1991 book *The Coming War with Japan*, which argued that because the two countries were pursuing such different strategies, they were on an inevitable

---

[41] White 1985. I thank T. J. Pempel for reminding me of the impact this article had. See also Horvat (2000) for a discussion of the importance of White's article.

[42] Neff 1989: 51. Okimoto and Raphael (1993), however, argue that American opinion toward Japan, though negative, was also more ambivalent throughout this period.

[43] Crichton 1992: 347. A much toned-down version of the book appeared later as a much criticized movie.

[44] I must admit that this is not a book that I could bring myself to read, so I rely on a review by Sheila Johnson: evidently, US trade sanctions cause Japan to

retaliate by crippling the US's Pacific Fleet, paralyzing its financial markets, reoccupying Saipan and Guam, and threatening it with a secretly acquired nuclear capacity... In the end, a full-scale war between the US and Japan is narrowly averted, although not before a kamikaze-like 747-pilot dives his airplane into the US Capitol, killing most of Congress and the President. (Johnson 1995c).

collision course. As a result, 'conflict will escalate in the next two decades to include the possibility—indeed probability—of an armed conflict, a second US–Japanese war in the Pacific.'[45]

Political scientist Samuel Huntington, perhaps the senior American realist scholar, also voiced similar sentiments. In a 1993 article, 'Why International Primacy Matters,' Huntington argued that America's international power position was being undermined because Japan had long been waging 'an economic Cold War.' As Huntington put it, 'since the 1950s Japan has pursued a strategy designed...to maximize Japanese economic power...Japanese strategy is a strategy of economic warfare'. Huntington also prominently cited statements such as Japanese politician Ishihara Shintaro that 'Economic warfare is the basis for existence in the free world...the twenty-first century will be a century of economic warfare...There is no hope for the United States.'[46] Huntington went on to compare the Japanese economic threat to past threats posed by Nazi Germany and the Soviet Union:

Japanese strategy, behavior, and declarations all posit the existence of an economic cold war between Japan and the United States. In the 1930s Chamberlain and Daladier did not take seriously what Hitler said in *Mein Kampf*. Truman and his successors did take it seriously when Stalin and Khrushchev said, 'We will bury you.' Americans would do well to take equally seriously both Japanese declarations of their goal of achieving economic dominance and the strategy they are pursuing to achieve that goal.[47]

Although Clancy was eerily prescient regarding 9/11, he got the nationality of the pilots wrong.

One popular culture counterpoint to these novels was a January 1992 absurdist poem by George Dawson (1992: A19), 'Blame the Japanese,' that was published on the *New York Times* op-ed page. In part, Dawson wrote:

> ...When the baby has the colic, and your dog is full of fleas,
> Don't complain to Washington—just blame the Japanese.
> ...When your son is quitting college, and your daughter's getting D's,
> Just do what Iacocca does—and curse the Japanese.
> ...When the temperature is falling, and your pipes are sure to freeze,
> Call upon your Congressman to bash the Japanese.
> When everyone around you is complaining of the news,
> And some condemn the Arabs while others blast the Jews,
> Stiffen up your lip, my son, and never bend your knees—
> Just be a true American, and blame the Japanese.

Perhaps reflecting the seriousness of anti-Japanese feelings at the time, I remember a fellow graduate student commenting that, 'I hope people understand this was meant to be ironic!'

[45] Friedman and LeBard 1991: book jacket. It must be noted, however, that Friedman and LeBard did not rely on revisionist arguments in coming to this conclusion, but rather stressed geopolitical conflicts of interests, especially after the end of the Cold War.
[46] Huntington 1993: 72 and 75.   [47] Ibid.: 76.

The revisionist prescription of managed trade was picked up by numerous analysts and policy pundits. In 1990, Bruce Stokes released a Japan Society monograph, *The Inevitability of Managed Trade*, in which he juxtaposed traditionalist free trade views with a revisionist rationale for managed trade. As Stokes put it, the US saw Japan as 'the principle culprit, indelibly [linked] with managed trade solutions to US trade problems.'[48] With the traditionalist approach clearly failing to deal with the trade problem, combined with the ascendancy of new thinking on trade, Stokes concluded that 'Time may be on the side of those who advocate managed trade.'[49] One of the clearest proponents of a government role in boosting America's high-tech, strategic industries was the BRIE economist, Laura Tyson. In a series of articles and then in her widely read 1992 book, *Who's Bashing Whom?*, Tyson had cautiously endorsed some form of market share agreement a la the 1986 Semiconductor Agreement. Tyson, who was to become one of President Clinton's top advisors on Japan, argued that the 'real Japan Problem' was that 'structural barriers to the Japanese market are rooted in the unique character of Japanese business organizations and their distinctive relationship with one another and with the Japanese government.' Thus, some form of managed trade was needed because 'in Japan something akin to managed trade is often required to achieve something akin to a market outcome.'[50] The call for a managed trade solution was also repeated by many others. In 1988, two former Secretaries of State, Henry Kissinger and Cyrus Vance, argued that the two countries should simply agree on an acceptable level of trade imbalance, and then leave it to Japan to decide how to achieve it.[51]

Once again it was the business community that most powerfully championed a managed trade approach; indeed, as argued in the last chapter, parts of the business community had been key architects of revisionist thought. The key actor now was the USTR's Advisory Committee for Trade Policy and Negotiations (ACTPN), which in 1989, for the first time, publicly endorsed a 'results-oriented' trade policy as the only way to assure access to the Japanese market. This influential group, dominated by internationalist, high-tech companies, had in the past been a strong supporter

[48] Stokes 1990: 7. It should be noted that Stokes defined managed trade broadly to include voluntary export restraints, voluntary import expansion, and quantitative targets (p. 5).
[49] Ibid.: 53.
[50] Tyson 1992: 55 and 263. It should be noted that Tyson was cautious in her support of managed trade, and also stressed that macroeconomic approaches were equally if not more important.
[51] Kissinger and Vance 1988: 913. I thank Richard Katz for pointing this out.

of a liberal trade philosophy. But over the course of the 1980s many ACTPN firms had become convinced of the revisionist conclusion that the Japanese market was so closed and different that this departure from orthodox policy was necessary.[52]

By 1987 the group had begun the process of setting out the intellectual case for a results-oriented approach. The committee that drafted this report, led by Tim Regan of Corning, drew heavily on revisionist thinking in detailing the numerous structural barriers that effectively closed the Japanese market.[53] As Regan put it at the time,

We have to be results-oriented. Endless negotiations over barriers and rules is like trying to peel an onion. The results have been pretty skimpy... We shouldn't be negotiating over how Japan's economy is organized, or telling Japan to remake itself in our free market image. Instead of talking about rules, let's agree to specific import results. Let Japan figure out how to achieve the result.[54]

ACTPN also pushed the argument that Japan was an outlier in terms of intra-industry trade: that is, unlike other industrial economies, which tended to import even where they had a competitive export industry, Japan seemed to only export. The bottom line for ACTPN was thus that 'the unique nature of the Japanese economy requires a results-oriented trade strategy.' Thus, where 'informal or invisible barriers exist, US nego-tiators should insist on appropriate sectoral import levels that properly reflect the international competitiveness of US suppliers.'[55]

Journalist Richard Katz at the time presciently noted that 'ACTPN's most important impact will not be on immediate Administration policy, but in building a consensus over the next few years.' Already it was significant that former free traders in ACTPN had shifted their views on Japan. As one participant put it, 'Four years ago, (ACTPN co-Chairman and American Express Chairman James) Robinson would have preferred to stick with the

[52] Of the 45 members of ACTPN, more than half were large internationally oriented high-tech companies. Key members included Motorola, IBM, Corning, Cray, Dow Chemicals, ATT, Allied Signal, Boeing and Hewlett Packard. The group also included representatives from numerous smaller firms, labor unions, and farm groups. One other member was Georgette Mosbacher, the 'glamorous wife' of Commerce Secretary Robert Mosbacher. Whalen 1990: 51; and ACTPN 1993.
[53] Interview with former Tokyo Embassy official, 4/7/97. Other chapter writers included Edward Lincoln and Marcus Noland. ACTPN had originally intended to submit this report to Reagan's USTR, Clayton Yeutter, who was thought to be sympathetic to the idea. But ACTPN did not finish it before the 1988 election, and thus presented it in January 1989 to Bush's just-nominated USTR, Carla Hills. ACTPN also called for a more coherent strategy of seeking market access for high technology industries, and stressed the importance of the macroeco-nomic approach as well as dealing with America's own economic problems.
[54] Quoted in Katz 1989: 4–5.   [55] Ibid.: 2.

more orthodox approach...The change comes from a recognition that Japan's economic structure and import behavior are different.'[56]

Revisionist ideas perhaps resonated most deeply in Congress, where anger and resentment had clearly reached a boiling point. Congress in this period was the repository of all of America's feelings of angst and frustration over its declining power and status relative to Japan. The harsh rhetoric coming out of Congress was also underscored by some dramatic displays of outrage—as, for example, Congressmen smashing Toshiba radios on the steps of the Capitol following the 1987 revelation that the Toshiba subsidiary had illegally sold sensitive submarine-related technology to the Soviets. As mentioned earlier, traditionalist thinking had never been as strong in the Congress as in the executive branch, so it is not surprising that Congress had become openly scornful of the traditionalist approach. With agreement after agreement having failed to open the market, and years of macroeconomic efforts having failed to reduce the trade imbalance, faith in traditionalist prescriptions had largely disappeared. Congress was thus in an activist, retaliatory mood when it passed the 1988 Omnibus Trade Act, which included the so-called 'Super 301' provision that required the President to retaliate against nations judged to be 'unfair traders.'

Congress in this period also adopted the language and arguments of revisionist thinkers. Revisionist ideas were adopted most actively by House majority leader Richard Gephardt (D-Missouri), described as a 'founding father of managed trade,' who now argued that 'we must break out of the outdated, outmoded ways of thinking about how trade affects our nation's economy.'[57] In a speech delivered on the eve of the fiftieth anniversary of the Pearl Harbor attack, Gephardt espoused a straight revisionist line in arguing that 'the unrecognized incompatibility of our economic systems is at the root of our current tensions and frictions,' the most important cause of which were the *keiretsu*. Furthermore, 'The United States has been handcuffed during the last ten years because of the Reagan and now Bush Administration's blind ideological adherence to the principle of free trade.'[58] Congress as a whole was thus receptive to the revisionist argument that efforts to remove specific barriers in the Japanese economy were essentially futile, and thus that unique trade remedies were required. In this sense, Congress viewed 'the Japan Problem' in much the same way

---

[56] Ibid.: 5–6. The speaker was a Robinson underling, the American Express Vice President for International Corporate Affairs, David Rich.
[57] Quoted in Whalen 1990: 38.   [58] Gephardt 1991: 3 and 6.

as revisionists in ACTPN and the Commerce Department, and thus was very receptive to the idea of negotiating market-share agreements. While Republican members of Congress were less enthusiastic about targets, due to their commitment to laissez-faire economics and also the desire to not openly contradict the administration's policy, more Republicans were now willing to deviate from these principles—but only in the particular case of Japan.

Revisionism struck such a deep chord in Congress in part because it provided a clear and simple explanation for all of the American problems with Japan, but Congressional members hardly needed any convincing. Nearly every member had heard horror stories about the Japanese market from their constituents, and by the late 1980s Congress as a whole had fully accepted the argument that Japan was inherently closed and structurally different, and now a threat to the US. In this sense, as one Congressional aide put it, the revisionists were 'preaching to the already converted.'[59]

Last but not least, an important shift was also occurring inside the executive branch, as a number of formerly traditionalist officials were now embracing revisionist assumptions, and were joining the struggle to overcome the remaining bastions of traditionalist thought. I need to emphasize again that government officials were not merely responding to ideas developed on the outside; rather, as had been the case from the 1970s on, a subset of government officials continued to be central developers of revisionist ideas. This role is perhaps best exemplified by the so-called 'Team B' concept. This referred to a subset of officials inside each of the government agencies who had become convinced that traditionalist approaches were futile and that the US needed to fundamentally reorient its policy along revisionist lines.

Commerce and USTR officials had been pushing for such a re-evaluation for a number of years, and continued to take the lead. Commerce Secretary Robert Mosbacher was one of the key figures in this group, described as leading the 'revisionist group within the Administration ... [which believed] that "Japan is different" and cannot be dealt with according to the same liberal trade principles as European trade partners.'[60] Career

---

[59] Interview with Japan-related Congressional staff member, 4/23/97. My sense is that Congress in this period was simply in an angry, retaliatory mood, regardless of the specific arguments about Japan. That is, Congress listened to the Trade Hawks and gladly stepped up its threats of retaliation, and later listened to the revisionists and again was quick to threaten punishment.

[60] Whalen 1990: 39.

officials Maureen Smith and Michael Farren were also important advocates of revisionist ideas. One analyst reports that Farren held to particularly strong revisionist sentiments; during the Structural Impediments Initiative (SII) negotiations, for instance, he argued that 'it is absolutely false to assume that we can't see results very quickly.'[61] One of Farren's colleagues remembers him often repeating the Chalmers Johnson quip that Japan 'was the only centrally planned economy that works.' Similarly, revisionist assumptions were strongly held in the USTR, although perhaps not as deeply as in Commerce. One analyst mentions both Deputy USTR Linn Williams and Assistant USTR Joseph Massey in this regard. Of the two, Massey was clearly the stronger advocate of the revisionist position.[62] One USTR official later insisted that the USTR staff did believe that Japan was closed and different, but most did not see it as a great threat.[63]

The most important development now was that similar shifts were underway inside the two Departments that formerly were most dominated by traditionalist assumptions, State and Defense. Inside the State Department, officials who had strong backgrounds in general economic and trade issues were the first to adopt revisionist views on trade policy toward Japan. These officials tended to be found in the economics-related bureaus and the trade-related offices within the Bureau of East Asian and Pacific Affairs. One key figure in this regard was Under Secretary of Economic Affairs Richard T. McCormack, a hard-liner who was the Department's lead negotiator on SII. In this period even career officials who had become specialists on Japan were finding it harder to maintain a traditionalist stance. In part, this reflected the rising criticisms aimed at these officials, and particularly the Office of Japan Policy, for being too quick to defend Japan; many of these officials had already been tarred with the obviously uncomfortable label of being members of the 'chrysanthemum club,' or those who had become too sympathetic to the Japanese government's position. In any case, even officials at the highest levels of the department were now arguing that the US should no longer treat Japan leniently for the sake of the political relationship. As one analyst put it, State officials 'are inclined to take a harder line on trade, especially toward Japan, with less concern than previously for long-range security and geopolitical concerns.'[64]

Team B members were also very active inside the Department of Defense. As discussed earlier, officials involved in technology issues were

---

[61] Quoted in ibid.: 52.   [62] Ibid.: 60–1.
[63] Interview with senior USTR official, 9/12/04.   [64] Whalen 1990: 44.

already concerned that Japan's industrial machine was poised to overwhelm America's technological base, and so were no longer willing to see technology issues relegated to secondary status. In this context, the publication in 1989 of Ishihara Shintaro's book, *The Japan That Can Say NO: Why Japan will be First Among Equals,* fed directly into these concerns. Here was a highly visible politician not only arguing that Japan should stop giving in to US demands, but also issuing the not so veiled threat that it should use its technological power as geopolitical leverage. What most caught the attention of the defense establishment was Ishihara's remark that 'we control the high technology on which the military power of both [the US and Soviet Union] rests.' Therefore, 'if Japan told Washington it would no longer sell computer chips to the United States, the Pentagon would be totally helpless. Furthermore, the global military balance could be completely upset if Japan decided to sell its computer chips to the Soviet Union instead of the United States.'[65] Such intemperate statements, coming in this period of American crisis and doubts, could only increase distrust of Japan. The US was now becoming worried that it was so heavily dependent on Japanese technology and capital.

Defense officials who were most wary of the Japanese were concentrated on the acquisitions and technology side of the department, rather than from the more traditionalist International Security Affairs. Some officials mentioned in this regard include David Tarbell, the Director of International Economic Affairs who was heavily involved in the supercomputer issue with Japan, and Stephen Breyer, Deputy Under Secretary for Trade Security Policy, who had taken a hard-line on the Toshiba case.[66] These officials also played a crucial role in the FSX controversy of 1989, in which the Bush administration came under intense pressures to reconsider the agreement to co-develop with Japan the next generation of fighter-bomber.

[65] Ishihara 1991: 43 and 21. This book was originally co-authored with Sony Chairman Morita Akio under the title *'No to ieru Nippon,'* but was quickly translated into English by (according to Ishihara) the Pentagon's DARPA. This version quickly made the rounds in the US government, and raised a firestorm. In the official translation that appeared in 1991, Ishihara (1991: 12 and 149) contends that the 'illicit version was full of mistakes, some laughable and some very serious,' while the translator, Frank Baldwin, referred to the pirated version as 'a contemptible piece of work.' The official version was minus the contribution of Morita, who was evidently uncomfortable with the controversy the book had stirred. Fallows later criticized 'the flamboyant nationalist politician' Ishihara for his racial views. As Fallows (1990: 54) put it, the original book was 'rich in the Japanese racial theorizing sometimes called Yamato-ism...The Japanese race, Ishihara has said, is now demonstrating its excellence—indeed, its superiority—through its economic achievements.'

[66] Whalen 1990: 66. As in State, there were thus signs of a split between the policy side, which still held to traditionalist assumptions about the importance of the relationship, and those parts of the Department that focused on economic or technology issues.

In the final months of the Reagan administration the two sides had agreed to co-produce the new aircraft based on the US-made F-16. But critics inside and outside the administration argued that Japan would take advantage of the advanced technology it stood to gain from the US to build up its own domestic aviation industry, which at that point was non-existent. The fear, voiced by officials in Commerce, the USTR, and State was that the US would thus lose 'the one remaining area of industrial technology where American leadership is still secure.'[67] Others in defense, for instance senior official Richard Perle, worried that Japan could not be trusted to protect advanced defense technologies. The deal was eventually renegotiated to insure that 40 per cent of the work on the new aircraft would be done by American firms, and set limits on the transfer of technology to Japan.[68]

In any case, members of Team B did meet a number of times for informal discussions, and occasionally brought in key revisionist thinkers to help clarify their ideas and arguments.[69] It is difficult to measure exactly how much of an impact the group had, but it was at least vocal and contentious enough to cause one State Department traditionalist to label the group as 'bomb throwers.'[70]

Revisionism and the Policy Process in the Bush Administration

The constant drumbeat of revisionist assumptions and prescriptions seemed to be resonating in all parts of American society—except at the top levels of the Bush administration, where traditionalist attitudes still predominated. As Dryden notes, the Bush administration 'at the very top at least, was much more pure in its devotion to free-market principles than its predecessor.'[71] It was around this time that a senior Bush administration official opined that 'A chip is a chip. It doesn't matter whether it is a semiconductor chip or a potato chip. It is the same thing for the American economy.'[72]

---

[67] Whalen 1990: 12. Strong critics included State Department official Kevin Kearns, Commerce Secretary Mosbacher, Hills, and Gephardt (Brock 1989: 30).

[68] Brock 1989: 30; and Kearns 1989. Laura Stone (1999: 261–4) offers a good summary of the evolution of Defense attitudes.

[69] Interview with State Department official, 3/24/97.

[70] Interview with veteran State Department official, 1/5/97.

[71] Dryden 1995: 357.

[72] Quoted in Fukushima 1994: 116. Fukushima (p. 16) notes that Intel Corporation head Andy Grove sent (the Bush) official a violin with a note attached saying 'You can fiddle as the American semiconductor industry burns just as Nero fiddled while Rome burned.'

This commitment to traditionalist assumptions was perhaps best illustrated by the administration's reaction to ACTPN's 1989 call for a results-oriented approach. In its initial meeting with USTR Carla Hills, some ACTPN members came away with the impression that she not only welcomed the suggestion, but was also quite enthusiastic about it. This impression was reinforced in her subsequent Congressional testimony, in which she did not directly disavow numerical targets, which prompted a *Washington Post* article that stated that 'the Bush Administration is considering setting targets for Japanese purchases of US products.' The stance was a short-lived one, however. As Dryden puts it, 'Even the suggestion that the administration was thinking about throwing free-trade dogma out the window enraged John Sununu, the fiercely conservative... chief of staff.' One of Hill's aides reported that 'she got a telephone call from Sununu... He just read her the riot act on managed trade.'[73] Hills soon met again with ACTPN officials and delivered a clear rejection of the call for numerical targets, prompting one ACTPN member to observe, 'we knew right then that there were still a lot of free trade, doctrinaire people in the administration.'[74]

Top officials in the administration were also opposed to a more active industrial policy role to counter Japan's competitiveness. This opposition was symbolized, according to Bruce Stokes, by the demotion of DARPA's director Craig Fields, 'the government's most ardent proponent of industrial policy.'[75] Top administration officials also pressured Commerce Secretary Mosbacher to tone down his support for industrial policy, most notably his backing of a government role in developing high-definition television (HDTV) technology.[76] This included a 'private rebuke' by Sununu over 'Mosbacher's blatant departure from free market principles.'[77] As Stokes put it,

The biggest obstacle to a new American approach to trade is the Bush administration, which remains firmly opposed to managed trade and industrial policy... [Its actions amount to] what *Business Week* dubbed a managed trade and industrial policy jihad led by director of the Office of Management and Budget Richard G. Darman, chairman of Council of Economic Advisers Michael J. Boskin and White House chief of Staff John H. Sununu, all of whom share a vehement opposition to government policies targeted to interfere in trade to help particular industries... As long as Sununu, Darman and Boskin hold the upper hand in the White

---

[73] Dryden 1995: 356–7. The aide was Linn Williams.
[74] Interview with former Tokyo Embassy official, 4/7/97.
[75] Stokes 1990: 11.   [76] Dryden 1995: 357.   [77] Whalen 1990: 50.

House, managed trade and industrial policy are likely to remain in the deep freeze.[78]

The administration was also reluctant to use the newly established Super 301 provision against Japan. In the spring of 1989, the US did name Japan under this provision, but limited its specific charges to supercomputers, satellites, and lumber. The Bush administration refused to go beyond this or to aggressively purse other retaliation policies. Rather, according to Stokes, 'Hills counted heads on Capitol Hill... and realized that there was no longer sufficient interest in Congress to force the administration to go after Japan. She called Congress' bluff—and got away with it.'[79]

The Bush administration realized that it needed to diffuse the growing anger being directed at Japan, but was motivated mostly by the traditionalist concern that the security relationship had to be insulated from trade frictions. According to officials with access to the President, George Bush himself never saw Japan as an economic threat as the revisionists did, but feared that failure to address the trade problem risked a domestic political backlash. One official recounts that just prior to Bush's meeting with Prime Minister Kaifu in Palm Springs in 1990, for instance, the President personally intervened to elevate trade issues on the agenda. Evidently, the President's original talking points, prepared by the NSC staff and National Security Advisor Brent Scowcroft, mentioned trade issues last, and only briefly. On the flight to Palm Springs, however, the President reversed the order of the talking points, indicating that although 'we didn't have a security problem with Japan, [there was] a hell of a trade problem,' and this had to be addressed, otherwise 'the entire relationship will suffer.'[80]

While the Bush administration saw the need to address the trade problem, it did not adopt the revisionist call for managed trade, market-share targets, and the like. The administration's most ambitious negotiations with Japan—the SII that began in July 1989—was essentially designed to remove barriers and thus to liberalize the market process in Japan.[81] The

---

[78] Stokes 1990: 46–7. [79] Ibid.: 46.
[80] Interview with senior USTR official, 9/12/04; see also Armacost 1996: 70.
[81] See Schoppa (1997) for the most in-depth analysis of administration thinking on the SII. The administration was also looking for some way to head off stronger action by Congress, which at the time was on the verge of passing the Gephardt amendment, which the administration saw as a protectionist bill largely aimed at Japan. Some new market-opening initiative was seen as necessary to preempt Congressional action. Fukushima (1991b: 21) cites a Bush official saying that the administration saw SII as a 'workable alternative to managed trade,' since there 'were more free-trade-oriented and more open-market-oriented ways to resolve our trade problems with Japan.'

difference was that the SII departed from the orthodox approach of simply looking at barriers and regulations; now, the US approach recognized that there were indeed *structural* barriers that worked to shield the economy from imports. Still, the SII talks were premised on the traditionalist assumption that once barriers were identified and removed, 'normal' market forces would be freed and imports would increase. To return to the onion metaphor, the feeling was that one may have to remove a few extra layers of (structural) protection, but once this was done, the core would end up looking reasonably like other capitalist economies.

The bulk of the rest of the Bush approach also reflected traditionalist assumptions that manipulating market signals through macroeconomic policy and exchange rate changes would eventually lead Japan to increase its intake of foreign goods. Perhaps even more so than under Reagan's leadership, the administration's approach held close to the traditionalist position. One of the Bush administration's main priorities was to strengthen the GATT, which was seen as the best way to ensure global economic liberalization, and thus engaged Japan to this end. One former USTR official thus described the Bush trade policy toward Japan as 'essentially a GATT-plus approach.'[82]

Even the sectoral agreements negotiated in this era moved further away from a managed trade orientation than had been the case with the Reagan administration. The one agreement that did include the mention of a market share target, the June 1991 renewal of the 1986 Semiconductor Agreement, was a 'softened' version of the original. Although the reference to the 20 per cent market share target was moved into the main text of the agreement, it was explicitly stated that it represented 'neither a floor, nor a ceiling, nor a guaranteed market share.' In addition, other 'quantitative and qualitative factors' would be taken into consideration.[83] One USTR official described this as a broader 'market access' objective that went beyond the market share concept, for instance in its encouragement of long-term business relationships between foreign and Japanese firms.[84] The US also agreed to drop the remaining sanctions that had been applied in 1987 to punish Japan for failing to live up to the original agreement.[85] For these reasons the 1991 extension was accomplished surprisingly

---

[82] Janow 1994: 58–9.   [83] Quoted in ibid.: 64.
[84] Dryden 1995: 372; and Janow 1994: 63–4.
[85] In 1987 the US had determined that dumping in third-country markets was continuing and that the 20 per cent foreign market share was not going to be realized, and thus leveled some US$300 million in retaliatory tariffs on selected Japanese imports. US$135 million in sanctions for dumping had already been removed at the end of 1987 (Janow 1994: 62–3).

quietly, given the heated controversies surrounding the first agreement and the subsequent sanctions.[86]

Even so, top officials in the Bush administration were clearly uncomfortable with this extension, reflecting what one USTR official describes as 'a sore point for senior members of the Bush administration,' and particularly for Carla Hills. It is significant that the administration did not even try to negotiate any other agreement that included a market share number.[87]

In the final stages of the administration the two countries did enter into three other sectoral talks in which VIE-related numbers were at least mentioned. In the 1991 agreement on government procurement of computers, the two agreed to various 'quantitative criteria' to assess progress. In the 1992 agreement on paper products, the final pact included seven 'quantitative and qualitative factors that will be used to measure progress' toward the goal of 'substantially increasing market access.'[88]

The numbers-oriented discussion that received the most publicity concerned trade in automobiles and auto parts. The 'Bush Auto Trip,' as the January 1992 summit in Tokyo came to be known, occurred in the context of deep American discontent over the declining state of the economy, as well as the recognition that the presidential campaign was heating up. The President therefore made the goal of this trip the creation of 'jobs, jobs, jobs,' and to underscore this goal decided to bring along a number of American CEOs, including the heads of major auto parts makers and all three of the 'Big Three.' Under pressure from MITI, the Japanese auto firms agreed to announce their intention to increase their purchases of US auto parts, and these numbers were totaled and included in the agreement, indicating that the firms intended to increase their purchases from the level of US$9 billion in JFY 1990 to US$19 billion by JFY 1994.

Although the 1992 'auto summit' is today remembered only for the incident in which President Bush became ill at a formal banquet and vomited on the lap of his host, Prime Minister Miyazawa, its importance for this story concerns these auto parts purchasing plans. At the time, both sides made it clear that the plans were private and voluntary, and did not represent any sort of commitment by the Japanese government. As discussed in Chapter 5, however, the numbers later became controversial

---

[86] Japan's MITI was still opposed to any sort of quantitative indicator, but agreed because it 'also wanted the 10 per cent market share requirement softened' (Dryden 1995: 372).

[87] Janow 1994: 65.

[88] Ibid.: 62 and 65. One of the seven factors was 'change in the level of import penetration.'

when the Clinton administration tried to interpret these numbers quite differently. Some outside observers also saw things similarly at the time; as Dryden put it, the numbers were put forward 'in the important political context of a presidential visit, and the pledges were announced at the same time as the official communiqué,' and therefore, 'expectations were established.'[89]

Although the auto summit seemed to come closer to the revisionist call for a 'results-oriented' trade policy, the Bush approach set clear limits in this regard. When Bush administration officials spoke of 'results' in describing their negotiating goals, they used this term in a generic sense, implying the simple desire to achieve some 'worthwhile outcome,' rather than the more specific guarantee of some share of the market. More importantly, the two governments agreed very clearly that the use of any sort of indicator would be only for the purpose of assessing progress, rather than as explicit and official Japanese government commitments that could be subject to retaliation. The commitments mentioned in these agreements were to be private and voluntary, rather than official and sanctionable. Thus, as one observer put it, 'Bush's numbers were on the "front end" only.'[90]

* * *

By the early 1990s the debate over how to resolve 'the Japan Problem' had increasingly become a battle over whether traditionalist or revisionist assumptions were more accurate or held out more promise. That this was in essence a battle of *assumptions* was nicely underscored in Tyson's 1992 *Who's Bashing Whom?*, in which she chose as an epigraph the famous quotation from Abraham Lincoln:

The dogmas of the quiet past are inadequate to the stormy present. The occasion is piled high with difficulty, and we must rise to the occasion. As our case is new, so we must think anew and act anew. We must disenthrall ourselves and then we shall save our country.[91]

---

[89] Janow 1994: 66; and Dryden 1995: 375. These purchase plans were appended to the joint communique that followed the summit. Japan was legally correct, however, in arguing that the auto purchase plans were part of an informal understanding, rather than a legally binding 'agreement.' This distinction was to return to haunt the two sides in 1993.

[90] Interview with State Department official, 9/4/97.

[91] Abraham Lincoln, Annual Message to Congress, 12/1/1862. As an ironic historical footnote, Lincoln (1992: 340) used these beautiful words not for the immediate and unconditional emancipation of the slaves, but rather to compensate the freed slaves to repatriate to Liberia or even to some future American colony in Central America, which he thought would appeal to the blacks 'especially because of the similarity of the climate with your native land.'. We should remind ourselves that not all new ideas are necessarily good ones. Prestowitz (1988: 25) put it more plainly when he argued that 'we must re-examine our assumptions.'

Judging from the growing acceptance of their arguments, the revisionists seemed to be winning this battle of assumptions. As described in this chapter, the repeated failure of traditionalist policy, combined with the simple and compelling alternative offered by revisionism, had allowed the latter to dominate the discussion of Japan in nearly every realm. Revisionist dominance was clearest in mainstream journalism, in Congressional debates, and within the business community. In academia, traditionalist voices still existed but were becoming very quiet, perhaps even cowed. Many formerly traditionalist academics had been put on the defensive, in some cases stung by accusations that they were naïve 'Japanapologists' or, worse, 'agents of influence.' Others had come to accept core tenets of the revisionist perspective, or were simply becoming uncomfortable arguing anything that sounded like a traditionalist line.[92] Even in the field of neoclassical economics, the favorite punching bag for revisionists, opinion had become split due to the rise of revisionism as well as strategic trade theory. And when it came to the case of Japan, it was becoming difficult to find academics who espoused strong traditionalist views.[93] Inside the US government the majority of career officials had adopted revisionist assumptions. This had been the case early on in the trade-related agencies, but by the beginning of the 1990s many in the more traditionalist agencies such as State and Defense were also beginning to shift in this direction.

Thus, by the end of the Bush administration revisionist assumptions had already achieved what Hall terms 'viability.'[94] It had achieved 'economic viability' in that it had demonstrated the 'apparent capacity to resolve a relevant set of economic problems'; it had achieved 'political' viability in that it certainly had great 'appeal in the broader political arena'; finally it had achieved 'administrative viability' in that the majority of career officials had come to adopt revisionist assumptions.

However, revisionist assumptions had not yet become adopted as the working policy assumptions of the US government. Although a growing number of officials had come to the conclusion that the revisionists were substantially right about Japan, there were enough officials, especially among the top political appointees in the administration, who were not

---

[92] In an incident unrelated to academics, but nevertheless indicative, Dryden (1995: 285) recounts a speech in which Japanese Foreign Minister Sakurauchi Yoshiro made the claim that Japan had 'one of the most open markets in the world'; this pronouncement was greeted with 'suppressed laughs and snickering throughout the hall.'

[93] See Johnson (1988) for his strong criticisms of neo-classical economic thinking applied to Japan. Two noted economists who held their ground through this entire period were Hugh Patrick and Jagdish Bhagwati, both of Columbia University.

[94] Hall 1989: 371–4.

prepared to reject traditionalist assumptions. Top officials remained committed to liberal trade principles, and more importantly placed a priority on the importance of Japan as a political and military ally. As one observer put it, despite the existence of internal splits, State and Defense especially 'continue to play traditional roles, attempting to balance increasing emphasis on economic and trade issues against diplomatic and strategic concerns.'[95]

There is no way to be certain what sort of policy approach a second Bush administration would have adopted. Given that traditionalist assumptions still held sway at the top, however, had Bush been re-elected the US probably would *not* have moved further down the managed trade road. Although the US may have continued to seek 'results' (as in worthwhile outcomes) it would most likely have stopped short of seeking hard, sanctionable numbers or targets. Carla Hills had put it clearly when she argued just before the election that 'I am against managed trade. I will not enter an agreement that stipulates to a percentage of the market.'[96]

Thus, in spite of the underlying changes in ideas and attitudes about Japan, the full translation of revisionist thought into policy assumptions, and then to policy change, had not yet occurred and was still not inevitable. Entering the election of 1992, the stage was set for a fundamental shift in US assumptions, but the final outcome was by no means already preordained.

[95] Whalen 1990: 40.
[96] Quoted in Dryden 1995: 371. Hills (1993: A10) later made similar arguments in a *Wall Street Journal* op-ed piece, 'Targets Won't Open Japanese Markets.'

PART II

The Clinton Transition

Institutionalizing Revisionist Assumptions

4

Out with the Old, In with the New

The question of whether the Bush administration would stick to a traditionalist approach to Japan was made moot by the election of Bill Clinton in November 1992. In the first few months of the new administration, US trade policy toward Japan underwent a visible, rapid shift toward the revisionist position. By the April 1993 summit meeting with Prime Minister Miyazawa, less than three months after the inauguration, the Clinton administration had made clear its desire for a 'results-based agreement,' by which it meant agreements that included hard, sanctionable numbers, and over the ensuing three months seemed to have persuaded the Japanese government to negotiate on that basis. This shift to a focus on concrete results occurred in a very short period of time, especially considering how long the US had stuck to its traditional trade policy.

This chapter focuses on the crucial first months of the new administration, tracing in detail the internal debate among Clinton's policy advisors. What is striking about this process of policy change was how enthralled these officials were with the revisionist paradigm. Almost immediately, the adoption of new assumptions about Japan—revisionist assumptions—had a visible and direct impact on this major policy shift.

The 1992 Campaign

Contrary to expectations, Japan trade policy was not at all a focus of Bill Clinton's presidential campaign. As described in the last chapter, there were considerable pressures building up in the US for a more decisive approach to the Japan problem, and the Bush administration's inability to deal with it seemed to be a glaring weak spot. Certainly other Democratic candidates, most notably Tom Harkin and Robert Kerrey, had tried to score political points by pledging a tougher approach on trade, as did the two populist candidates, Pat Buchanan and Ross Perot.[1] The political opportunity the issue offered was also not lost on Clinton or his advisors, one of whom acknowledged that the candidate himself realized at the time that 'Japan was very unpopular.'[2]

The Clinton campaign's laser-like focus on the country's economic problems also made the Japan problem a seemingly natural issue. The public had come to associate America's economic problems with its foreign trading partners, with Japan the most visible target. Clinton's emphasis on expanding exports, as a way of fostering domestic growth, and his pledge to elevate international trade policy in terms of national security, were both at least implicitly directed at Japan. But Clinton chose to refrain from harping on the Japan problem, instead casting his position on international trade issues in a more positive light—that the US needed to 'compete, not retreat,' and that in order to become more competitive it first needed to put its domestic house in order.

The fact that the Clinton campaign chose not to raise the Japan issue is best explained as a variant of the now famous phrase, 'it's the economy, stupid'—the strategy of placing the blame for America's economic problems squarely on George Bush's shoulders. Clinton's advisors felt that focusing on international trade problems would have shifted part of this blame toward foreigners and away from the Bush administration's failings. Raising the Japan problem would have diluted the message that the election was all about Bush's mishandling of the domestic economy.[3]

The candidate himself was also not originally inclined to take a harsh line toward Japan. Bill Clinton entering the campaign was not known as a critic of Japan and certainly cannot be classified as a revisionist. If anything, Clinton's record as governor of Arkansas demonstrated the opposite, in that he had actively sought Japanese investment as a means to foster economic development. Indeed, Clinton was later criticized for being willing to lower his state's already low environmental standards in order to attract more foreign investment. As governor he had made three trips to Japan for the specific purpose of drumming up interest in investing in

---

[1] Political analyst Norman Ornstein, however, noted at the time that 'Japan-bashing provided early notoriety and an emotional boost, but few votes in primaries and caucuses' (Ornstein 1992, quoted in *JEI Report* 8/21/92: 3).

[2] Interview with campaign advisor and senior DC member, 4/29/97.

[3] Interviews with senior Clinton campaign advisor, 4/17/97, and senior DC member, 4/29/97. One of the few times that the Clinton campaign criticized foreign companies was over the issue of whether they were paying their fair share of taxes, but this was a general criticism, not directed solely at Japan, and was in any case dropped relatively quickly. Interview with senior Clinton campaign advisor, 4/17/97.

Arkansas. The Japanese press also reported that Clinton had developed friendships with certain local businessmen.[4] While the governor did voice his frustration over the protected market, these complaints were not an indictment of the Japanese system as a whole, but rather focused on two of Arkansas' potential exports, rice and poultry.

Clinton's campaign statements on Japan were surprisingly standard, no more revisionist in tone than President Bush's more traditional position. In a *New York Times* interview in late June 1992, Clinton called the bilateral tie 'our most important bilateral relationship now,' and that the two needed to recognize their 'shared understanding of our acknowledged relationship, of our respective national security and multinational and multilateral responsibility and our responsibilities for the developing world.'[5] In the few times that Japan was even mentioned during the campaign, it was usually in a positive or exhortatory sense—that Japan had done better and that the US (given better leadership) could do just as well. Clinton's focus on the importance of exports made at least some criticism of Japanese protectionism inevitable, but the tone was by no means as strong as the revisionists. Clinton favored pressuring the Japanese to lower its trade barriers, warning that 'Japan must open the doors of its economic house or our partnership will be imperiled.'[6] He also demonstrated his intention to enforce compliance with trade agreements, including his support for reviving Super 301: 'Although the US has negotiated many trade agreements, particularly with Japan, results have been disappointing. I will insure that all trade agreements are lived up to.'[7] Most of Clinton's statements, however, were aimed less at Japan than his rival, as when he said during his convention acceptance speech in July that, 'We've fallen so far, so fast, that the Prime Minister of Japan actually said he felt "sympathy" for America. When I am your

---

[4] *Japan Times,* 11/5/92, and *Yomiuri Shimbun,* 11/5/92, both accessed through the Nikkei Needs Database <http://www.nikkeieu.com/needs/>. Clinton (2004: 270) later noted that the trip was part of the 'first Arkansas trade mission to the Far East.'.

[5] *New York Times* 6/28/92: 7.

[6] This and 200 of Clinton's other campaign statements and position papers can be found on the National Public Telecomputing Network website <http://SunSITE.sut.ac.jp/pub/academic>. A search through these materials found only 13 references to Japan that can be deemed even remotely critical, mostly that Japanese markets should be more open. All other references to Japan—all passing references—either praised it or were used to exhort the US to catch up. Clinton, moreover, was not perceived as a hard-liner on Japan. In a poll conducted by the *Nihon Keizai Shimbun* in July, Clinton was picked as the least likely to be the toughest negotiator with Japan. Perot was first with 42 per cent, followed by Bush at 23.3 per cent, and Clinton last at 11.5per cent. *Nihon Keizai Shimbun* 7/13/92 (Nikkei Needs Database <http://www.nikkeieu. com/needs/>).

[7] Quoted in Lincoln 1999: 123.

president, the rest of the world won't look down on us with pity. They'll look up to us with respect.'[8]

Inside the campaign, however, policy discussions of Japan had begun to take on a different tone. This process of 'educating the candidate' was one that was increasingly dominated by revisionist ideas. The campaign official who was initially most strident in pushing the issue was Derek Shearer, a professor at Occidental College, and a somewhat enigmatic figure in the Clinton campaign. During the early days of the campaign Shearer seems to have taken it upon himself to serve as the unofficial 'coordinator' of Japan policy, arguing that the campaign needed to confront the issue more squarely. Shearer clearly advocated revisionist assumptions, and also evidently consulted with Clyde Prestowitz to draw up a heavily revisionist-oriented 'syllabus' for the candidate to read. Clinton appears to have read these materials avidly, and according to one report 'enjoyed the hawkish line, even delighting in Michael Crichton's latest novel, *Rising Sun*.'[9]

During the remainder of the campaign the information that reached the candidate was increasingly dominated by revisionist thinkers. Given the campaign's focus on other issues, there were not many briefings on Japan, but almost all of these were conducted by revisionists, with Prestowitz and former USTR official Glen Fukushima being the most well known. Prestowitz, for instance, forwarded two memos to the transition team that followed a revisionist line. In one, he argued that the past 'assumption that the two countries' economies are essentially similar was false,' and that the US now had a chance to 'dramatically... alter the terms of its relationship with Japan.' Specifically, Prestowitz called for the 'negotiation of targets for

[8] Miyazawa, the Prime Minister in question, later said that the Japanese term he had used, *dōjō*, implies more an understanding of the US situation—empathy, rather than a more condescending feeling of sympathy or pity (*Nikkei Weekly* 10/26/92: 1).

[9] *US News and World Report* 7/12/93: 28. Other materials included Clyde Prestowitz's *Trading Places*; Laura Tyson's *Who's Bashing Whom?*; Robert Kuttner's *The End of Laissez-Faire*; and writings by Glen Fukushima (ibid.: 24).

Shearer had evidently developed his ideas on Japan from his ties to a group of revisionist thinkers in Southern California, including Chalmers Johnson and Steve Clemons, as well as to Mike Mochizuki, then at USC. Shearer was also involved in a Japan Society sponsored trip to Japan in 1991, which included revisionist thinkers James Fallows and Bruce Stokes, that evidently had an impact on his views of Japan. Shearer's impact on the campaign's Japan policy is disputed by other advisors, and it appears that he played a role only in the early stages of the campaign. As more heavyweight advisors joined the team, most notably Robert Rubin and Roger Altman, Shearer became increasingly marginalized (interview with transition team official, 4/2/97). Although these two would later play a role in hardening Japan policy, they did not push the Japan issue in the campaign, preferring instead to maintain the focus on domestic issues. Shearer came under fire early in the campaign for his political leanings, described by one conservative as a 'socialist' on domestic economic policy. He was later given a relatively low ranking job in the Commerce Department, which he left very shortly, to become Ambassador to Finland.

market shares or sales volume of certain US goods in the Japanese market,' especially in autos, auto parts, and certain electronics. In a second memo he noted that this would require 'negotiations for market shares or other concrete objectives that are at odds with traditional notions of free trade.'[10] The campaign's only formal briefing on Japan, held at Clinton's *alma mater* (Yale) on September 8, was given by Mike Mochizuki, a close friend of Shearer.[11] Mochizuki described himself at the time as somewhere in between the traditionalist and revisionist positions, but his message on the Japanese economy was strongly revisionist in orientation. Mochizuki argued first that the system was so structurally different, operating on different principles, that we should not expect convergence to a US-style economy. Mochizuki stressed the importance of a results-orientation, as standard approaches such as manipulating exchange rates or liberalizing the market would have a limited impact. He also argued that Japan had a propensity to accept managed trade—repeating Fallow's line that the Japanese negotiators themselves often asked 'how much do you want' in terms of market shares. Mochizuki also argued that agreements such as the SCA and the agreement on autos, with their heavy emphasis on numerical targets, were likely to be the most effective.[12]

Toward the end of the campaign, insiders felt that the candidate was surprisingly knowledgeable about Japan and aware of the problems of access to that market. He had also reportedly come to the opinion that the Japanese business community behaves differently, and that we should not expect their behavior to converge with ours. One advisor reported that Clinton had told his team that the Japan issue needed to be addressed more sufficiently.[13]

---

[10] The two unpublished memos were entitled 'Proposal for a New Japan Policy,' and simply 'Japan Policy,' which he later shared with a Carnegie-sponsored study group.

[11] Shearer had lobbied for the choice of Mochizuki. The hour-long briefing was held in Yale's Quinnipiac Club. The other briefers on Asia were Winston Lord and Richard Holbrooke. For an interesting account of these briefings, see Karube 1996: 51–2.

[12] Mochizuki also argued that these agreements were effective because they encouraged US investment in the Japanese market (interview with Clinton campaign advisor, 5/15/97; Karube 1996: 53). Clinton evidently listened for most of the briefing, not asking many questions. One of the few times he interrupted was when Mochizuki mentioned that the Japanese government preferred to see Bush re-elected; Clinton is reported to have asked if there was anything the Japanese could do at that late stage to help Bush.

Mochizuki later reiterated his revisionist-oriented position in a public forum: 'I think we need to focus on targets...I think its fundamentally wrong to think that [Japan] is becoming a capitalist system like that of the United States...Japan will stick to its keiretsu system of organizing business. So what we should do is get away from generic negotiations like SII and focus on results-oriented policies' (Economic Strategy Institute 1993: 33).

[13] Interview with Clinton campaign advisor, 5/15/97.

Yet to the very end of the campaign this shift in views was not reflected in official rhetoric, and the spotlight remained off of Japan. Although the Japanese government and media looked closely for signs of criticisms from the Democratic candidate, Japan was not that important to the campaign. As one advisor put it, because of the focus on the domestic economy, 'Japan was simply not on the radar screen.'[14]

The New Administration's Early Months

The Japan issue continued to take a back seat during the transition period, as the President-elect's advisors scrambled to put the new administration in place, and then to establish its approach to domestic economic policy, which was even then seen as the key to whether the administration would last more than four years. The administration devoted the bulk of its attention and political effort on domestic economic policy, in particular the passing of its initial budget proposal.

Prior to the end of February, when the administration initiated a review of Japan policy, virtually no official work was done on the issue.[15] However, the parameters of the administration's new policy were being laid down on an informal basis, first indirectly through the political appointment process, and then as key figures in the incoming administration began informally to consider the Japan issue.

The political appointment process in the first Clinton administration was more intriguing than usual because the Democrats had been out of office for so long. After the dust had settled, two things for our story were clear: none of the well-known revisionists was offered an important spot in the new administration, and yet every key appointee dealing with Japan policy came in holding strong revisionist inclinations.

The fact that Clinton and his transition team decided to pass over the prominent revisionists did not reflect a conscious decision to maintain a traditionalist Japan policy. There is very little evidence that Japan was a deciding or even an important factor in any of these appointments—this single issue was simply not an important litmus test. This is not surprising given the vast number of policy issues each official would have to deal with,

---

[14] Interview with campaign advisor and transition team member, 5/12/97.

[15] Some staff-level meetings, including a preliminary meeting of an interagency working group on Japan, were held to prepare for visits by the Ministers of MOFA and MOF, scheduled for early February, but these meetings did not discuss major policy changes (*Inside US Trade* 2/12/93: 4; interview with veteran USTR official, 5/2/97).

and also because of the low priority the Clinton campaign had put on Japan. In addition, the political appointee process is always one in which politics, both partisan and personal, are as important as policy, and the Clinton transition was no exception.

Media speculation at the time, however, was that the direct influence of the revisionists was bound to increase, as certain officials with revisionist backgrounds were rumored to be in line for top trade positions. The most visible of these figures was Clyde Prestowitz, who was actively considered for the USTR spot, an appointment that would have sent a clear signal to Japan that the US was going to get tough on trade. As fellow revisionist James Fallows put it, this would have been taken by Japan as 'a declaration of war.'[16] Another revisionist thinker rumored to be in line for a top trade job was Glen Fukushima, who was mentioned in the press as also being considered for the top USTR job, and also perhaps for a position in the newly created National Economic Council (NEC). Chalmers Johnson was mentioned, at least briefly, as a possible candidate to replace Michael Armacost as Ambassador to Japan.[17]

The one individual associated with the revisionist camp who did receive a high-level appointment was Laura Tyson, appointed as chair of the CEA in November. Even in this case, however, it seems that her appointment was less because of her views on Japan and more because of her advocacy of a domestic industrial policy. In any case, her appointment as chair of the CEA meant that her impact on trade policy would be no more than indirect.[18] The only other revisionist to join the administration was Derek Shearer, but his position was as a relatively low-ranking official in the Commerce Department that would have little impact on Japan trade policy.

Clinton's decision to pass over the more prominent revisionist candidates was taken as a lost opportunity by the revisionist camp. Clinton was criticized for giving most of the posts related to Asia to people more

---

[16] *Washington Post* 12/19/92: C1. The new administration evidently shied away from Prestowitz in part because of his controversial background. One Senate insider was quoted as calling a Prestowitz appointment 'a fantasy' precisely because of his controversial views (*Los Angeles Times* 12/15/92: D-1).

[17] *Washington Post* 12/19/92: C1; and *Financial Times* 2/11/93: 4. Fukushima had long been an advocate of creating a high-level office in the White House devoted to Japan trade policy, so a position in the NEC seemed a natural for him. He was offered a mid-level position in Treasury, which he declined for 'personal reasons' (*Tokyo Business Today* 5/94).

[18] Tyson herself seems to have believed that she was not picked for her expertise on Japan (*Washington Post* 12/19/92: C1). According to Bob Woodward (1994: 73–5), Clinton did not even raise the Japan issue in his interview with Tyson for the CEA chair.

Tyson herself later commented that her position in CEA was 'not the same as being the USTR. I get asked a lot of questions about how trade policy is going to change, and I sometimes say, "well, you'll have to talk to the USTR about that" ' (Economic Strategy Institute 1993: 95).

knowledgeable about China, as was the case with the top Asia spot in State, which went to China hand Winston Lord.[19] Other appointments were also disappointing to the revisionists, for instance the choice of Bowman Cutter to head the administration's Japan policy review group; as one put it later, 'we had never even heard of Bo Cutter.' Revisionists criticized the Clinton administration for not having enough expertise on Japan—or perhaps, more accurately, for not enough revisionist-oriented expertise.

Clinton's choices of two inexperienced candidates for the top trade spots met with the harshest reaction. The appointment of the chair of the Democratic National Committee, Ron Brown, to head the Commerce Department was seen as motivated by patronage rather than policy. It was, however, the selection of Mickey Kantor, an international lawyer with very little trade policy background, as the new USTR that came as the most profound disappointment to revisionist thinkers. The common wisdom was that his selection was due to his role as Clinton's campaign chair and because he was a long-time friend of Hilary Clinton, and certainly not because of his expertise on trade policy. As Chalmers Johnson derisively put it, Kantor 'was chosen explicitly because he knows nothing about trade.'[20]

That no open advocate of revisionism was given a prominent trade policy position is significant in terms of how directly their ideas could be translated into policy. As Haas and others have pointed out, outside ideas can most easily influence policy making if proponents become direct participants in the policy process.[21] In this, the revisionists found themselves shut out.

It should be stressed, however, that while Cutter, Brown, and Kantor were not associated with the development of revisionism, none of the three was a blank slate when it came to the Japan problem. All were aware of revisionist arguments about Japan, and none was a traditionalist in any sense. To put it differently, almost everything that the three knew about Japan was based on revisionist assumptions. Their exposure to revisionism was to deepen over the course of their subsequent involvement with the issue, as did their understanding of, and commitment to, the revisionist line. But it was clear from the start that they brought revisionist proclivities with them.[22]

As it turned out, then, all of the individuals who were appointed to positions that touched on the Japan issue either already espoused

---

[19] Lord then chose China specialists as his key assistants, and was able to place a China hand in the key NSC/Asia slot (Ennis 1993a: 10). Cutter was named as the top assistant to Robert Rubin, the NEC head; one of Cutter's tasks was to run the Deputies Committee, which was tasked with the Japan policy review; see Destler 1996 for details.

[20] *The Strait Times* 1/5/93: 4.   [21] Haas 1992.

[22] These points were made in numerous interviews, and especially confirmed in an interview with senior DC member, 4/29/97.

revisionist assumptions or were strongly leaning in that direction. While this unanimity of views was not part of a conscious policy strategy, it is an indication of how widespread revisionist assumptions had become, particularly in the business community, from which the Clinton people drew heavily in making their appointments.[23] Put another way, not one of Clinton's appointees held to a traditional view of Japan or the bilateral relationship. Further, I have found little evidence that any individual who was a proponent of traditional views was even considered for any of these positions—traditionalists seemed to be a dwindling breed at the time.[24]

What is notable about the Clinton administration's Japan policy team is the high degree of unity, top to bottom, around a revisionist-oriented view. Unlike in the Bush years, when revisionist-leaning career officials had to overcome resistance from more traditional-leaning political appointees, now there was greater receptivity to these new ideas about Japan at the highest level of the policy making process.

* * *

In the months leading up to the inauguration, the political appointees in the new administration set out to address pressing international economic issues, and the Japan problem more specifically. The steady stream of revisionist advice that had begun during the campaign continued, and indications are that Clinton and his advisors were coalescing around revisionist assumptions about Japan.

Administration officials continued to solicit briefing memos from key revisionist thinkers. In at least two confidential memos to the transition team, Prestowitz argued very strongly that the Japanese economy did not, and would never, operate on similar principles as the US, and thus that the US should therefore seek to negotiate market shares in key sectors.[25] During the Little Rock economic conference on December 14 and 15, for instance, all of the Japan-related discussions took on a distinctly revisionist tone. Significantly, the main official briefers on Japan were the two

---

[23] Clay Chandler of the *Washington Post* (2/22/91: A1) argued at the time that the new team had deep business experience with Japan and that 'they acknowledge primarily that their experiences have left them fed up with Japan's restrictive business practices, wary of Japanese assurances and convinced of the need to precisely quantify Tokyo's progress in opening its markets.'

[24] The one exception may be former ITC Chair Paula Stern, who was not known as a hardliner on Japan. Stern, however, was mired in controversies of her own, including a fax campaign that accused her of lobbying for Japanese companies, and for making judgments as ITC chair that allegedly hurt US business (*New York Times* <http://nytimes.com/>) 12/27/92.

[25] Interview with transition team official, 4/2/97.

revisionists then still rumored to be in line for administration posts, Prestowitz and Fukushima. The central theme of the discussion was that any domestic economic recovery depended on solving problems with the international economy, which in turn depended on solving the Japan problem. The central message about the Japanese economy was that it was indeed a different one, operating on different principles, and that the US thus needed 'something different' in terms of its policy approach. The possibility of seeking numbers or quantitative targets was also broached, although not pushed as strongly as observers had expected.[26]

Revisionist ideas also dominated the informal discussions being held by Clinton's new group of trade policy officials. Soon after the inauguration, Mickey Kantor took the initiative in gathering the newly appointed economic officials on an informal basis, in a series of meetings that later became known as 'The Saturday group.' This group discussed many issues, but Japan policy was one of its central topics, and it was here that the early parameters of eventual policy began to take shape. Membership in the group was limited to the political appointees, thus cutting off the career bureaucracy. Key figures besides Kantor were Laura Tyson, Roger Altman, Bo Cutter, Larry Summers, and Joan Spero, all of whom became key architects of Clinton's Japan policy. Furthermore, these meetings began so early in the new administration that these appointees had not even been fully briefed by their career staffs. In fact, the career officials were so completely shut out that some complained that the only clues they had about the discussions were when they were tasked with gathering some set of numbers or other information.[27] The initial direction of Japan policy in the new administration was clearly being set by the political appointees.

The central figure in this group was Laura Tyson, the Berkeley professor who was known as an advocate of managing trade with Japan. While her appointment as chair of the CEA was probably motivated more by her activist stance on industrial policy, reports are that during the campaign Clinton 'devoured' her book, *Who's Bashing Whom?*[28] As mentioned earlier,

---

[26] Interview with US Embassy official, Tokyo, 4/7/97. In addition, other key presentations on international trade included prominent advocates of a new approach to trade policy, including Laura Tyson and Alan Blinder. It was basically Gene Sperling who determined who would be asked to give these briefings, although both Bo Cutter and Mickey Kantor played key roles in putting the meetings together. Interview with campaign advisor and transition team member, 5/12/97.

[27] These meetings are discussed in detail in Karube (1996: 65–71). Much of the analysis in this section draws on that book.

[28] *US News and World Report* 7/12/93: 28.

Tyson's most quoted phrase summed up her results-oriented approach: 'In Japan something akin to managed trade is often required to achieve something akin to a market outcome.'[29]

Tyson presented the group with a memo on Japan policy that made the case for a results-oriented approach, and discussed the criteria to determine which industry or sectors should be the target of negotiations.[30] This memo became the focus of early discussions, and thus appears to have helped shape the parameters of later policy decisions. Also discussed in this informal rump group was the possibility of pushing for benchmarks for Japan to reduce its overall trade surplus, an idea pushed most heavily by Lawrence Summers.

The Saturday group discussions were also shaped by an influential outside source: ACTPN. On February 10 the group publicly presented its new report on Japan trade policy to Kantor, in which it repeated its support for a 'results-oriented' approach, and now endorsed the use of temporary quantitative indicators (TQIs) as a way to force open the market. At this point, ACTPN's real impact was in providing what one observer termed 'intellectual input' into the process; ACTPN's argument for a new understanding of how the Japanese economy operated, and its compelling image of a Japanese market that was nearly impenetrable, dovetailed with the early thinking of the administration.[31] Kantor was evidently affected by this portrayal of the Japanese economy and the logic of their policy position. Kantor, according to one colleague, was 'really revved up' by the report, while another recalled Kantor often carrying around the ACTPN report, 'all dog-eared and tagged.'[32] During a well-publicized meeting in early February that lasted for nearly an hour, the leadership of ACTPN presented their report directly to President Clinton, who was reportedly 'seized by' ACTPN's analysis and conception of the Japanese economy.[33]

A number of those I spoke with cite the ACTPN report as being a key influence on the thinking of both Kantor and Clinton. Certainly the impact

[29] Tyson 1992: 263. Tyson (1991: 139) was even more explicit in an earlier academic article in which she argued that 'it may prove necessary for the US to negotiate a minimum share of the Japanese market for foreign suppliers . . . such managed trade arrangements may be better than nothing at all.'

[30] Others remembered this memo to have included advocacy of a market share approach, but this has not been confirmed (interview with veteran Commerce official, 4/14/97).

[31] Lincoln 1999: 124. According to Lincoln (p. 124), ACTPN was not seeking managed trade since TQIs 'were not intended to produce cartelized outcomes in Japan, would not be an automatic trigger for American retaliation when not realized, and should simply be thought of as a "benchmark." ' In this sense, then, the administration went well *beyond* what ACTPN was asking for.

[32] Interview with very senior DC official, 4/29/97, and USTR official 4/23/97, respectively.

[33] *Tokyo Business Today* 7/93: 8; interview with veteran Commerce official, 4/14/97.

was there, and the group's timing was perfect, as it weighed in precisely when the administration was just beginning to consider its Japan policy. But, again, this is not a simple case of decision makers taking outside policy advice and implementing it. ACTPN was not just an interest group pushing for a favored policy, but rather an advocate of a different conception of the Japanese economy. Furthermore, Clinton's informal Japan team was already strongly taken by the revisionist paradigm that ACTPN was endorsing. It was here, I believe, that ACTPN had its real impact, in that it reinforced the revisionist drumbeat the administration was already internalizing. And the reason its policy recommendations were endorsed in 1993—after being rejected four years earlier—was precisely because the new administration itself was already adopting similar assumptions.

These background developments on Japan policy remained hidden from public view before early March 1993. In the meantime, the administration's approach to trade policy in general was gradually taking shape, as reflected in Clinton's American University speech, given on February 26. Clinton carried through on his pledge to be a 'different kind of Democrat,' as his new approach largely avoided calls for protection against imports, and instead focused on the need to expand exports and opening markets abroad—the notion that the US needed to 'compete, not retreat.'[34]

More significantly for our story is that there was as yet no indication that the US was interested in seeking a different approach to Japan. Clinton's speech stressed the need for opening the Japanese market, but still in more traditional terms of identifying and removing protective barriers. Similarly, other official statements by the administration, for instance in the confirmation hearings of Mickey Kantor and Laura Tyson, reflected a desire to be tough with Japan on trade, but nothing in the way of advocating results,

---

[34] Clinton's continued support for NAFTA and for following through on negotiating a successful Uruguay Round, also broke out of the traditional Democratic mold.

Clinton also carried through on his pledge to elevate the international trade issue by creating a White House-level coordinating agency, the NEC. Although some saw the NEC to be designed with Japan policy in mind—in the general sense that the US needed to solve the Japan problem if it was going to turn its economy around—the creation of the NEC was a broader attempt to create a more coherent economic policy in general. Also, the fact that the NEC had responsibility for domestic economic policy also meant that any focus on Japan would be diluted. Interview with NSC official, 3/12/97, and Department of Defense official, 5/13/97. Clinton's deep concern for economic policy was also shown by his choice of close advisor Robert Rubin as the first head of the NEC. This appointment gave the NEC instant legitimacy and high-level access—a great deal of momentum at a key juncture. This proved to be the case while Rubin was NEC head. Others were critical that Rubin ran the NEC on an informal, almost personalized basis. Once he left, the NEC did not have strong mechanisms in place to replace his personal access to the President (interview with senior NSC official, 4/14/97).

numbers, or any form of managed trade. While a great many in the media in both countries were already speculating that numerical targets would be part of Clinton's new approach, this speculation was still idle: the fact is that the administration was only then getting around to formally considering what to do about the Japan problem.

Revising Japan Policy: The Deputies Committee

Once the administration turned its attention to the Japan trade issue, however, the shift in policy assumptions came quickly—literally in a matter of weeks. Policy discussions, which began in earnest in the last week of February, were spurred on by the administration's decision to agree to Japan's request to hold an early summit meeting with Prime Minister Miyazawa, scheduled for mid-April.

The administration's early policy making structure centered on a subcabinet interagency body co-chaired by Cutter from the NEC and Sandy Berger of the NSC. As seen in Table 4.1, the Japan policy review was divided into two tracks, with Berger and the NSC overseeing the review of the security relationship and Cutter and the NEC in charge of economic issues. This group then reported its findings up one level for approval, to the Principals Committee, made up of the cabinet-level officials, which in turn passed their recommendations on to the President.[35]

Deliberations on Japan trade policy were handled by the economic side of this body, a working-level group of 13 officials who were known as the Deputies Committee for Economic Policy, or simply as the DC. It was in the DC that the administration's new approach to Japan was shaped. The DC's role was especially crucial in the initial stages of policy making, as it served as the driving force for the shift in trade policy towards a result orientation.

The DC deliberations took place in the context of an administration that seemed quite receptive to revisionist views of Japan. As described above, the President and some of his top advisors had been heavily influenced by revisionist thinking, and no doubt laid out the broad parameters of the group's deliberations. Tracing the exact role that the President played is a difficult and sensitive task, but from my interviews of DC members it

[35] Ennis (1993a) and Destler (1996) discuss the Deputies Committee's deliberations in some detail. The dividing line between the two tracks was never absolute, however, since Cutter and Berger coordinated policy recommendations, and could weigh in with the other on issues that concerned them. Furthermore, some officials on economic policy were members of both staffs (Destler 1996: 11).

Table 4.1 Japan policy review in the Clinton administration, March 1993

Deputies Committee for Economic Policy (DC)	Security policy

Chair: Bowman Cutter (NEC)
Members:
  Council on Economic Advisors
    Laura Tyson (Chair)
    Alan Blinder
  United States Trade Representative
    Charlene Barshefsky (Deputy USTR)
    Ira Wolf (Assistant USTR for Japan)
    Ellen Frost (Counselor)
  Department of Commerce
    John Rollwagen (Deputy Secretary)
    Marjory Searing (Deputy Assistant Secretary)
  Department of the Treasury
    Roger Altman (Deputy Secretary)
    Lawrence Summers (Under Secretary,
      International Affairs)
  Department of State
    Joan Spero (Under Secretary, Economic Affairs)
    Joanna Shelton (Deputy Assistant Secretary)
    Dan Tarullo
  National Economic Council
    Robert Fauver (Assistant for International
      Economics)
    Robert Kyle (Assistant for International Trade)
	Chair: Sandy Berger (NSC)
	Members:
	  National Security Council
	    Kent Wiedemann (Asian Affairs)
	  Department of State
	    Winston Lord (Assistant Secretary)
	    Thomas Hubbard (Deputy Assistant
	      Secretary)
	    Rust Deming (Japan Desk)
	  Department of Defense
	    William Pendley (Assistant Secretary
	      for Regional Affairs)

Source: Ennis 1993a and Destler 1996.

appears that as the group began its meetings, Clinton was now known to favor a tougher trade policy toward Japan, and had expressed to some senior members his skepticism that simply manipulating macro variables or the exchange rate would be sufficient. The President later recounted that sometime in early 1993 he instructed Mickey Kantor 'to find a way to open the Japanese market more,' after a meeting with the Big Three and the UAW. In addition, DC members reported that presidential aides George Stephanopoulos and Rahm Emanuel would occasionally sit in on DC meetings, although they usually did not actively participate. Clearly, the President put some importance on the Japan trade issue, and on the automotive industries in particular.[36]

---

[36] Interviews with very senior DC official, 4/29/97; and senior DC member, 4/29/97. The Clinton quote appears in Clinton (2004: 462). Clinton (p. 502) also listed Japan trade policy as one of his biggest early foreign policy priorities—what he called 'barking hounds'—following Bosnia, Russia, Somalia, Haiti, and North Korea.

However, President Clinton does not seem to have been involved in deciding the specifics of the new policy approach, and in this critical period seems to have delegated this task entirely to the DC. This is not surprising, given that he and his administration were preoccupied early on with the domestic economic program.[37] Quite naturally, the DC participants were trying to 'anticipate the reactions' of the President, and so some sort of more aggressive approach was inevitable. But because these policy parameters were so vague the group could have chosen from a broad range of policy options. Indeed, even those who thought they were anticipating reactions could only guess what it was that the President really wanted.[38] The policy discussions of the DC in those crucial first weeks, where the groundwork for the shift in policy was put into place, were thus not subject to a great deal of high-level political control. The attitudes—and assumptions—that the Deputies brought with them thus had a huge impact on the formulation of Japan policy.

There was also a strong meeting of the minds between the political appointees and most of the career bureaucracy. As described in the last chapter, a growing number of officials in the economic agencies had become strong advocates of revisionist assumptions, and during the Bush administration parts of the pol-mil agencies had moved in that direction as well. Many revisionist-oriented officials were initially quite happy with the new group of political appointees, in that they were seen as already revisionists or at least receptive to revisionist assumptions. These revisionist-oriented career bureaucrats had been waiting for the previous eight years for just this sort of shift at the political level, and were now close to ecstatic.[39]

Somewhat ironically, therefore, the DC showed considerable independence from the career bureaucracy, carrying out their policy deliberations without heavy input or guidance from the career officials. In part, this was because the political appointees brought with them a certain wariness of the career bureaucrats. It is not uncommon for the two groups to have a

---

[37] See Woodward (1994) for a detailed inside account of the administration's first year focus on its economic recovery program and health care; and Clinton (2004: 451–63).

[38] Some also had the sense that the President was looking for policies that would differentiate him from Bush, a natural desire for any new President (interview with senior NSC official, 4/14/97).

It should be stressed that over time the role of the DC receded and the President and top cabinet members became more involved. Barshefsky later praised Clinton for his deep involvement in policy, at least after the April 16 summit: 'he was deeply involved in reviewing the drafts, and I assure you that he focused directly on things like "highly significant," and the results, and the measurements, and the qualitative and quantitative measurements and the objective indicators and so forth. His mind is on the economic side of this' (US Senate 1993: 21).

[39] Interview with veteran USTR official, 5/2/97.

certain level of mutual discomfort at the beginning of an administration, and in this case the discomfort level was still high in February 1993.[40] The political appointees distrusted some bureaucrats because of their reputation as being 'Japan hands,' and thus co-opted by, or sympathetic to, the Japanese position. This is also ironic, as most bureaucrats by this time were closer to the revisionists than to the Chrysanthemum Club. However, Clinton's new people were coming in from outside the government, and thus unfamiliar with how thinking in the agencies had already shifted. The prevailing rhetoric of the late 1980s certainly influenced the new administration: as one outside observer put it, to the Clinton people, 'anyone who knew something about Japan was suspect.'[41]

Perhaps more important in this case was that the new appointees were wary of the career officials because the latter had been working with Republican administrations for more than a decade, and thus had had a hand in creating the 'failed' policies that now needed to be corrected. Even if the economic bureaucrats were not thought to be sympathetic to Japan, they might be resistant or unwilling to reject the more traditional policy approach they had helped to develop.[42]

In addition, however, Clinton's political appointees brought with them a great deal of confidence that they understood Japan and knew how to deal with it. It turns out that this group of political appointees had had extensive personal experience with the Japanese market in their previous occupations. These experiences gave them confidence that they had a better understanding of 'the real Japan' and its economy than the career officials. A number of DC members had direct business experience with Japan. For instance, Roger Altman, the head of the economic policy side of the DC had worked for the Blackstone Group, and these experiences had shown him just how closed the market there really was, and that a different sort of approach was necessary.[43] John Rollwagen had been the CEO for the supercomputer firm Cray, which had been at the center of a number of disputes with Japan. In addition, Joan Spero had dealt with Japan in her

---

[40] Interview with DC official, 4/18/97. The distinction between the political appointee and the career official is a constant one in decision making in the White House, with the former closer to the President and thus more sensitive to the political implications of policy, while the career official is usually more experienced with policy matters, and more attuned to the objectives of their particular agency. By early 1993 the two groups still had not had sufficient interactions to develop a smooth working relationship. Indeed, many of the new appointees had not even been fully briefed on Japan by their own staffs before the start of the DC meetings.

[41] Interview with former NSC official, 4/9/97; see Fallows 1989a; and Choate 1990.

[42] Interview with DC official, 4/18/97.   [43] Interview with senior DC member, 4/29/97.

position with American Express, as had Charlene Barshefsky in her law practice.[44]

For these reasons the DC participants relied on their own experiences and understanding of Japan, rather than simply following the policy advice of the career bureaucrats. Because the DC participants were not yet strongly tied to the bureaucracies they represented, they were relatively free to advocate policy positions that may not have fully reflected their own agency's thinking. In fact, some of the political appointees turned out to be even more revisionist-oriented than the career bureaucrats, and started out advocating positions that went beyond even what the career officials in the economic agencies felt comfortable with.

The political appointees in the DC were later criticized by both revisionists and traditionalists for not understanding Japan well enough. In speaking with the majority of these officials, however, I found their level of knowledge to be generally high, even if their expertise was understandably narrow, since they had dealt with Japan mostly through their dealings with the business world. For the purposes of this story, it is less important to judge their competence. Rather, the point is that their experiences with the Japanese market filtered their understanding of Japan, and made them strong advocates of the revisionist critique.

At the same time, because the political appointees had virtually no experience in negotiating with the Japanese government, their independence from the career officials led to some basic mistakes. One astute career official noted later that while there were some good, smart people in this group, they did not know many of the details or background to these issues—knowledge that they could have had if they had more fully utilized the experience of their staffs, and knowledge that would have helped them avoid some of the mistakes that were made leading up to the Framework.[45]

A central characteristic of this group was their near total agreement on a revisionist-oriented view. This group agreed, to a person, on a new set of assumptions that differed notably from what prevailed in the Bush administration, and that made the need for a new policy direction clearly and painfully obvious to all. The consensus around this new set of assumptions was so nearly total, it was as if the group could not imagine how previous

---

[44] Craib 1994: 5.

[45] Interview with senior NSC official, 4/14/97. This situation was in stark contrast to the traditional way that trade policy had been made, where the career bureaucrats had a very important role to play. Under Bush, trade policy centered on the interagency Trade Policy Review Group (TPRG). In this structure, concrete policy discussions usually percolated from the bottom up, with recommendations passed upwards only after being fully vetted at lower levels of the bureaucracy.

administrations could have thought or behaved differently. As Charlene Barshefsky put it later:

When we all walked into the room for the first time, we walked in with largely a unanimity of views with respect to Japan. We all come with very broad commercial experience and we are all very bottom-line oriented. And when we walked in, it was more a question of resolving nuances than resolving or jawboning each other on ... the way in which we thought we should approach the Japan relationship.[46]

The fact that the US policy approach shifted so clearly and in such a short period of time makes tracing the deliberations of this policy group crucial, but also very difficult. As scholars interested in the impact of ideas know, actually tracing ideational factors is always a difficult task, but it is especially challenging in this case. First, none of the group's deliberations are in the public domain, so I have had to rely on extensive interviews with the group's members.[47] Second, the consensus within the group on revisionist assumptions was not contested, but rather existed from the beginning. A contentious and drawn out debate between the contending schools of thought would have made it easier to identify the triumph of the new assumptions.[48]

Third, the group met for many more hours, in total, than is usually spent on a single policy issue at the White House level. The meetings, usually attended by the deputies plus one career official, were scheduled for twice a week for two hours at a time. During the period leading up to the April Miyazawa Summit the group often met on a daily basis, and the meetings usually went on for well over two hours, at times taking up much of the working day.[49]

Finally, the discussions in this forum took on a distinctively meandering style, which made it more difficult for participants to recall the exact

[46] US Senate 1993: 21. In part, no doubt, this unanimity of views had been hammered out in the early discussions of the shadowy 'Saturday Group.'

[47] Furthermore, while at NSC I did not access any classified documents related to these discussions. I pointedly avoided accessing any materials on this group, or any other internal debate on Japan policy that appears in this book. I have pieced together this account solely from my interviews, published reports, and my intuition as to how policy is made in the White House.

[48] The fact that the deputies and their principals all seemed to be on a similar page makes determining causation even more complicated, as it is more difficult to tell whether the DC members drove the process or were 'following orders.' As argued above, however, the parameters of policy were so vague that the DC had a huge amount of leeway.

[49] Interview with veteran USTR official, 5/2/97. Ennis reports that the group engaged in 40 hours of planning sessions. In addition, the NEC's Cutter provided twice weekly breakfast briefings for NSC head Anthony Lake and NEC chair Robert Rubin. Destler (1996: 38) cites one participant calling the number and length of these meetings 'surreal.' The member went on to say that it was 'incredible to think of the brainpower and political power being spent in one-and-a-half-hour meetings (on Japan).'

parameters of the debate or to identify precise decision points; many of their accounts of the group's discussions were thus impressionistic. Also, because the meetings were so long and featured what one participant characterized as 'endless discussions,' decisions were not made, but rather evolved. More than a few of the officials I spoke with attributed the DC's informal style to its chair, Bo Cutter, who reminded at least one participant of an academic who ran the DC discussions as a loosely organized seminar rather than a tightly run decision making body. The drawn-out and repetitive nature of these discussions became something of a joke among the career officials, one of who likened the DC meetings to a television soap opera—even if you missed a few sessions, you could come back and they would still be debating the same issues.[50]

Despite these difficulties, it is important to trace the policy deliberations of this group, the task of the remainder of this chapter. After speaking with most of the DC participants, I believe it is possible to reconstruct the different positions taken by key individuals, and the parameters of the policy debate that emerged. In piecing together the different elements that made up the DC's eventual consensus position on Japan, it seems to me that this is one case where we can almost see, and trace, how the adoption of new policy assumptions led directly to an important shift in policy.

The DC Deliberations

The DC began its discussions with the unspoken consensus that the traditional emphasis on the security side of the relationship was inappropriate and needed to be changed. Almost to a person the group felt that past administrations had not taken the Japanese economic threat seriously enough, and thus had failed to pursue policies that were sufficiently forceful or aggressive. The group also agreed that attempts to solve the trade problem through tough measures in the past had been hamstrung by excessive concern for the security side of the relationship. Altman later testified that one of the key accomplishments of the DC was to shift the priorities of Japan policy:

Let us not underrate the degree to which the focus is now economic. . . . It is quite remarkable the degree to which [past administrations] were not economic or trade oriented. They focused on issues of security. They focused on global political issues.[51]

---

[50] Interview with senior NSC official, 4/14/97. Destler (1996: 38) also cites 'Cutter's 'fluid' management style.'

[51] US Senate 1993: 12.

In contrast to previous administrations this group believed that US policy had to focus on the economic side of the relationship. This consensus view was captured in the metaphor of the 'three-legged stool,' in which both the security and political legs were strong and sturdy.[52] Indeed, the security track within the DC had little to discuss, as the US–Japan alliance was deemed to be in good shape, with few problems or even disagreements. In contrast, it was only the economic leg that was weak and in need of repair. In fact, some felt that this leg was so weak and unstable that it was in danger of collapsing—and perhaps damaging the entire relationship as a result.

The group's attitude toward the traditional approach was clearly revealed in its first action—the decision to disregard a set of briefing papers that embodied standard traditional assumptions about Japan and the bilateral relationship. These policy papers had been prepared under the direction of State official William Clark in the fall of 1992, after the election but before any of the new appointees had taken their positions. The Clark materials were based on the traditional assumption that the security relationship was paramount, and thus that economic tensions needed to be 'managed.' The economic side of the analysis did not consider non-traditional policy approaches, such as a results orientation or numbers, as an option.[53] The Clark papers were further doomed in part because of Clark's image as a member of the Chrysanthemum Club. Clark had had a long career in the East Asian bureau, and was described by associates as a traditional, 'old-line' foreign policy veteran who clearly valued the security side of the relationship.[54] In this context, the Clark papers were seen by some in a doubly negative light—as a not so veiled attempt to lock the new administration into a traditional policy approach. To some, this effort only confirmed the DC's suspicions about the career officials.[55]

The Clark memos, and the traditional assumptions they represented, were taken off the table and almost literally thrown away.[56] Indeed, there was barely any fight in the DC to have them rescued, as even

---

[52] This metaphor was evidently the idea of the Deputy National Security Advisor, Sandy Berger. Interview with senior NSC official, 4/14/97; see also Lincoln 1999: 121–2.

[53] Interview with State Department official, 4/8/97.

[54] Others put it less charitably: 'Bill Clark would not have known an economics issue if it had bit him.' Interview with senior NSC official, 4/14/97; and State Department official, 4/8/97.

[55] Interview with senior NSC official, 4/14/97.

[56] In one interview a senior DC official (4/29/97) made the hand gesture of picking up a pile of papers, dropping them into an imaginary waste-basket, and wiping his hands.

representatives of the State Department gave them little or no support. All agreed that traditional assumptions were already a dead letter.

This was a crucial shift in assumptions that was nearly instantaneous and occurred with little or no debate—in some ways it was a 'non-decision' that reflected the group's near total consensus that made additional debate unnecessary. The DC was already determined to redefine Japan policy from scratch, based on a different set of assumptions. The only issue was how the new assumptions were to be operationalized.

The DC spent almost all of its time discussing the economic side of the relationship, and it was here that revisionist assumptions had their clearest impact on policy. Through the long meetings and 'endless discussions' of this group, more concrete consensus positions gradually emerged, all culminating in the conclusion that the US needed to focus on concrete 'results.'

First, the group took the 'Japanese threat' very seriously, and argued that the US needed to take a more aggressive and sustained policy approach. The DC members seemed to have stopped short of viewing Japan in alarmist terms, or at least did not go to the extremes of some revisionist analysts, that the US economy was about to be swallowed up by the Japanese juggernaut, or other such rhetoric. But even if the group did not voice such extreme views, their deliberations took place in a broader context of alarm and concern over Japan's growing economic strength.[57] At another level all agreed that failure to increase access to the Japanese market would threaten the revival of America's export capabilities and competitiveness, and thus the revival of the US economy—which after all was the administration's top priority. The group also agreed that Japan's growing competitive advantage in high-tech industry was potentially damaging to key US industries and to the US economic future. Tyson's impact on this issue was central, as all in the group were familiar with her published support of the strategic trade argument. Failure to open the Japanese market for US high technology firms would have two consequences: it would allow the Japanese to take advantage of economies of scale afforded by a protected, safe-haven domestic market, and it would deny these same benefits to American firms, which needed access to the second largest economy in the world to achieve leading edge competitiveness. Failure to open the Japanese market would put a long line of future technologies in the same position as

---

[57] Although Japan's economic downturn had been ongoing since 1990, it appears that no one in the DC believed it would last much longer. All assumed that the Japanese economy would soon re-emerge, leaner and meaner.

computers and semiconductors, all of which were seen to be at risk from Japanese competition.[58]

The group also agreed that gaining access to the Japanese market through conventional means was next to impossible. There was no doubt in any-one's mind that the economy was heavily protected, and perhaps inher-ently so. Most of the DC members had had first-hand experience trying to crack that market, and so all scoffed at the Japanese government's insist-ence that its market was the most open in the world. The group also shared the sense that the Japanese economy was uniquely structured, with insti-tutions that differed dramatically from the US model. Much of the group's discussions touched on the role of market structures such as the *keiretsu*, cross-shareholding, cartels, and business–government collusion. In addi-tion, all in the DC had had to deal with the Japanese government and its bureaucrats in their own efforts to crack the market, so were quite receptive to assertions of bureaucratic dominance.

Finally, the group coalesced around the notion that the Japanese econ-omy should be thought of as operating on a different set of principles than what pertained in the US. The key voice in this discussion again appears to have been Tyson, whose recent book made this argument in easily under-stood terms. The view of the Japanese economy as operating on other-than-market principles was also strongly held by those who had had direct business dealings with Japan, including Altman, Rollwagen, Spero, and Wolf, and by the other academics in the group, Summers and Blinder.

The group's rejection of traditionalist assumptions led naturally to a rejection of the policies based on those assumptions. The DC first concen-trated its fire on the process-oriented approach of the SII talks, an approach that the group felt was exhausting and overly complicated, and that was futile as well. The group rejected the pursuit of any more SII-type negoti-ations, or any other process-oriented approach aimed at changing the nature of the Japanese system, as this would be time-consuming, would create a great deal of animosity and, given the system's resistance to change, would most likely lead to nothing positive.[59] The group's repudi-ation of process-oriented negotiations soon hardened to include virtually

---

[58] Tyson 1993. The other academic in the group, Larry Summers, also backed the strategic trade view.

[59] Interview with senior NSC official, 4/14/97. Other career officials rejected it without even understanding it (interview with DC official, 4/18/97). In part, criticisms of Bush policy also reflected a new administration's presumption that its predecessors had failed and that its job was to put things right. Some of my sources stressed this point, noting that the new political team was naturally open to ways to differentiate themselves from the Bush administration (interview with senior NSC official, 4/14/97).

any market-based negotiation. Early on, the group's consensus shifted to the position that all past negotiations with Japan had failed, that not one of the numerous trade agreements had borne any fruit.

It should be noted that the argument about the futility of all past negotiations clearly stemmed from the DC participants rather than the career officials. In fact, the DC's sudden public statements dismissing all past agreements took the career officials by surprise, and they found themselves in the awkward position of having to scramble to find some evidence to back this argument up.[60] Some career officials in fact warned that a blanket repudiation of all agreements would undermine US objectives: if the goal was to make sure that future agreements were to be successful, we should seek to strengthen the enforcement of current agreements, not repudiate them across the board.[61]

The DC essentially concluded that the market liberalization approach itself was flawed, as simply negotiating away market barriers would do nothing to insure access to Japan's uniquely structured markets—Bush's traditional approach was futile because the US was dealing with an 'untraditional' economy.

More particularly, the group criticized the Bush approach for not being concrete enough on both the 'front end' and 'back end' of its trade negotiations—that is, Japan needed to be forced into specific commitments on market access, and held to real consequences if those commitments were not fulfilled. On the front end of the equation, demands for access had usually been unspecified and vague, and it was felt that this gave the Japanese government too much leeway in deciding how to implement an agreement. Too often, because goals were unspecified, the Japanese side would pronounce an agreement a success, while the US trade agencies and Congress saw only a lack of real progress—which was then usually attributed to bad faith on the part of Japan. The group also felt that past agreements did not have effective enforcement mechanisms built in, either in terms of sanctions or even simply some monitoring arrangements. Given unspecified demands and the lack of an enforcement mechanism, it was not surprising that agreements were not yielding any results.

* * *

What quickly emerged from the DC discussions was a clear—and uncontested—consensus that concrete 'results' had to be included in any future

---

[60] Interview with veteran USTR official, 5/2/97; USTR official 4/9/97; and USTR official, 4/15/97.

[61] Interview with veteran USTR official, 5/2/97.

negotiations. Essentially, the US had to more clearly specify, up front, what goals each agreement was designed to achieve, and that these goals needed to be somehow made enforceable. This consensus was most strongly supported by the representatives of the USTR and Commerce—not a surprise as this had been the longstanding position of both organizations. What was different this time around was the shift of two other agencies, CEA and Treasury, that had previously been the staunchest opponents of deviations from a market-based approach.

Tyson, the new chair of the CEA, was the leading intellectual voice calling for the need for a results-oriented approach, a policy position that her CEA predecessors would have found to be unacceptable. Another unique aspect of the role she played was her participation in the deputies-level deliberations—normally, a cabinet-level official such as Tyson would not be involved in such discussions so directly. Her participation in this group reflected both the informal nature of policy making in the early Clinton administration, but also her own strong intellectual stake on the Japan trade issue. Similarly, the Treasury representative, Lawrence Summers, took the unorthodox position in favor of a results orientation, a substantial deviation from Treasury's normally free-market approach. Some participants recall a memo from Summers that endorsed the argument that the Japanese economy was unique and thus that the SII approach was likely to fail. Summers also deviated from Treasury's traditional market-oriented position on macroeconomic issues, and instead surprised many by his support for some sort of target on the macro side— the idea that Japan should reduce its trade surplus below a fixed percentage of its GDP. Summers was also in support of the sector-specific approach to negotiations.[62]

The significance of the role played by Tyson and Summers goes beyond their specific policy positions. Equally important was that the representatives of two usually free-trade oriented agencies were now willing to back policies that were 'previously considered to be off limits.'[63] With the two agencies most likely to oppose a results approach now among its proponents, the balance in the DC had clearly shifted toward the revisionist line. It should also be noted that both were clearly operating on the basis of their own understandings and assumptions about Japan, rather than the positions of their career bureaucrats.

[62] Interview with senior DC member, 4/29/97; and Treasury official, 5/14/97. Summers did not advocate numerical targets for these sectoral negotiations. Summers, like Tyson, later backed away from his support of the macro target, as described later.
[63] Interview with Commerce official, 4/9/97.

The group's new assumptions about Japan, and their call for a more results-oriented approach, found a receptive audience at higher political levels in the administration. Robert Rubin, the NEC head who enjoyed very strong ties to the President, had also had extensive dealings with Japan while on Wall Street. Although Rubin did not have a public record in terms of his position on Japan, he turned out to be one of the most hard-line of any of Clinton's top advisors and quite amenable to a revisionist view. As one career official put it, 'Rubin didn't see a tradeoff between the alliance and trade—he didn't value either!'[64] Rubin was clearly in favor of a harsh and aggressive approach. Treasury Secretary Lloyd Bentsen was originally seen as a strong critic of Japan, but does not appear to have played a central role in formulating policy in this period. There are few public records of his policy position, but the Japan Economic Institute relates the story that Bentsen told one Japanese official in a private meeting that 'since the Japanese economy is not a free-market system, Japanese bureaucrats should not worry about the substance of the agreements they make but instead should focus on outcomes.'[65] Two close political allies of the President, Ron Brown and Mickey Kantor, who had both been criticized for their lack of experience on trade matters, also turned out to be strongly in favor of revisionist-oriented policies toward Japan. Although neither was a known revisionist when they first took their positions, almost everything they knew about Japan came from the revisionists; furthermore, their on-the-job training was entirely revisionist in orientation. From his first day on the job Brown was tutored on Japan by his key deputies, and soon was espousing a perfect revisionist line.[66] Kantor turned out to be the senior official who most clearly embraced the revisionist position, becoming a 'true believer,' according to one deputy.[67]

While the DC had clearly concluded that it would be seeking results-oriented agreements, the group was not yet ready to operationalize exactly what this meant, and thus was not able to explicitly define would it would demand of the Japanese. This indecision reflected a disagreement between two camps in the DC, known later as the 'hard-liners' and the 'moderates,'

---

[64] Interview with senior State Department official, 4/24/97; see Woodward 1994. Destler (1996: 37) reports that 'Rubin considered himself a hawk on [Japan], having had unhappy experiences with Japan at Goldman Sachs.'

[65] *JEI Report* 10/14/94: 10.

[66] John Rollwagen and Derek Shearer were Brown's key advisors on Japan (*Inside US Trade* (4/30/93: 11).

[67] Most others I spoke with agreed that Kantor truly believed the revisionist logic, but some felt that he was mostly motivated by political considerations—a standard image of Kantor that the media has embraced.

that was hardly visible at the time but that was to hamper the US all the way through the end of the Framework talks.

On the one hand the hard-liners argued that the only way to solve the Japan problem was to insist on concrete, sanctionable numbers. That is, on the front end of the negotiations the US had to achieve something close to quantitative targets, including at a maximum a clear commitment by the Japanese government to set aside an explicit share of the market for foreign products. The hard-line camp also argued that on the back end of the negotiations the Japanese government had to be made accountable or liable to achieve the agreed upon goals. For the hard-liners this meant making it clear that the Japanese government would have to take responsibility to ensure that the numerical targets would be achieved; no longer would vague promises of expectations be enough. Furthermore, the hard-liners felt that any agreements needed to be made enforceable under US trade laws, including the explicit threat of sanctions. Only agreements that included some 'teeth' had any hope of success.

The hard-line position reflected the majority opinion in the DC. Tyson was initially identified as a key proponent of numerical targets, with one DC participant remembering her as a 'tigress who came in pretty hard on numbers.' Others recall that a version of the memo she had written for the Saturday group served as the critical concept paper in the DC, this time explicitly including the idea of numerical targets.[68] The precise impact of Tyson and her memo is subject to some controversy, as some participants felt she was not so strongly in favor of numbers, or that they had expected her to be even more aggressive.[69] But all of the DC members were familiar with her book, which they interpreted as a clear call for market share targets. Regardless, what was crucial is that supporters of a numerical target approach coalesced behind her. Another strong advocate of a numerical approach was Deputy Commerce Secretary John Rollwagen. In addition to being the CEO of Cray, Rollwagen was a prominent member of ACTPN, where his strongly revisionist views on Japan's market structure and government role helped to shape that group's advocacy of numerical targets. Rollwagen continued to advocate his revisionist view of Japan and the need for numerical targets while he was a member of the DC.[70] The USTR,

---

[68] Interviews with senior NSC official, 4/14/97; veteran Commerce official, 4/14/97; and Commerce official, 4/9/97.

[69] Interview with DC official, 4/18/97. This may also have reflected Tyson's later change in position.

[70] His role, however, was cut short because of his involvement in a political scandal, which caused him to resign from his post in May 1993.

represented by Charlene Barshefsky, was also a strong advocate of numerical targets. Barshefsky was to play a more prominent role later in the Framework, becoming one of the strongest proponents of pushing America's maximum trade demands. Finally, Summers of Treasury was initially seen as a member of the hard-line camp, in part because his support for a macroeconomic target was so different from anything that Treasury had ever endorsed. It does not appear that Summers ever advocated numerical targets on the sectoral side, however, but neither did he oppose the pursuit of such targets.[71] In terms of the President's cabinet-level advisors, USTR's Kantor and Commerce's Brown became the most visible proponents of seeking numerical targets, a position they maintained through the end of the Framework. None of the other cabinet members were as vocal as Kantor or Brown on this issue; more significantly, none took a stand rejecting the numbers approach.

The hard-line position favoring numerical targets got an unexpected boost on 19 March when it was announced that the US share of the Japanese semiconductor market had suddenly risen above the 20 per cent level in the fourth quarter of 1992, the deadline specified in the Semiconductor Agreement. While the Japanese government and some economists sought to explain this as being caused by market forces, the message that the DC took was clear: the only agreements that work are those that include concrete numerical targets. DC hard-liners increasingly touted the Semiconductor Agreement for its inclusion of clearly defined results, and because it contained concrete enforcement mechanisms. Some officials took to labeling the SCA as the *only* successful bilateral agreement. Overnight, the hard-line position in the DC in favor of numbers was clearly strengthened. The semiconductor announcement and its timing were thus, according to one US official, 'MITI's worst nightmare.'[72]

In contrast, a smaller group of DC officials, known later as the moderates, while still committed to achieving results, were not entirely convinced that this required explicit numerical targets, or that they had to be legally sanctionable. On the front end of the negotiations, the moderates felt that instead of market shares, it might be enough to define a series of

[71] Colleagues of Summers recall him often arguing two sides of an issue, in typical academic fashion. Combined with his impressive intellectual style, this perhaps confused listeners as to where Summers actually stood (interview with Treasury official, 5/14/97). Also, because Summers later defected from the hard-line camp, it is even more difficult to pin down his exact initial position.

[72] Interview with USTR official, 4/15/97. The fourth quarter figure of 20.2 per cent was well above consensus projections; officials up to that point were focused on how the US should respond if the target was not met (*Inside US Trade* 3/19/93: 14).

numerical or quantitative indicators that could be used to verify that American exports to Japan were actually increasing. Furthermore, the moderates were not convinced that the agreements needed to be made explicitly sanctionable under American trade law. Rather, so long as the Japanese government was willing to politically commit itself to achieving results, then suasion, cajoling, and pressure might be enough to ensure compliance.[73]

It should be stressed that even the moderates never disputed the need for a results orientation in negotiating with Japan; in this sense, this group was also driven by revisionist assumptions. They in fact considered themselves to be allied with the hard-line camp, and later preferred to describe themselves as 'moderate hard-liners.' Their moderation was thus more in terms of the specifics of the approach—how strongly to insist on actual numerical targets, and whether to force the Japanese government to be legally liable for their enforcement. The underlying goal of achieving results was never disputed.[74]

Initially, the moderates were in the minority, with only three DC officials clearly identified in this group from the beginning—NEC head Bo Cutter, Joan Spero from State, and Alan Blinder, Tyson's deputy at CEA.[75] Surprisingly, however, it appears that it was only Blinder who spoke out most explicitly against numerical targets.[76] Also, many of the career bureaucrats supported the moderate position, but as theirs was a support role they were less able to vocalize their discomfort with the maximum hard-line position in the DC meetings.

[73] These officials were also aware that provisions such as Super 301 would likely be found illegal under existing trade rules, especially in the soon to be inaugurated WTO, and did not want to risk having this tool rejected outright.

[74] Other moderates in the group had more practical reasons for being skeptical about numbers, for instance the issue of how to identify sectors for negotiation in a non-politicized way. Others felt that the numbers approach would be no more than an artificial solution, met by government fiat rather than a real change in market access. If US industry was not prepared to follow up by focusing on gaining true access to the market, these negotiating efforts would not be enough to solve the problem (interview with senior NSC official, 4/14/97).

[75] Again, it is not clear when their discomfort with numbers first appeared. Others remember both as being in favor early on (interview with NEC official, 4/21/97).

[76] Interview with DC official, 4/18/97. This is a bit ironic, given that Blinder (1990) had earlier contributed to revisionism with his article, 'There are Capitalists and Then There are the Japanese.'

As discussed in Chapter 7, over time a number of formerly hard-line officials did defect to join the moderates, including notably Tyson and Summers, in part reflecting the realization that the US was not going to be able to achieve its hard-line demands. Put another way, after the US had backed away from its initial hard-line goals, it became harder to find officials who wanted to be known as advocates of a position that had failed.

However, because Cutter was the head of the DC, it was inevitable that his views would carry extra weight in determining the US bargaining position. At this point I must admit that I found Cutter and his position to be one of the most enigmatic parts of the DC process, in that I heard as many versions of his position as the number of interviews I conducted. From what I can gather, Cutter was not comfortable with officially demanding market shares or numerical targets, and seems to have vetoed some of the language of the hard-liners. Thus, the US never publicly presented the maximum hard-line demands as *official* US policy.

Yet Cutter was not willing or able to take these maximum hard-line demands completely off the table. There were a number of reasons for this. First, Cutter seems to have seen his role as a moderator or consensus builder for the group, and thus was reluctant to decisively impose his own viewpoints. Also, because the hard-line view was the initial consensus, Cutter felt that he could not override it completely. Second, as a negotiating tactic, Cutter and the other moderates saw some benefit in approaching the Japanese with something close to its maximum demands, even if there was little chance that those goals could be achieved. In fact, some felt this tactic might make the fallback position easier to attain later on.

Finally, the relative quietness of the moderates may have reflected something close to wishful thinking: there was at least some chance that the Japanese government might be willing to accept numerical targets or, more likely, some form of an agreement that would include enough quantitative indicators so as to be the functional equivalent of targets. In this sense, the prevailing attitude was, as John Kunkel notes, 'to get as much as you can.'[77] The moderates also seem to have had some confidence in their own ability to come to a compromise with their Tokyo counterparts; the moderates thought themselves to be reasonable people, and thus believed that they could get Japan to be reasonable as well.

For these reasons the initial US approach to Japan that was unveiled in March 1993, as discussed in the next chapter, appeared to be very close to the hard-line position of achieving some sort of quantitative agreement with Japan, perhaps even including a market share target. At the very least, any agreement had to include numerical indicators that would be used to ensure that Japan was faithfully implementing its commitments—in other words, the US needed *real* results.

---

[77] Kunkel 2003: 167. The phrase actually came from Commerce official Marjory Searing, cited in ibid.: 172.

The split in opinion in the DC on this score was thus not made public, and did not become evident until much later. One reason for this is that the DC tried very hard to maintain an outward appearance of unity by deliberately keeping all internal disagreements under wraps. One of the DC's earliest decisions was to try to 'speak with one voice' when it came to negotiating with Japan. In the past it often seemed that Japanese officials were able to use a divide-and-conquer strategy to exploit internal divisions in the US government. Thus, even if the moderates were still skeptical, they were persuaded to swallow their misgivings and get behind the hard-line consensus. In reality, however, the US was less unified than it appeared to be on the surface, and had not truly come to a consensus on what it was going to try to achieve in the negotiations.

At the time, however, the DC as a whole did not believe that this lack of consensus would really matter. That is, both hard-liners and moderates took an incredibly cavalier attitude toward the upcoming negotiations: the prevailing view was that once the DC made up its mind exactly what to ask for, the Japanese government would eventually be forced to go along. True, the Japanese might protest, but in the end they would be forced to cooperate. Kantor later summed up this underlying attitude when he exclaimed during one frustrating phase of the Framework negotiations, 'we're the US, damn it,' as if that should be enough.[78]

This overconfidence and lack of concern was to prove fatal. With the benefit of hindsight it is clear that the division between the two camps hampered the US negotiating position throughout the Framework. Not only was the US unable to define clear initial objectives, it was also never able to reconcile the two contending camps. Most importantly, the moderates were never able to fully control or rein in the hard-liners. Thus, even though the official US position did not embrace the quest for numerical targets, the hard-liners were able to work behind the scenes and outside of the formal negotiating process to try to achieve their objectives through what one participant later described as 'guerilla tactics.' Furthermore, because the DC was never able to completely and sincerely disavow these hard-line demands, this also allowed the Japanese side to characterize the complicated American position as simply 'managed trade,' which was a relatively easy target to shoot down.

The inability of the DC to reconcile these two camps—or what Cutter later described as an 'unstated and undigested disagreement' on what exactly the US was seeking—explains a great deal of the later dynamics of

[78] Interview with senior NSC official, 4/18/97.

the Framework talks.[79] That is, all of the later conflicting and confusing statements that were to come out of the Clinton team, and their many seemingly contradictory negotiating positions, can be traced back to this internal division. Not only did the US fail to 'speak with one voice,' the two camps later acted independently to try to undermine each other in order to achieve their own favored policy. In the end, this lack of unity was a major cause of the US not only failing to achieve its maximum hard-line demands, but also failing to even achieve the moderates' fallback position.

* * *

The policy process in the early Clinton administration was also notable for the very quiet position taken by the usually more 'traditional' agencies— State, Defense, and NSC—none of which spoke up in opposition to the shift in emphasis to the economic side of the relationship, the decision to seek results-oriented negotiations, or on the debate about asking for targets. In part, this lack of voice was due to the structure of the process, which made it difficult for these agencies to weigh in on the specifics of the economic debate. This arrangement did increase the autonomy of the economic group, giving 'officials concerned with defense and security issues...far fewer chances to quell debate over economic conflicts with Japan.'[80] But the two tracks were not completely separate, as both groups could make inputs on the other, and since both issues were being jointly coordinated by Cutter and the NSC's Sandy Berger. These agencies, had they wished to, could have made their opposition to the new policy approach felt.

A combination of factors explains why they did not. The most important is that the pol-mil community basically saw the security relationship with Japan as fairly solid, and agreed that it was the economic side of the relationship that needed to be fixed. Security officials did not object strongly to a hardening of the economic line so long as the security side was not put in jeopardy or used as leverage to gain economic concessions. Indeed, some in the pol-mil agencies shared the sense that addressing the economic problems might serve to strengthen, not undermine, the overall relationship.

There were also dynamics within each of the agencies that contributed to their low-profile reactions to the economic debate. As described in the last chapter, in the case of the State Department, the internal battle had been

---

[79] As Cutter put it to Kunkel, 'probably from the beginning there was a different point of view...but it was not very much debated in those early months because I think it was assumed by everyone that words were being heard in the same way' (Kunkel 2003: 170).

[80] Ennis 1993a: 9. This decision to discuss the two issues on separate tracks also seems to have been made without much debate. It also made some organizational sense, as the meetings were under the co-direction of the NSC and NEC.

shifting, putting traditionalists clearly in the minority. This was true even at the top of the Department: although Secretary of State Warren Christopher cannot be described as a revisionist, he was known as a supporter of a very hard economic line. He was evidently not willing to see trade issues ignored for the sake of protecting the alliance, a stance some officials believed stemmed from his frustrating experience with Japan during the Textile Wrangle in the 1970s.[81] Throughout the Department many Japan specialists were themselves adopting revisionist assumptions, including the need for a more results-oriented approach. Even those who did not push this line felt under pressure not to be caught on the wrong side of the debate—being labeled a member of the Chrysanthemum Club could be fatal to one's career.

In the Department of Defense, there was growing support for a more activist Japan trade policy. As described in the last chapter, the struggle between the acquisitions side of the Department versus the Japan policy side had been ongoing for years, with the former gradually gaining ground, particularly after the end of the Cold War. Further, Clinton's new appointees on the acquisitions side brought with them an even stronger concern that America was becoming technologically dependent on Japan, and this policy thrust dominated the Department's thinking for the first two years of the administration.[82] In the case of the NSC, it was the creation of a new rival organization, the NEC, that helps explain why it did not play its customary role of coordinating and mediating between economic and security concerns. Early in the administration the NEC enjoyed a great deal of momentum, in part because it was the administration's new creation, and also because NEC head Rubin was so close to the President.

Personnel decisions also played a role in why the traditional agencies had little influence on economic policy. In the case of State, the East Asia Bureau was dominated by China experts, while the Department's top Japan experts were all shifted to other duties. In any case, the DC tapped the Economics Bureau to participate in the group, rather than the East Asia Bureau. This meant that it would be generalists, Joan Spero and her deputy Dan Tarullo, rather than Japan specialists, who would have the most direct impact on policy. The Department of Defense seems to have been slow in getting its personnel in place, and was thus at a huge disadvantage compared to the other agencies; often, the Department would be represented by a desk officer, two or three ranks below the other members of the DC. In the case of the NSC, none of the Directors for Asian Affairs was an expert in

---

[81] Interview with US Embassy official, Tokyo, 4/7/97. Christopher was a career official in the State Department at the time.
[82] Interview with Department of Defense official, 4/1/97.

dealing with Japan relations, and certainly did not espouse a strong traditional position.

Finally, there was an element of bureaucratic strategy at work as well: many pol-mil officials could see that the administration was clearly going in a new direction on trade policy, and felt that it would be foolhardy to get in the way. As one official put it, none of these agencies wanted to 'get rolled' on this issue.[83]

Whatever the reasons, the traditional agencies did not play their traditional roles. Veterans of past policy debates were surprised that there was so little debate in the DC about the possible tradeoffs involved in a more aggressive economic approach.[84] As one DC participant put it, 'this was the first time in 40 years the NSC supported a tougher trade line.' Another participant put it more bluntly: the traditional agencies 'were not able to check the shrill stuff . . . They let the economic guys have their way.'[85]

---

[83] Interview with Department of Defense official, 5/13/97. Ennis (1995: 19) cites a Pentagon official that 'there was a fear early on in the Clinton Administration that defending US–Japan security relations would be political suicide . . . People were afraid that if they spoke up they would get killed.'

[84] Interview with Commerce official, 4/9/97.

[85] Interview with NEC official, 4/21/97, and Treasury official, 5/14/97, respectively.

5

Implementing the New Japan Policy

In a matter of months, beginning with the education of candidate and then President Clinton to the emergence of the consensus on results in the Deputies Committee in March 1993, new assumptions about Japan and its economy had been institutionalized in the US government. These new assumptions led directly to a dramatic shift in America's trade policy approach. In this new era of bilateral negotiations economics would trump security, and results would overshadow process. From now on, the US would avoid market access negotiations that were process-oriented, but rather would only consider agreements that would guarantee some sort of concrete results. Because 'diffuse reciprocity' would not work with the Japanese, what was needed was some form of 'specific reciprocity.'

The next task for the DC was to get the Japanese to agree to the results-oriented approach. It seems that during the long discussions in the DC, the one question that was not considered seriously enough was whether the Japanese government would be willing to 'play ball.' The unspoken assumption was that the Japanese might not like numbers or a results orientation, but that once the US government decided what it wanted, and was willing to get behind it, the Japanese would eventually come around.

The US Signals its New Approach

The first official signal of an emerging shift in US policy came on March 9, 1993, when Mickey Kantor testified before the Senate finance committee that as the result of the ongoing Japan policy review the US had decided 'to find a better approach for dealing with Japan trade issues.' In this context Kantor mentioned that the DC was 'actively considering' the use of some sort of quantitative indicators that would require Japan to commit to a level of market penetration that would pertain if its markets were open, and that the US was particularly interested in strategic industries.[1]

Indications that the US was about to shift toward a results orientation were reinforced at a widely publicized public forum on March 17 sponsored by Clyde Prestowitz's new think tank, the Economic Strategy Institute. Here the panelists discussing Japan displayed an 'unprecedented willingness to adopt a results-oriented approach.'[2] Most notably, two administration officials voiced their support for a results orientation, at least unofficially. Laura Tyson, the new CEA chair, explicitly endorsed the pursuit of market sharing arrangements:

We've had the greatest successes . . . in areas where we have taken a very specific sectoral approach . . . I think of the semiconductor agreement (which if you look at its history) you would judge that agreement in terms of its market-access provisions to have been a successful agreement . . . [In the sectoral approach] you occasionally deal with looking at a market-sharing arrangement—which we did in the semiconductor market access agreement—that's an important approach.[3]

Although Tyson was careful to argue that market share arrangements were only one facet of a multi-track approach that should include structural and macroeconomic negotiations, the endorsement by a high ranking official of this new trade approach was taken by many as a signal that the administration had already decided to change policy.[4]

Another official, Derek Shearer, the campaign advisor who had been designated Deputy Commerce Undersecretary, presented an explicitly revisionist argument:

We should be clear that Japanese capitalism is different than American capitalism . . . I think its clear that they operate on some different principles, different forms of organization [and so] we should also be somewhat humble about our ability to change that society from the outside . . .

So I think we should junk SII, and I'm for results-oriented policy . . . [We should tell Japan] Here is the results we would like. You know your business and your people, you figure out how to get the results. If it involves changing how you operate, that's up to you. If you want to allocate the market share differently and

---

[1] *Inside US Trade*, 3/12/93: 6.
[2] *PR Newswire* 3/18/93, Nikkei Needs Database <http://www.nikkeieu.com/needs/>.
[3] Economic Strategy Institute 1993: 99.
[4] The mere fact that administration officials would attend an ESI meeting was taken by some in the media as significant in itself. Commerce official John Rollwagen was also present, but evidently did not speak (*Inside US Trade* 3/19/93: 6).

include American firms, that's fine. We've given you clarity, we would like these results, but we leave how you implement it up to you.[5]

The administration was also making it clear that it would hold the Japanese responsible for the fulfillment of all existing trade agreements, an area where it charged that the Bush administration had failed completely. As Kantor put it in a speech to the SIA on March 3, in reference to the Semiconductor Agreement and other bilateral deals, 'we will enforce those agreements. We have to or we shouldn't have entered into them in the first place.'[6]

A more controversial indication of the new approach was a March 26 letter from Kantor and Ron Brown addressed to MITI Minister Mori Yoshiro, that pressed the Japanese government to fulfill its 'pledge' to increase US sales of auto parts that it had made during Bush's January 1992 visit. As described in Chapter 3, during that visit the major Japanese auto firms had announced their plans to increase purchases of US-made auto parts to US$19 billion by the end of 1994. However, the Japanese government had made it clear that these plans were voluntary, private ones, and thus not a commitment made by the Japanese government, and this understanding was later acknowledged by USTR Carla Hills. Yet, the Kantor-Brown letter now took a harsh tone in criticizing Japan for not doing enough to fulfill its commitment, and demanded to be informed of 'the steps Japan intends to take to meet its pledge to expand US auto parts sourcing.' Kantor later told reporters that 'the letter speaks for itself,' and that 'we expect the Japanese government to live up to its commitments.'[7]

As will be described in detail in the next chapter, this letter had an enormous impact on the policy deliberations that were at that moment taking place within the Japanese government. Officials at that time were scrutinizing every clue as to the Clinton administration's likely policy approach, and were already becoming convinced that the US would seek some form of numerical targets, and would then try to hold the Japanese

---

[5] Economic Strategy Institute 1993: 28 and 32. Shearer was here making an analogy comparing the Japanese economy to the Tsukiji fish market, where he believed market shares were allocated 'very subtly... using hand signals and ways that only anthropologists can decipher.' It should be noted that Shearer was not a member of the DC, and his impact on it was indirect, through his boss, John Rollwagen. Shearer's exact role was not known to the audience at the time, however, and because he had been known to be an inside advisor to Clinton on Japan trade policy, it was assumed that he was speaking for the administration.

[6] *Inside US Trade* 3/5/93: 1.

[7] Ibid.: 4/2/93: 9. The letter is reprinted on page ten of the same issue. The letter was given to Mori during a March 26 meeting with Kantor. Kantor had previously hinted about his position on Japan's auto 'pledge,' but only informally, as in a February 26 statement to reporters (ibid.: 3/5/93: 4).

government accountable for achieving those targets. These officials were also concerned that any government role in setting even informal and vaguely defined goals, a la the 1992 auto agreement, would later be twisted by the US into something more formal and specific. Essentially, the message of the Kantor-Brown letter—and its less than diplomatic tone—confirmed all of their worst fears. This letter helped to shift the balance in the policy debates in Japan by undermining those officials who favored some sort of compromise, and strengthening those who insisted that Japan needed to reject any form of numerical targets once and for all.

Considering the later impact that this letter had, it is interesting that it did not fully reflect the consensus of the DC, which had still not made a final decision on how hard to actively push for numerical targets, and on whether to make these numbers sanctionable. Rather, the letter appears to have been initiated more by Kantor, and to a lesser extent by Brown, as a way to preemptively push Japan toward a market-share approach.[8] It also reflected the hard-liners dissatisfaction with the tone of the DC discussions, which reflected Cutter's more moderate position. In this sense, the letter was the first of the 'guerilla tactics' employed by the hard-liners to move the process in their direction. Furthermore, the letter evidently was not cleared through the normal White House process, in which concerned agencies are consulted and given the chance to comment on any such communication. In part this was because the NEC, which should have been the central clearinghouse for a letter such as this, was not yet fully established with all of its systems up and running. According to a senior NEC official, 'we were still in disarray.'[9] In any case, all of the officials outside of USTR and Commerce I spoke with say that they never saw the letter until after it had been sent out; indeed, most knew of it only after it appeared in *Inside US Trade*.

Once they saw the letter, however, all of these career officials understood the impact it would have on the Japanese government, knowing that it would indicate that Clinton was indeed seeking to negotiate along the lines of the Semiconductor Agreement, and that it would galvanize MITI resistance. One US career official put it more bluntly: 'We knew MITI would go nuts.'[10]

---

[8] Evidently, Kantor had wanted to use even stronger language, including making a reference to Japan's 'commitment' in the auto parts talks of January 1992. Kantor agreed to delete this wording, but insisted that the harsh tone of the letter remain as is, despite some objections of career officials in both the USTR and Commerce (interviews with veteran USTR official, 5/2/97; and veteran Commerce official, 4/14/97).

[9] Interview with very senior DC official, 4/29/97. Destler (1996: 37) describes the letter as an 'early glitch' on the part of the NEC.

[10] Interview with veteran Commerce official, 4/9/97; and USTR official, 4/15/97.

* * *

President Clinton unveiled the new policy approach during his summit meeting with Prime Minister Miyazawa on April 16, in which the two leaders agreed to initiate within the next three months a new 'framework' for economic relations. In his public statements following the meeting, Clinton made the gist of the new approach clear. First, the President argued that the economic side of the relationship needed to be elevated:

During the Cold War, security relations often overshadowed other considerations— especially economic concerns . . . [But during the summit] economics were at the heart of our discussions. I stressed that the rebalancing of our relationship in this new era requires an elevated attention to our economic relations.

Later, in response to a reporter's question, Clinton made it clear that the US approach would be results oriented:

What I asked the Prime Minister for was a change in the direction of our relationship so we could focus on specific sectors and specific structures, with the view toward getting results . . . I think when we focus on specific areas, even though we may differ about specifically how we should do that, we tend to make progress.

I would like to have a focus on specific sectors of the economy, and I would like to obviously have specific results. We had a semiconductor agreement which gave some hope that this approach could work. There was also a more general commitment in the area of auto parts which has shown some progress.[11]

While the President evidently did not mention targets in his private discussions with Miyazawa, Bo Cutter in his subsequent press briefing confirmed that the President had asked for an agreement that included 'measures' and 'indicators of success.'[12]

As the US team got down to hammering out its initial Framework proposals, it still assumed that even if Japan protested against a results orientation or numerical targets, it would eventually give in. More specifically, the US understood that Japan was extremely sensitive to phrases such as 'numerical targets' and 'market shares,' but felt that if the US were to tone down its rhetoric and refrain from using these controversial terms, then the Japanese would eventually be persuaded to give in. The US thus discounted or reinterpreted Japan's opposition to 'managed trade' as simply a rejection of hard market share targets. For instance, Prime Minister Miyazawa himself during the April 16 summit stressed that resolving the

---

[11] Office of the Federal Register 1993: 442. (The President's News Conference with Prime Minister Kiichi Miyazawa of Japan, April 16, 1993.)
[12] Ibid.: 5.

trade issue 'cannot be realized with managed trade nor under the threat of unilateralism.'[13] The Japanese government, in late May, issued a formal statement of the principles under which it would negotiate with the US. This document ended with a section entitled 'No Managed Trade,' that came to the pointed conclusion that 'measures amounting to managed trade will not be taken by either [governments and that] there will be no discussion of establishing numerical targets.'[14]

As a result, the DC in the month following the April summit dropped the phrases 'targets' and 'market shares.' At the same time, the DC remained committed to making sure that the agreements came very close to achieving verifiable results. The task now was to include enough numbers and quantitative indicators, and to make these sufficiently enforceable, so as to achieve a concrete bottom line. Still undecided was just how concrete the numbers and indicators needed to be.

The DC now turned its attention to the structure of the new round of bilateral negotiations, which the two heads of states had agreed to initiate by the G-7 summit in Tokyo in July. The result of this round of discussions was a document entitled 'US Proposal for Bilateral Framework with Japan,' which was approved by the DC on May 14, the cabinet on May 18, and ultimately by the President.[15]

Revisionist assumptions clearly lay behind the provisions of the US proposal. The DC rejected a process-oriented approach as unlikely to be effective. Similarly, on the macro side, the group decided that manipulating macro variables and leaving it to the market to generate outcomes was futile. Rather, the group called for a specific reduction of Japan's current account surplus, leaving it to Japan to figure out how to achieve this goal. Specifically, the US proposed a 'basic bargain,' in which the Japanese government would:

1. Reduce its current account surplus to a range of 1.0 to 2.0 per cent of GDP within three years; and
2. Increase its manufactured imports by one-third as a share of GDP within three years.[16]

---

[13] Ibid.: 441.

[14] Reprinted in *Inside US Trade* 6/4/93: 9. Japan's positions are described in detail in Chapter 6.

[15] *Inside US Trade* 5/21/93: 18 and 6/11/93: 13–14. The 'US Proposal' is reprinted in *Inside US Trade* (6/11/93: 14). This proposal was delivered to Ambassador Kuriyama Takakazu on June 7.

[16] In return, the US would agree to (1) reduce its budget deficit, increase public investment; and (2) maintain an open market, but only so long as Japan made 'satisfactory progress' in opening its market.

This results-oriented proposal on the macro side meant that Japan would have to decrease its current account surplus, which stood at US$118 billion, or about 3.1 per cent of GDP in 1992, by one-third to two-thirds within three years. Its manufactured imports that year totaled US$117 billion, and this would rise by about US$40 billion. Summers later testified that the demand thus generated would account for the creation of one and two million jobs worldwide, and 'several hundred thousand' in the US.[17]

The DC had also concluded that a central focus of the Framework was to be sector-specific negotiations, but had not yet decided exactly how to determine which sectors should be included. There was no question that the Japanese government's procurement practices would be one subject of the Framework talks. As discussed in Part I, a long list of competitive US industries had for decades complained that these procurement policies favored domestic firms, even when US goods were cheaper and more attractive. Here the DC decided to focus primarily on telecommunications, medical equipment, computers, and satellites.

How to choose which private sector industries to include in the negotiations was a more complicated matter. Here the DC discussed strategic as well as political rationales. Tyson was the most influential voice on the strategic side, and focused on industries with cutting edge technologies that were deemed to be important for the overall economy, and that showed a high level of competitiveness on a global basis. Based on these criteria, a small number of industries, including supercomputers, were discussed as candidates for negotiations. The political criteria included such things as the overall size of the industry, its potential for job creation, and its importance to the trade deficit. In addition, the US was looking for 'good allies' who were willing to take their own steps to enter the Japanese market, and who were willing to provide the administration with needed information on market conditions.[18]

It is thus interesting that the only industries that were specifically mentioned in the US Proposal—autos and auto parts—did not meet the DC's strategic criteria, leading a number of DC participants, most notably Summers, to oppose inclusion of them.[19] But everyone in the DC understood the political realities. Given the size of the industry and the oft-used argument that the automotive trade deficit accounted for more than

[17] US House 1993: 7.
[18] *Inside US Trade* 5/14/93: 13. The author of the article was paraphrasing 'a key Administration official.'
[19] Interview with veteran Commerce official, 4/14/97.

one-half of the bilateral imbalance, there was no doubt that autos and auto parts met the group's political criteria. The auto-related industries were then applying steady pressure on the Clinton administration to include autos in the new talks. For these reasons, all in the DC understood that the upcoming trade talks could not proceed without autos.[20]

Finally, the DC was of one mind that the agreements would have to include some sort of quantifiable or concrete ways to measure results, and that these would have to be somehow enforceable. Here, however, the DC could not decide the extent to which it was demanding explicit market-share numbers or numerical targets. The hard-line faction still wanted negotiations to be aimed at achieving specific targets, and that these needed to be enforceable through explicit sanctions for non-compliance. Ron Brown, for instance, in an April 23 press conference in Tokyo, argued that 'the only logical way' to reduce the trade deficit was to seek 'measurable results, to in fact have some targets.'[21] In contrast, moderates such as Cutter continued to indicate their reluctance to endorse hard numbers. At the press conference following the Miyazawa Summit, for instance, Cutter hesitated to clarify the US position on numerical targets, and instead continued to stress that results could be measured in a variety of ways. In the end, the group was not able to come to full agreement on hard targets; instead, the US proposed the boilerplate language that 'multiple benchmarks will be established in order to monitor progress in improving market access.'

Still, even the moderates in the group had not changed their commitment to a results orientation: according to DC observers, the group's 'commitment to measurable results has not been questioned,' and these

---

[20] It should be noted here that the automotive industries were certainly in favor of being included in the Framework, and had come to back the emerging DC coalescence around a results orientation. In mid-February, for instance, the Auto Parts and Accessories Association (APAA) went beyond its long-standing support of the January 1992 effort to have Japan's auto firms increase their purchases of US auto parts, and submitted a paper to Congress arguing that Clinton should 'seek enforceable, verifiable agreements measured by new sales' of auto parts (*Inside US Trade* 3/5/93: 5). At the end of February the Big Three were also beginning to voice support for a results orientation (ibid. 2/26/93: 11).

But it also seems to me that the two industries were not actively advancing either the revisionist argument, or calling for revisionist-style managed trade solutions. That is, up until early 1993, the automotive industries were much more concerned with limiting Japanese exports to the US. It was only when it appeared that the administration was moving in a new direction that the automotive industries began to back the managed trade approach. Later, in mid-1994, Andrew H. Card, Jr., then the president of the AAMA, supported a numerical target approach while at the same time arguing in favor of generic market opening: 'Let's open the Japanese auto market—really open it up the way the US market is open—and stand back and let the (Japanese) consumer decide this decades-long debate' (Barranger 1994: 17).

[21] *Inside US Trade* 4/30/93: 11.

results had to be defined 'concretely and quantitatively.'[22] Furthermore, all still hoped that the US would be able to achieve a more explicit quantitative approach in the upcoming negotiations, even if these were no longer called numerical targets.

Negotiating with Japan

As soon as the two sides sat down at the bargaining table, however, the US discovered that achieving its initial goals was going to be more difficult than had been assumed. As will be discussed in Part III, the Japanese government was during this period developing a consensus that it had to say 'no' to all of Clinton's managed trade demands. The US team remained blithely unaware that when Japan was saying no to managed trade, it was trying to reject not only the hard-line market share targets, but also the moderates fallback position of quantitative indicators that would ensure results. These developments, however, were not at all apparent to American policy makers at the time.

Indications of the new Japanese position came during a series of negotiations in June 1993, when the Japanese delegation signaled its resistance to any hint of managed trade.[23] On the macro side the Japanese, at the insistence of MOF, refused to specify a numerical target for reducing its current account surplus, or the inclusion of a specified, three-year time frame. Here, the Japanese side was willing only to consider a much looser commitment to boost domestic demand as a means of reducing its trade surplus—hardly a new offer, as Tokyo had been promising to do this for close to two decades.

As expected, the stickiest issue involved what indicators would be used to measure results on the sectoral side. As mentioned, the US team was careful not to use the term 'numerical targets,' but did try to find some phrasing that would be less explicit, but that would amount to the same thing. Over the course of negotiations this led to a push for more concrete indicators than the multiple benchmarks it had called for in its initial proposal. Among the many phrases discussed, the US side evidently focused mostly on 'objective criteria,' including 'quantitative criteria.'

[22] *Inside US Trade* 5/14/93: 13, and 5/21/93: 18.
[23] Talks were held in Washington on June 11–12 and in Tokyo on June 27–28. The US deputies-level delegation was chaired by Bo Cutter, and included Altman from Treasury, Barshefsky from USTR, and Spero from State. The Japanese team was chaired by MOFA's Matsuura, and consisted of the vice ministers of the three main ministries.

To the US negotiators, these terms seemed much less objectionable than 'numerical targets.' But this distinction was largely lost on the Japanese, who by then were hearing 'market share target' every time the US said 'quantitative criteria.'

This resistance was evident even in the area of Japanese government procurement. The Japanese were willing to discuss these issues, since its own procurement decisions were clearly its own governmental responsibility. However, the Japanese side indicated that it would continue to resist any proposal that some sort of numerical or quantitative target be established.[24]

It was on the question of the automotive trade that the Japanese tried to take their strongest stance. Here, Japan resisted the idea of specifically mentioning efforts to increase sales in the auto and auto parts industries, largely at the insistence of MITI. The Japanese side argued that the automotive firms were completely private entities, and thus not subject to control by the government. Japan thus continued to resist any discussions of private industry behavior that went 'beyond the reach of government.'

The two sides were unable to resolve any of these issues over the course of two negotiating sessions in June. After a two-day series of talks in Tokyo on June 27 and 28, the US negotiating team had come to the conclusion that they would not be able to budge the Japanese bureaucrats in time for the July 10 summit. The US team left Tokyo on June 28 with no agreement, and basically resigned themselves to waiting until after Japan's upcoming elections, set for July 18.

At this point, Prime Minister Miyazawa intervened to break the deadlock. On June 30, Miyazawa sent a personal letter to Clinton in which he indicated that Japan was prepared to compromise on all of the points then holding up negotiations.[25] On the macro side, Miyazawa would not specify an explicit target for reducing its trade surplus, but agreed that Japan would commit itself to significantly reduce its trade surplus. And while Japan still would not agree to setting any numerical targets in either the sectoral or government procurement talks, Miyazawa was willing to discuss some 'illustrative set of criteria,' either qualitative or quantitative, to

[24] In an April 2 letter to MITI Minister Mori, Kantor had argued that 'any Japanese economic stimulus package... include a specific allocation for foreign goods and services by the Japanese governments as a way to ensure implementation of government procurement agreements... [particularly including] computers, medical equipment, supercomputers, and telecommunications equipment' (*Inside US Trade* 4/23/93: 6).

[25] The letter was delivered by Ambassador Kuriyama to Clinton on July 2 (*Asian Wall Street Journal* 7/12/93: 22; see also *JEI Report* 7/16/93: 6).

measure progress and results. The clear message here was that if the US would disavow numerical targets, some deal on results was still possible.

With Clinton due to arrive in Japan for the G-7 summit in a matter of days, there was not much time to resolve the remaining issues. But the US side felt that the letter indicated Miyazawa's readiness, even eagerness, to cut some deal, and thus had its negotiators return to Tokyo on July 5. Negotiations continued at the bureaucratic level from July 6 to 8, during the G-7 summit. The main negotiations were between Cutter and MOFA's Matsuura, but as the latter was also heavily involved with the G-7 meetings, progress was slow.[26] Although the two sides were able to resolve some of the issues during these day-long talks, they remained deadlocked on two basic points: whether the illustrative set of criteria should be made more specific, and the extent to which these would constitute a commitment on the part of the Japanese government.

With talks bogged down, the Japanese side requested that the talks be raised to the political level, and as a result, a new round of talks opened on the July 8. The Japanese side was represented by a single official, Owada Hisashi, a MOFA bureaucrat who was seen as being very close to the Prime Minister, and thus able and willing to make compromises that the other bureaucrats refused to consider.[27] Owada faced a US team composed of NSC's Lake, Altman from Treasury, and Rubin and Cutter from the NEC. During these meetings, held all day on July 8 and 9, some progress was made on all of the remaining points of contention.

However, with Clinton scheduled to leave Japan on the morning of July 10, it appeared that these last-minute negotiations would simply run out of time. At the last moment, the President and Prime Minister met for dinner at the Hotel Okura on the evening of July 9, in what later became known as the 'sushi summit.' It was here that Clinton and Miyazawa were able to come to a series of compromises on the remaining issues that left both sides professing to be pleased.[28] These compromises were, however,

---

[26] Matsuura was Japan's G-7 'sherpa.' Cutter was backed by a team of Altman and Summers from Treasury, Barshefsky from USTR, Spero from State, and Blinder from the CEA.

[27] Owada also happened to be the father of Japan's newly named crown princess.

[28] Prior to the dinner a reporter asked if they expected to reach an agreement by dessert, to which Miyazawa replied: 'No dessert with sushi' (*Asian Wall Street Journal* 7/12/93: 22). Clinton (2004: 529) later remembered that 'Miyazawa always joked that the sake we drank contributed more than the sushi to the final outcome.' The dinner was a '1 plus 1' meeting, and included Japanese Ambassador Kuriyama and National Security Advisor Tony Lake. The substantive compromises, however, were done by Cutter and Owada. After dinner ended at 11 p.m., bureaucrats had to work all night to put the compromises into final language, and only got final approvals from the heads of state early the next morning. The Japanese delegation then had to rush to have the agreement typed and printed in time for the joint press conference that had been scheduled for 10 a.m.

Table 5.1 The Framework's sectoral and structural 'baskets'

1. *Government procurement.* Measures 'aim at significantly expanding Japanese government procurement of competitive foreign goods and services, especially computers, supercomputers, satellites, medical technology, and telecommunications.'
   Of these, medical equipment and telecommunications were later defined as 'priority sectors,' to be concluded in the first six months of negotiations. Commerce took the lead on medical equipment, while all others were negotiated by USTR.

2. *Regulatory reform and competitiveness.* Subgroups included financial services, insurance, competition policy, transparent procedures, distribution, and export promotion to Japan.

3. *Other major sectors, including the automotive industries.* 'Efforts . . . will have the objective, inter alia of achieving significantly expanded sales opportunities to result in a significant expansion of purchases of foreign parts by Japanese firms in Japan and through their transplants, as well as removing problems which affect market access, and encouraging imports of foreign autos and auto parts in Japan.'

4. *Economic harmonization.* Subgroups in this basket included investment, technology, and buyer–supplier relations, chaired by State, and intellectual property rights, led by Commerce.

5. *Implementation of existing arrangements and measures.* This basket called for close monitoring and implementation, including commitments made under the SII.

Source: 'Joint Statement on the US–Japan Framework for a New Economic Partnership' 7/10/93. Reprinted in *JEI Report* 7/16/93: 7–9.

interpreted very differently by the two sides. As will be discussed in the next three chapters, this division of interpretations would complicate the Framework negotiations for the next two years.

* * *

The initial Framework document thus divided the upcoming negotiations into five 'baskets' of issues, further divided into 16 subgroups, as outlined in Table 5.1. Of these baskets, only the first (government procurement) and especially the third (autos and auto parts) proved to be highly contentious, as they were the only ones that involved issues of results or, as Japan charged, managed trade. These were the issues that received nearly all press attention, and thus will be the focus of the analysis in the rest of the book.[29]

There were four key issues involving the Framework's results orientation: the question of a numerical target to reduce Japan's macroeconomic surplus; numerical indicators in the sectoral negotiations; the question of

---

[29] The Framework document also included the 'Common Agenda for Cooperation in Global Perspective,' which included discussions of the environment, technology, development of human resources, population, and AIDS. The final section was 'High-Level Consultations' which called for biannual Heads of Government meetings. Thus, Lincoln is correct when he argues that 'the common perception that the Clinton administration abandoned a structural approach is not correct,' in that issues such as intellectual property rights, distribution, and competition policy were included in the negotiations (Lincoln 1999: 128). With that caveat in mind, I focus only on the more controversial aspects of the negotiations.

enforcability, or whether the agreements would be subject to sanctions; and whether to specifically include the automotive sector as a target of negotiations.

The essence of the final compromise was that the US would drop its insistence on a numerical target on the macro side in exchange for a Japanese agreement on a results orientation on the sectoral side. As Altman later testified:

We began by seeking outright numerical commitments in terms of the degree of reduction in the current account surplus. In the last analysis, we concluded that there was a bargain to be struck where we would get, in effect, what we primarily sought on the microeconomic side—results commitment, measurement, the time table, and so on—in exchange for a very strong commitment from them, but short, yes, short of a numerical one on the macroeconomic side.[30]

As a result, the US agreed to drop any mention of numbers or a specific time frame on the macro side, accepting instead Japan's willingness to promote domestic demand 'intended to achieve over the medium term a highly significant decrease in its current account surplus...[and] a significant increase in global imports.'

This phrasing later became controversial as the two sides continued to disagree on exactly what the two phrases meant, despite hours of discussion and debate. The negotiators had even debated at length the distinction between 'significant' and 'highly significant.' The US team interpreted the inclusion of the latter phrase to mean that Japan had agreed to the proposal that it would reduce its surplus to 1–2 per cent of GDP, which the US described as the historical level over the previous 20 years. As Altman testified,

We think on the macroeconomic side the measurement is a rather clear one...We interpret the term 'highly significant' to mean that they will get down at least below 2 per cent. They have also committed to do so over the 'medium term.' That is a period which we interpret to be in the vicinity of 4 years.[31]

Kantor also endorsed this view in testimony right after the Framework was initialed, saying that the US interpreted this phrase to mean that the surplus would drop to its 'historical level of 1.5–2% within 4 years,' although Kantor also argued that the ultimate goal was to get the deficit down to zero.[32]

The US side was very pleased that Japan had agreed to a results orientation in the sectoral baskets. The Framework document stated that the

---

[30] US Senate 1993: 20.   [31] Ibid.: 10–11.
[32] *Inside US Trade* 7/16/93: 9.

negotiations would be assessed 'based upon sets of objective criteria, either qualitative or quantitative or both as appropriate,' which the US took to imply an official commitment to achieving results. This phrasing stopped short of numerical targets, but was much more specific than the original proposal of multiple benchmarks or Miyazawa's phrase 'illustrative criteria.' The US believed that it was the more concrete specification of the 'front end' of the trade negotiation that was significant. As Barshefsky testified,

It is the results orientation of the Framework that sets it apart from past agreements. The Framework establishes, as a principle, the use of objective criteria, both qualitative and quantitative, to evaluate progress toward market access in each sectoral and structural area.[33]

The exact form of 'objective criteria' was left undefined, in part because this would differ according to the sector involved. But the US team was confident that it could force the Japanese to agree to something sufficiently concrete. Furthermore, if Japan would not agree to a mutually acceptable definition, the US was prepared to define it unilaterally. As Barshefsky put it, 'We have made it very clear to the Japanese that, to the extent we cannot agree on the appropriate indicators to utilize, *the United States will, if it must, unilaterally apply indicators and assess progress on that basis.*'[34]

The US was also confident that it had made some progress on the 'back end' as well—holding the Japanese government responsible for enforcing any new trade agreements. First, the US was able to reject Japan's proposal to include the phrase that 'the criteria should not be used as targets or commitments for the future,' which it saw as a Japanese attempt to disavow all responsibility for following through on its agreements.[35] The final Framework language was more to the US liking, although still vague: 'The two Governments are committed to implement faithfully and expeditiously all agreed-upon measures.'

More importantly, the Framework raised the political stakes in the negotiations by making them subject to review at the presidential level. The Framework called for heads of government meetings to be held twice a year, at which time the two sides 'will issue public statements that include reports of results achieved.' Here, the US side felt that by bringing the President more explicitly into the negotiating process, it would make it

---

[33] US Senate 1993: 8.   [34] US House 1993: 16; italics mine.
[35] *Asian Wall Street Journal* 7/12/93: 22.

more difficult for Japan to either refuse to compromise, or to be negligent in carrying through on its commitments. As Spero put it, 'the strong political momentum, we believe, will place additional pressure on negotiators to produce tangible results.'[36]

The US further assumed that, if presidential-level scrutiny was not enough, then the Framework agreements would be fully enforceable under US trade law. Barshefsky testified that:

if tangible, measurable progress toward market access is not evident, we will not hesitate to use other approaches that Congress has provided. These prerogatives have been fully preserved in the framework...

This substantially distinguishes this effort from, for example, SII, under which the United States agreed that measures achieved within the SII would not be considered actionable under section 301. We have not done that with this framework.[37]

The following day, Barshefsky further testified that the US has 'no reluctance to utilize our trade laws as enforcement mechanism...this administration is not going to be bullied by Japan or by other trading partners.'[38] In retrospect, it is not clear exactly what trade law remedies the Clinton administration was prepared to invoke. All in the DC assumed that the mere threat of using US trade law would be enough to move the Japanese. Furthermore, by raising the issue to the presidential level, it was felt that Japan would be forced to make sufficient concessions.

Inside the White House, however, Kantor wanted to go even further in pinning the Japanese down in terms of the enforceability of the agreements, and seems to have feared that the US had already given away too much leverage.[39] Kantor attempted to rectify this only days after the Framework had been signed, by sending a letter in which he formally declared that the US 'reserves the right to enforce Japan's compliance with market access agreements.'[40]

The US also claimed victory on the final contentious issue, whether to include autos and auto parts as part of the private sector negotiations. By making the auto talks an explicit basket under the Framework, the US was assured that this sector would receive its due attention. Some career officials, however, also recognized that the US team had made a significant concession when it agreed to include a paragraph that stated that

---

[36] US House 1993: 8.   [37] Ibid.: 12 and 18.
[38] US Senate 1993: 16–17.
[39] Interviews with USTR official, 4/9/97; and USTR official, 4/4/97.
[40] *Inside US Trade* 7/16/93: 10. The letter was addressed to Ambassador Kuriyama.

'Consultations will be limited to matters within the scope and responsibility of government.' This was evidently a phrase that Miyazawa himself insisted on inserting.[41] It was also a phrase that USTR career officials objected to, correctly foreseeing it as a 'bear trap' that would allow Japan to deny responsibility for enforcing *any* private sector agreements.[42]

As seen in Table 5.1, the US was able to include in the final agreement a specific reference that the negotiations on autos and auto parts would aim at 'achieving significantly expanded sales opportunities to result in a significant expansion of purchases of foreign parts by Japanese firms in Japan and through their transplants.'

Here it was the Japanese team that had reason to be upset. The specific mention of 'a significant expansion of purchases' had been resisted by MITI through all of the previous negotiations. Although MITI welcomed the inclusion of the language limiting 'government scope and responsibility,' it wanted to maintain a very hard-line on any private sector negotiation. Owada's agreement at the last moment to include the reference to expanding puchases therefore infuriated MITI officials. MITI Vice-Minister Okamatsu Sozaburo, upon hearing of the agreement, rushed to the Hotel Okura well after midnight of July 9 to try to re-open talks, arguing that MOFA did not have the authority to make that particular concession. The US team, in the midst of its final briefing to the President, sent Barshefsky (later nicknamed 'Stonewall') down to the lobby to intercept and rebuff Okamatsu. In a now well-publicized incident, Okamatsu and MOFA's Matsuura afterwards angrily confronted each other in the Okura lobby. This confrontation ended in a heated shouting and shoving match, witnessed by some in the US delegation, between two of Japan's most senior bureaucrats.[43]

The Early Framework Dynamics: The American View

The dynamics at work in the initial Framework talks led some astute observers at the time to see a 'reversal in roles.'[44] In particular, the

[41] *Asian Wall Street Journal* 7/12/93: 22.
[42] Interview with veteran USTR official, 5/2/97. See also *Asian Wall Street Journal* 7/12/93: 22. The phrase had been used at least once before—in the January 1992 communique on auto parts—and this had allowed Japan to argue that its only responsibility was to collect data from the industry (interview with DC official, 4/18/97).
[43] Ennis 1993b: 57; *Asian Wall Street Journal* 7/12/93: 22; interview with USTR official, 4/9/97.
[44] Ennis 1993b.

normally unified and coherent Japanese negotiators seemed to be in disarray, with the politicians and bureaucrats seemingly working at cross-purposes, and with the central ministries not only disagreeing, but literally coming to blows.

In contrast, the US team appeared to be uncommonly unified. The US insistence on negotiating on results seemed unwavering, even if the exact specifics were not yet clear. And Japanese negotiators were finding that the more traditional agencies, State, Defense, and the NSC, were not receptive to the familiar argument that trade issues should not be allowed to poison the overall relationship. The US government's strategy of 'speaking with one voice' seemed to be working, leading Cutter to express gratitude to officials from the more traditional agencies, particularly NSC head Tony Lake, for not undermining efforts to address the economic issues. Japan was thus hearing a consistent message: the economic side of the relationship had to be fixed first, and any trade agreement had to be results oriented.[45]

In the aftermath of the Framework agreement Clinton's negotiators appeared confident, almost euphoric. They all of course understood that the initial Framework agreement only set the parameters of the upcoming negotiations, and that it was not a final agreement in itself.[46] But they also felt that getting the Japanese to agree in principle to a results orientation was the hard part. The prevailing feeling was that because the US had already won on the principles of the new negotiations, it should be relatively easy to reach an agreement.[47] Cutter put it most strongly, arguing that the US had 'accomplished every one of its negotiating goals in the creation of the Framework.'[48]

The US side was also sure that the Japanese government would eventually come to accept a results oriented agreement. That the US made this assumption was perhaps not unreasonable at the time, given Japan's past negotiating behavior. The few discussions in the DC on this subject led the group to conclude that the Japanese government was in the habit of protesting until the final moment, at which point they could be counted

[45] Ibid.: 56.
[46] In later testimony, the negotiators referred to the Framework as 'a directional document' or a 'rule book' that would govern subsequent negotiations.

Clinton himself seems to have been the most circumspect noting during his remarks at the Framework announcement that 'We should have no illusions. We announce today a framework to government specific agreements yet to be negotiated. Negotiating those agreements will surely be difficult.'
[47] Interview with USTR official, 4/9/97.
[48] *Inside US Trade* 7/16/93. Barshefsky later made the same point in her testimony on the Hill (US House 1993: 11).

on to give in. All that was needed was a bit of pressure. Even though Japan's resistance to 'results' seemed quite strong, there was little evidence that it would hold this line to the bitter end. Furthermore, the dynamics of the initial Framework talks seemed to confirm the assumption that Japan could be counted on to make last-minute compromises, if pushed hard enough. The US side saw little reason to take Japan's protests all that seriously.

This was an assumption that was shared not only within the US government, but also by most observers of Japan. Indeed, it was an assumption shared even within the Japanese government, where Japan's own hard-line faction, who I label the 'rejectionists,' was convinced that the rest of its government would eventually bow to US pressures. As described in the next chapter, this rejectionist faction in the summer of 1993 worked feverishly to make sure the Japanese government adopted a firmer line opposing managed trade. It turned out that the Japanese government not only maintained this hard-line, it actually strengthened it over the course of the Framework negotiations.

Reaching agreement under the Framework was thus to prove far more difficult than anyone in the US government imagined. The basic problem was the growing internal rift in the DC between hard-liners and moderates, which many in the DC did not even recognize at the time. In retrospect, the clear unhappiness of the hard-liners with some of the compromises made in the Framework on numerical targets and enforceability was an early warning sign. Already the hard-liners were engaging in guerilla tactics to make sure that any final agreement would include numbers and results.

However, none of this was apparent in July 1993. Within the US government, all assumed that its internal rift could be papered over or overcome, especially since both camps still agreed on the bottom line—the need for a results orientation. The US also continued to assume that Japan would yield if it was able to maintain its outward unity and was willing to play some 'hard ball' if needed. The US side held to these assumptions all through the Summer of 1995, when the Framework talks ended in Geneva without the concrete results orientation the US had initially so strongly desired. As one veteran negotiator put it, 'it wasn't until after Geneva that we realized that the Japanese were not going to give in.'[49]

---

[49] Interview with DC official, 4/18/97.

PART III

Contested Norms, Rejected Norms

6

Getting to No

The Evolution of Japan's Rejectionist Line

Up to this point I have focused on how the US policy making community shifted its assumptions about the Japanese economy, and how this led to different policy choices. In this chapter, I take a step back and retrace some of the same history, only this time from a Japanese perspective. I have organized the material in this way precisely because events were perceived so differently in the two countries, with interpretations in many ways running along parallel tracks, *Rashōmon*-style. Like its US counterpart, the Tokyo government in the decades leading up to the Framework was internally split between two different schools of thought: a political-military community that stressed the political benefits of the bilateral relationship, and economic bureaucrats who were increasingly resentful over having to yield to what seemed to be ever-escalating American trade demands. By the late 1980s a growing portion of the Japanese bureaucracy, the 'rejectionists,' argued that Japan's interests would be better served if it stepped up and finally said 'no' to increasingly unreasonable demands.

It is thus ironic that just as the US was adopting new assumptions about Japan, leading to the conclusion that trade negotiations had to focus on results, the Japanese government was moving in the opposite direction, girding itself to reject any trade demands that smacked of targets or results. US officials at the time, however, were oblivious to the shift underway in Tokyo—as well as the impact their own actions were having in hastening that shift. The two countries had thus set themselves up for a confrontation from which it would be very difficult to back away.

The explanation of why Japan was so adamant about rejecting Clinton's new trade demands includes an important normative dimension. Japanese government officials realized that if the US succeeded in achieving its managed trade objectives, it would thereby establish a new international norm—a new standard of appropriate behavior—as to how the world should henceforth deal with Japan. If Japan accepted America's demand for a new norm of 'specific reciprocity,' it could not plausibly deny similar agreements with other trading partners.

Furthermore, Japanese officials clearly recognized that because the legitimacy of US demands depended on revisionist assumptions, so too did the new norm of specific reciprocity. That is, if the world adopted the view that the Japanese economy was unique and inherently closed—a deviant case, or an outlier to which normal trading rules did not apply—then the international trading community would be justified in applying a unique and unorthodox trade approach. Put another way, if Japan agreed to accept revisionist *prescriptions*, it would at least tacitly be acknowledging that the underlying revisionist *assumptions* were valid as well. Thus, as this new paradigm grew in resonance in the US, the Japanese government increasingly sought to discredit and de-legitimize not only revisionist arguments, but also the revisionists themselves. The stakes here were high: Japan simply could not let revisionist assumptions become entrenched.

Contested International Norms

Japan's reaction to the new trade approach provides an interesting case for IR scholars who focus on international norms as a determinant of how states behave. In this approach, an actor's behavior is not driven solely by consideration of power and wealth but also by values and normative judgments of right and wrong. As enough states adopt a particular norm, commonly defined as 'collective expectations about proper behavior,' norms can constrain action by defining what is considered right or acceptable behavior. At a deeper level, norms can lead actors to define or re-define themselves—their very identity or the identity of others. Thus, interests and behavior can change because norms lead actors to adopt a new understanding of their identity and interests.[1]

---

[1] Katzenstein 1996: 5; Checkel 1998. The literature on constructivism is a vast and rapidly growing one. Other representative publications include Finnemore (1996); Klotz (1995); and Finnemore and Sikkink (1998). To the constructivist, non-material factors such as ideas, beliefs, and values also play a role in helping to shape how an actor *understands* his or her situation and interests. North Korea with one nuclear bomb is considered a greater threat than the United Kingdom with 500 not because it has more power capabilities but rather because it is perceived to be a rogue state willing to upset the status quo Wendt (1992). Similarly, Japan's

One persistent criticism of norms scholars is that they do not take power and power relations seriously enough. This criticism is not always warranted, and is certainly not an inherent problem with the constructivist approach.[2] But the criticisms persist in part because so much of constructivist analysis seems to focus on the consensual process through which actors come to intersubjective understandings, rather than instances where the strong impose their definitions of norms on the weak. While power and politics may be present, the creation of new norms often seems to occur without the apparent exercise of power.[3]

There also seems to be an element of self-selection at work. The bulk of constructivist research has focused on 'good' norms, or norms that very few disagree with—for instance, the illegitimacy of genocide, slavery, or other gross human rights violations. However, unqualified positive norms, which few actors have good reason to oppose, often are uncontested and thus do not need to be imposed—they may be appealing and accepted precisely because of their essential goodness. When norms are this compelling—not many would today argue that genocide is acceptable behavior—it may be relatively easy for actors to reach consensus, agree on, and implement a course of action *without* the overt exercise of power or coercion.

Furthermore, constructivist research has focused on successful norms—those norms that are implemented and have an important, long-term impact. But successful norms are, by definition, those that have been accepted by relevant actors. Focusing on these may thus introduce what might be called a 'survivor bias'—norms that have survived what Finnemore and Sikkink have termed a 'norms life cycle' of emergence, acceptance, and internalization, may have done so precisely because they were not opposed by significant actors (and perhaps, as mentioned above, because 'successful norms' so often are also 'good norms'). While

security policy commitment to non-aggression is not simply a reflection of constitutional constraints or domestic politics, but rather has become a part of the country's national identity, even 'culture' (Berger 1996).

[2] As some recent work by the so-called 'conventional constructivists' illustrate, power relations need not be ignored Katzenstein et al. (1998). The volume edited by Peter Katzenstein has gone a long way in dispelling another former criticism that the norms/constructivist approach is best suited for 'soft' issues rather than the 'hard' issues of national security and military affairs. The articles in that volume show that a focus on culture and norms can indeed help to explain certain aspects of security studies.

[3] Part of the explanation for this is that the constructivists have had to demonstrate that norms and identities *divorced from power* play an important role in international politics; the need to convince the realists that norms can have an important independent impact has perhaps channeled their research away from a focus on how norms interact with power.

Finnemore and Sikkink recognize that the 'completion of the life cycle is not an inevitable process,' not enough constructivist research has discussed norms that fail to make it out of the emergent stage.[4]

More attention needs to be paid to 'contested norms'—including norms that fail. There are countless cases where norms are highly contested, are not at all consensual, and very often involve resistance, bargaining, and outright conflict. Norms accepted by the international community may not be at all acceptable to those countries that may be their target. Norms can be actively resisted by significant actors who may try to undermine a new norm, or prevent it from being adopted. When norms fail, it is often precisely because of the exercise of power, where actors resist the definition and imposition of norms that run counter to their interests.

It is this class of norm that needs more investigation. Norms that are controversial are more likely to lead to contention, disagreement, and resistance; here is where the importance of power and bargaining may still be crucial. Such cases are more likely to bring us back down into the trenches of international politics where emerging norms have not yet reached the transcendent position of consensual intersubjective understandings.[5] Attention to this class of norms may give us better insights into the interactions of norms and power.

The case at hand is one example of such a contested norm, in that the US version of how Japan should be treated was one that was vehemently resisted by its intended target. On the surface, one might have expected the US to have a relatively easy time imposing this new standard. After all, the call for specific reciprocity had already reached what Finnemore and Sikkink call the 'acceptance' phase; indeed, such calls were even stronger from key nations in Europe and Asia. But, as will be discussed in the following chapters, the Framework negotiations boiled down to a battle

---

[4] Finnemore and Sikkink 1998. It is perhaps natural for analysts to have focused on successful ideas and norms, since these scholars have wanted to demonstrate how profound and important these concepts can be. And while constructivists are careful to note that norms can also be 'bad,' their almost uniform focus on the good is not just a coincidence; constructivists so far have tended to be those who desire to transcend the negative, gloomy world of the realists—both in theory and in practice—and this proclivity has been reflected in their work. Checkel (1998) also argues for the need for more attention to 'bad' norms.

[5] A focus on contested norms might also allay the suspicions of scholars who study 'non-Western' states that, in practice, current norms are largely defined by the West, which then compels or 'socializes' others to accept its definition of what is right and wrong; in other words, norms are perceived by some as a mere mask for power and recreating Western dominance. Perhaps this perception is due to the fact that so many of the central examples of constructivist research *seem* to be focused on Anglo-American conceptions of what should be acceptable behavior. Even if true, however, this is not a flaw of the constructivist approach but rather a problem with the type of research that has thus far been carried out.

over whether this new norm was to be established or rejected; in this sense, norms obviously mattered to both governments.

To a considerable extent the Framework struggle revolved around the accuracy and legitimacy of the revisionist assumptions that provided the logic for the new norm of specific reciprocity. In the end, Japan built a highly effective negotiating position, and was able to rebuff or otherwise discredit the revisionist paradigm. In the end, it was Japan that prevailed. While the US attempted to receive the intersubjective understanding of the international community that Japan should be treated as an outlier, it was the US that ended up isolated in the international debate and eventually beaten at its own norms game.

Japan's Growing Discontent with the Cooperationist Approach

The Japanese policy making story runs parallel to the American story described in Part I, in that it reflected an increasingly contentious debate between competing schools of thought over how to define the nation's interests in the bilateral relationship. As outlined in Table 6.1, in contrast to a 'cooperationist' camp that believed it important to accommodate US trade demands, a rejectionist camp advocated a tougher response— basically, that Japan at some point needed to say 'no.' As in the US, this new thinking had been gaining in resonance during the 1980s, but it was only in the early 1990s that it was able to dominate Japanese definitions of its interests.[6]

The cooperationist camp in the Japanese government shared many similarities with traditionalists in the US, most notably its focus on the importance of the security relationship. With Japan's national defense strongly tied to the Security Treaty with the US, the insulation of this tie was seen as a fundamental national interest and indeed the very core of Japan's postwar foreign policy.

Cooperationists also recognized that Japanese export industries, and indeed the economy as a whole, benefited enormously from access to foreign markets. This school of thought furthermore was aware that its export successes were causing considerable and painful economic adjustments in foreign markets, which in turn were leading to growing calls for

---

[6] Most of the source material for this section is derived from numerous interviews with Japanese government officials who were directly involved in the Framework talks, carried out in 1997–8. For an earlier version of this chapter, see Uriu 1999.

Table 6.1 Cooperationist and rejectionist views of the US

I. Cooperationist views of the US	II. Rejectionist views of the US
A. Cooperationist assumptions	**A1. Deterrence school assumptions**

– The US is a crucial political and military ally
  • The US is the cornerstone of Japan's defense and foreign policies
– Japan is dependent on maintaining access to the US market
  • In net terms, Japan benefits from international trade
  • Japanese exports are causing political damage in the US
	– The main cause of the trade problem lies with America's budget deficit, low savings rate, etc.
	– Japan has been very cooperative with US demands, even when demands have been unreasonable
	– Japan is rising in terms of economic power relative to the US
	– America's demands, unless deterred, will continue to escalate

B. Cooperationist policy prescriptions	**A2. WTO fundamentalist assumptions**
– The military and political relationship should be insulated from economic frictions – When the US makes trade and economic demands, Japan must make at least some concession – Japan should increase its contributions to support the alliance relationship	– US–Japan relations should be governed by the norms and principles of multilateralism: non-interference in the market, equal treatment, etc. – American 'aggressive unilateralism' is a threat to the international trading system
	B. Rejectionist policy prescriptions
	– Japan needs to say no to unreasonable US demands, and stick to it – Any form of 'managed trade' is no longer acceptable – Japan should deal with the US only in multilateral, not bilateral, settings

some form of retaliation. Japanese cooperationists believed that these economic frictions needed to be contained lest they explode and damage the overall relationship. In order to manage these tensions the dominant strategy was one of accommodation: Japan needed to do whatever was necessary to placate American trade and economic demands so that these disputes would not become overly politicized or confrontational.

Cooperationist thinking was the dominant view throughout the Japanese government through the mid-1980s. This was certainly true of the political leadership, the ruling Liberal Democratic Party (LDP), which had from its inception relied heavily on the political relationship with the US. The very parameters of Japan's foreign policy—the reliance on the US military and the focus on economic development through an export-led growth strategy—depended on a cordial bilateral relationship. The LDP thus had strong incentives to ensure that this relationship was managed and maintained. Therefore, when trade disputes threatened to get out of hand, party politicians had on numerous occasions intervened to force recalcitrant bureaucrats to offer just enough concessions to placate trade demands. Given the LDP's stake in preserving the relationship, these political pressures were at times direct and overbearing.[7]

Cooperationist views were also deeply held in the Japanese bureaucracy. Certainly the Ministry of Foreign Affairs favored protecting the bilateral relationship; this was MOFA's most important mission through the 1980s. Inside the ministry's North American bureau, officials in charge of the security relationship worked with those in charge of economic issues to forestall the buildup of tensions. Through this period this bureau was considered to be one of the more prestigious within the ministry, reflecting the priority given to the relationship. Even within MITI cooperationist thinking remained the dominant mode of thought through the mid-1980s. MITI officials were realistic enough to recognize that Japan's industries depended on continued access to international markets, and this in turn depended on maintaining a cordial relationship with the US. MITI recognized that an overly intransigent stance that invited American retaliation would lead to enormous costs—to individual industries, to the Japanese economy as a whole, and to MITI itself. MITI might resist trade pressures, but not to the point of risking a breakdown in relations.

---

[7] For much of the last decade Japan scholars were obsessed with the question of whether the politicians or bureaucrats actually ran the country. While that debate has quieted down, one thing is clear: when the LDP politicians felt strongly enough about an issue, they were able to intervene. Many of the most notable cases of this came in the trade and foreign relations realm, where key LDP politicians often assumed the role of 'political fixer' (Destler et al. 1976).

Japan's business community in general, and especially the politically powerful exporting industries, was also supportive of this cooperationist approach. Most recognized the critical importance of maintaining access to the US market, and thus had strong incentives to at least appear to support concessions. Japanese exporters were also acutely aware of changing US attitudes towards Japan, both in official circles as well as in the population at large. Given the depth and strength of US anger over trade issues, Keidanren realized that making concessions was far better than risking across-the-board trade retaliation or some significant closure of the American market.[8]

Not all those involved in the policy process favored accommodation, of course. Sectors such as agriculture and construction had long been adamant opponents of the cooperationist school's willingness to make trade concessions. These industries had few international activities or interests, and were therefore not so concerned about the possible closure of the American market. Conversely, these preferred to keep the Japanese market closed, since they would have been swamped by significant liberalization. The same goes for many of the less competitive industries: the domestic side of Japan's dual economy, many of which were under the jurisdiction of MITI.[9] In addition, the political power of these industries meant that their interests could not be ignored completely. However, policy makers had to take into account the interests of the overall economy, and clearly understood that the interests of these less competitive industries did not outweigh the overarching need for access to international markets. Instead, these 'losers' from trade were compensated in other ways.[10]

Cooperationists in the Japanese government were of course not happy with American pressures, especially as US criticisms became harsher and more vitriolic. In addition, many also recognized the growing strength of Japan's economy, and thus felt a deepening sense of pride in what Japan had accomplished. Cooperationists were also dismayed at the weakening of the US; many preferred America to be strong enough to continue to play its customary leadership role. Yet they also recognized that it was in part Japan's economic successes that were causing pain and dislocation in its

---

[8] Even particular exporting industries that were the focus of these trade concessions often still supported the cooperationist approach. Most of these industries recognized that some cooperation was better than being shut out of the US market entirely. In any case, most such industries were also compensated by the Japanese government in some way. At least one industry, automobiles, ended up in a stronger position because of the VER, which allowed the firms to shift into the higher profit end of the industry.
[9] Katz 1998b.   [10] Uriu 1996.

foreign trade partners. In the debate in the 1980s over how Japan could fulfill its international responsibilities, cooperationists argued that Japan had an obligation to rein in its exports or to open up its domestic market. Further, it needed to take these steps precisely because it was now in a position of strength: many felt that the stronger party should help the weaker to adjust. Japan needed to make concessions not only because it was rational to do so, but also because it was the right thing to do.

In sum, in the decades prior to the Framework the cooperationist school of thought maintained that Japan had to continue to make concessions in the face of American trade demands. The costs of failing to do so—the negative impact on the overall security and economic relationship—were simply too high to contemplate. While this school was increasingly resentful of American criticisms and finger pointing, and concerned with the continued escalation of demands, the consensus remained that it had no choice but to continue to make concessions: Japan simply could not afford to say no.

* * *

The cooperationist approach to the US and its trade demands came under increasing question in Japan during the 1980s—precisely at the time that the traditionalist approach in the US was under attack by the revisionists. This change was certainly evident among economic bureaucrats, but could also be seen throughout the government and in society as a whole. The shift in Japanese thinking basically stemmed from a combination of its resentment at not being given credit for being cooperative enough in meeting US trade demands, changing perceptions of Japan's relative strength, and anger over America's rising unilateralism.

In analyzing the bilateral trade relationship, one striking aspect is the extreme difference in how policy makers in both countries assessed their respective policy actions. I chronicled in Part I the deepening and sincere conviction among US officials that the Japanese economy was unique, closed, and a potential threat to the US economy and the international trading system. In contrast, I describe in this chapter how Japanese policy makers saw things in very different, but similarly heartfelt, terms: essentially, that the Japanese economy had already been substantially liberalized, and that the cause of the trade deficit lay more with the US.

In response to US charges that the Japanese economy was essentially closed, Japanese officials constantly pointed out that it had already removed most of its official tariffs on manufactured imports. Thus, 'openness' depended on the definition of the term; using the standard of overt tariff levels, officials often argued that it was one of the most open in the world. Japan was 'playing by the rules,' or at least the existing rules, and so the problem had to be that US firms were 'not trying hard enough' to crack the market—a countercharge repeated so often that many Japanese came to take it as gospel.

Many Japanese policy makers also bridled at the American claim that it was the main beneficiary of the open trading system. Japanese officials certainly recognized that the country did benefit, but argued that they were not unique in this—many others throughout the world had also enjoyed similar access. Further, despite the huge trade surplus, the argument was made that the US benefited as well, not only from trade, but also from the massive inflow of Japanese capital that was helping to finance the US trade and budget deficits. The US further benefited from access to the military bases in Japan, which allowed the US to project its power more effectively worldwide. If one looked at the relationship as a whole, it seemed clear that both sides benefited. To put it differently, this was a relationship of mutual dependence in that the US also needed Japan's support, even if this support so often was taken for granted.

Many Japanese officials were strongly resentful of the American charge that they were being uncooperative and intransigent. To the contrary, most believed that they were doing their best to accommodate US trade demands. Through the 1980s cooperationist thinking had led Japan to undertake a long series of steps designed to minimize the impact of its exports on the American economy.[11] Not only had it removed most of its tariffs, it also cooperated in regulating the outflow of Japanese exports—the long series of 'voluntary' export restraints, including steel, consumer electronics, and, from 1981, automobiles. On the macro side the government agreed to a series of efforts to increase aggregate demand that would increase domestic demand for all goods, including foreign imports. The Japanese government also agreed to try to influence the value of the yen–dollar exchange rate so that Japanese exports would become less competitive and American exports more so.

As the US shifted its focus in the 1980s to the selective liberalization of the Japanese market, the Japanese view was that it had continued to cooperate. Throughout the 1980s the two had concluded a long series of sector-specific, bilateral market liberalization agreements designed to remove specific barriers against imports.[12] In the early 1980s Japan was also taking steps to encourage increased imports that at times went beyond

[11] See, for example, Destler et al. 1976; Blaker 1977; Calder 1988; and Schoppa 1997.
[12] The ACCJ (1997) counts some 112 separate trade agreements reached during the 1980s.

its previous efforts to manipulate market forces. Rather, these were 'extra-market' measures to increase foreign imports—the precursors to later voluntary import expansions, or VIEs. Many of these measures were largely symbolic, as in Prime Minister Nakasone's 1985 'action program,' which called for all citizens to 'buy American'—the idea that if each person bought at least 10,000 yen (around US$100) of American-made products, the trade surplus would shrink dramatically. More concretely, the bureaucracy also occasionally gave specific encouragement to certain sectors to import more, and in particular from the US. In the early 1980s, for instance, top MITI officials encouraged Japanese semiconductor users to purchase more American products and to seek out longer term relationships with American producers.[13]

In sum, the Japanese government felt it had been making some sort of concession every time it was approached with a new proposal to alleviate trade tensions, no matter how difficult these demands were to meet. Even as the US became more aggressive in its trade demands, the Japanese government always seemed willing to offer some sort of concession or compromise.

Furthermore, Japanese economic officials were acutely aware of the domestic costs of having to constantly bow to pressures for trade concessions—costs that the US side never seemed to appreciate or even acknowledge. The Japanese government was not so strong as to be able to ignore political pressures from industries that were forced to bear the pain of trade concessions. Rather than simply letting the market take the hindmost, some sort of compensation had to be given to these industries, proportional to their political leverage.[14] But instead of appreciation for these efforts, US officials were becoming even more critical, laying the blame for the trade problem squarely at Japan's doorstep. As chronicled in Chapters 2 and 3, American rhetoric in the 1980s took on an increasingly strident tone, castigating Japan as an unfair trader whose economic structures were designed to insulate it from imports while it launched massive export assaults on others. In essence, Japan was being blamed for taking a 'free ride' at the expense of the world. Whatever the merits of these arguments, to the Japanese it seemed that their country was being made a scapegoat due to its very success.

The shift in Japanese attitudes was further spurred on by the amazing growth in its economic power in the mid-1980s, as well as the perceived

---

[13] Prestowitz 1987.

[14] As I have argued elsewhere (Uriu 1996), MITI as a political organization was very sensitive to the complaints and demands of nearly all of the industries under its jurisdiction, and would do whatever it could to help those industries avoid the costs of economic adjustment.

decline in America's economic strength. As the Japanese economy emerged as a dominant one—'Japan as number one'—it was only natural that pride in its accomplishments also rose, but in this period many were also getting caught up in the heady feeling of being a new economic super-power. Many were now pointing to the superior nature of its economic system and the Japanese way of doing things, focusing on what it must have been doing right in order to be so successful—from industrial policy, to business organization and practices, and so on. In this, there was a considerable degree of overlap with the early arguments being made by the revisionists in the US: the Japanese system was not only different, it was also *better*.

A related attitude that appeared over time was that Japan needed to behave in a way that befitted its new economic stature. In particular, it was simply inappropriate for a major economic power like Japan to be submitting to external demands all of the time. As Len Schoppa argues, a more powerful Japan desired a more equal status with the United States, and this made heavy-handed US demands more difficult to swallow.[15]

At the same time, it appeared to many that America's economy was in a secular decline, and in Japan there were mounting criticisms aimed at all aspects of America: the quality of its leadership and labor force, low savings rate, excess consumption, government deficits, the lack of quality control, racial and societal problems, and the like. In this period state-ments by senior politicians often made headlines in the US, as when ex-Prime Minister Nakasone criticized American racial relations, and when Kajiyama Seiroku, a senior LDP politician, questioned the quality of American workers. To many Japanese, America's angry reaction to these statements seemed excessive, as they felt that they were only stating the obvious. Besides, they had been saying similar things for some years, both privately and publicly, but were only now finding their statements show-ing up in the US press.

Nowhere were Japan's changing attitudes more strongly symbolized than Ishihara Shintaro's argument that his country needed to become a 'Japan that can say no' to trade demands, as described in Chapter 3. Rather than forcing Japan to change, perhaps the US needed to make the crucial adjustments, try harder, or to adopt Japanese government and business

---

[15] Schoppa 1999. In his usual comprehensive and solid manner, Schoppa points to many of the important elements of what he calls the 'social context' of the bargaining relationship that have undermined the effectiveness of US coercive bargaining strategies. While not refuting Schoppa's core arguments, the argument here focuses on the contest over a specifically defined norm—whether Japan should be treated according to revisionist prescripts.

practices, and the like. In terms of the trade relationship it was time for Japan to stop making all of the concessions.

In this context of shifting attitudes in Japan, American policy behavior in the late 1980s had a doubly negative impact. Most alarming to Japan was evidence that the US was becoming increasingly punitive and unilateral. In particular, the passage of Super 301, in which the Congress required the President to retaliate against foreign partners judged to be 'unfair traders,' became the symbol of what Bhagwati and Patrick called 'aggressive unilateralism.' While the Bush administration was careful to name others besides Japan as unfair traders, to the Japanese there was never any doubt that the provision was aimed at them. Japanese officials now complained that the US was essentially authorizing itself to serve as prosecutor, judge, and jury on the issue of unfair trade practices. Stacking the deck like this meant that Japan was going to be found guilty regardless of the merits of their case.

For Japan, though, the seminal event was America's imposition of trade sanctions in 1987, stemming from its alleged failure to live up to the commitments it had made in the Semiconductor Agreement of the previous year. As described in Chapter 2, in that agreement Japan committed itself to stopping the dumping of chips into the US market and also agreed, secretly, to try to raise the ratio of imported semiconductors to 20 per cent of its domestic market. The issue came to a head in January 1987, when the US gave Japan a two-month deadline to halt the dumping and increase market access. On March 26, 1987, the US imposed '100 percent tariffs on US$300 million of Japanese exports of computers, machine tools, and colour televisions—the first major sanctions against Japan since the Second World War.'[16] Even after the US was satisfied that dumping had stopped, sanctions continued because the US deemed that Japan was not making sufficient progress in expanding the market share of foreign semiconductors.

Again, views of what was going on here differed in the two countries. In the US, Japan's failure was another example of it reneging on its promises, or being unwilling to take promised actions; once again, the Japanese were acting in bad faith. In Japan, MITI officials argued that halting dumping of an easily transportable commodity like semiconductors was not an easy task, especially when much of the dumping was being done through third-party suppliers, where MITI's influence was especially tenuous. Furthermore, MITI felt that it had made a sufficient effort to encourage domestic producers to purchase more foreign, and specifically American, chips.

---

[16] Kunkel 2003: 99.

In any case, during the four years in which these sanctions were in effect, the parameters of the policy debate in Japan shifted significantly. The sanctions tested the willingness of many cooperationists to continue to give in to the US, and convinced many others in the government that the time had arrived to stand up to American trade demands. While cooperationists had been constantly warning of the dangers of saying no, the semiconductor sanctions demonstrated that Japan could be punished even when it tried to say yes.[17]

The Development of Japan's Rejectionist Line

By the end of the 1980s the Japanese government was on the brink of shifting toward a harder line against American trade demands. Rejectionists coalesced around two separate schools of thought, as outlined in Table 6.1. The main group, known as the 'deterrence school,' argued that past cooperation was not effectively placating US trade demands. If anything, it was having the opposite effect, encouraging the US to push for trade concessions that were increasingly harsh, intrusive, and more difficult to meet. This school believed that it was now in Japan's national interest to limit future pressures. While this school recognized the importance of the US and did not desire a breakdown in the relationship, it argued that unless Japan took a firmer stand, American demands would be constantly expanding. Japan was just going to have to dig in its heels at some point and just say no, and then would have to make it stick.

The deterrence school was, not surprisingly, strongest in MITI, since this ministry had borne the brunt of trade pressures. MITI bureaucrats had long been unhappy with making constant concessions, but it was the experience with the semiconductor sanctions that made it dead set against

---

[17] In the antiseptic language of cooperation theory, this widening attitude gap can be described as a fundamental disagreement over the definition of 'cooperation' and 'defection' and the issue of how to characterize each other's behavior. As described earlier, American revisionists argued that the US had paid a heavy price by keeping its markets open to Japan, but had been constantly thwarted in its efforts to open the Japanese market. In game theory terms, the US had been receiving the 'sucker's payoff,' in which it cooperated while Japan 'defected,' by keeping its markets closed. In this situation a 'tit-for-tat' strategy of retaliation to force open the Japanese market—aggressive unilateralism—was fully justified in order to move the situation back to one of mutual cooperation.

But in the Japanese view, it had already been cooperating with US demands to open its markets, in exchange for continued openness in the US market; from Japan's point of view, then, the situation had long been one of 'mutual cooperation' in which both sides were benefiting. Furthermore, Japan had gone out of its way to meet American demands, even when it was the US that should have been adjusting. In this situation, as the US ratcheted up

further concessions. Once the sanctions were imposed, MITI was roundly criticized in the Japanese media and by the party politicians, who blamed MITI for negotiating an agreement that had turned out so disastrously. As one former MITI Vice-Minister put it, the feeling was equivalent to being branded a 'Class A War Criminal'; this official remarked, somewhat resignedly, 'no one likes being called a war criminal!'[18]

These criticisms were especially galling because many of the MITI bureaucrats had been opposed to the Semiconductor Agreement in the first place, but had felt forced to come to some agreement by the LDP party politicians. The semiconductor disaster thus further cemented the resentment MITI bureaucrats felt toward the party politicians. Despite the clear need for a tougher response, the ruling party insisted on making concession after concession, forcing negotiators to come to some sort of accommodation with even the most unreasonable of demands. By the end of the 1980s, MITI officials resolved to do whatever they could to resist such agreements in the future, or any agreements that opened it up to sanctions. The motto inside MITI became 'never again.'[19]

The semiconductor sanctions also led to a shift in attitudes within MOFA, or at least within parts of the ministry. MOFA had been previously criticized by MITI officials for operating without any principles, making concessions just to placate the US, regardless of the consequences of these concessions.[20] But the semiconductor sanctions led to a division of opinion within the ministry. Two bureaus, Economic Affairs and Treaties, were now less interested in insulating the US relationship and instead were becoming more concerned with the multilateral implications of trade demands. The prestige of these bureaus, already high, was rising in part

---

its trade demands and threatened punitive actions, its behavior was increasingly perceived as unwarranted and aggressive—close to a unilateral 'defection' from mutual cooperation. In this case, if Japan continued to cooperate, it would then be receiving the sucker's payoff. As some have noted, when both sides cannot agree on the basic definition of what constitutes 'cooperation,' it becomes nearly impossible to reach cooperative solutions. In such situations a tit-for-tat strategy stands a very strong chance of causing a conflict spiral. This is precisely the outcome that pertained beginning in the late 1980s (Milner 1992).

[18] Interview with very senior MITI official, 10/22/97.

[19] While all MITI bureaucrats were influenced by the semiconductor sanctions, it seems that all of the MITI bureaucrats who played a key role in developing Japanese policy during the Framework were directly involved in the semiconductor negotiations. These included Hatakeyama, Toyoda, Sakamoto, and especially Okamatsu, all mentioned later. Hatakeyama later put it, 'We have learned a lesson . . . Once reference is made in a trade agreement to numerical figures, then these figures will get a life of their own. So we will never repeat this type of thing to avoid misunderstandings and managed trade' (*Washington Post* 4/25/93, Nikkei Needs Database <http://www.nikkeieu.com/needs/>).

[20] Interview with MITI official, 4/16/97.

because they were involved in the multilateral arena, an increasingly important dimension of Japan's foreign policy.[21]

In this period another important dynamic was underway inside both ministries: the emergence of a second group of bureaucrats who later became known inside the government as the 'WTO fundamentalists.' This group is important to our story in that key members became the main architects of Japan's rejectionist policy position during the Framework talks, and played the crucial role in making sure that it finally said no to US demands. The group consisted of a small cadre of government officials, mostly from MITI and MOFA, who were directly involved in the negotiating process during the Uruguay Round. Through this common experience this group of bureaucrats forged strong personal links and a common commitment to the multilateral approach. Initially, their endorsement of multilateralism was based on rational grounds, as the best way to combat American unilateralism. But as their name implies, this school of thought eventually developed a deep, nearly religious commitment to the principles of multilateralism, a commitment that went beyond rational calculations—as I will discuss in later chapters, this group stuck to its commitment to principles even when it was recognized that the costs of doing so outweighed its benefits.[22]

Essentially, the WTO fundamentalists agreed with the deterrence school that Japan had to say no: but they also felt that Japan should negotiate only in a multilateral setting. Their argument was that bilateral talks constantly put Japan at a power disadvantage, whereas a multilateral approach would de-politicize trade disputes and offer a more advantageous way to deal with trade frictions.

A little noted victory for Japan in a 1991 GATT case, involving allegations of dumping of auto parts into Europe, convinced many that multilateralism could be an effective approach. This was the first time Tokyo had requested a dispute settlement panel, since most officials had assumed that these panels operated with at least one eye toward international politics, which meant that their judgments would invariably go against Japan. Proponents of this approach were thus elated when they were able to convince the rest of the government to even pursue this case, and even

---

[21] Yasutomo 1995. There was also growing dissension even in the North American Bureau, which was in charge of the overall US relationship. On the one hand, the 1st North American division, which was in charge of political relations, continued to be relatively cooperationist; in contrast, the 2nd North American division, which was in charge of economic issues, advocated a much harsher approach. These officials, who also reported to the Economic Affairs Bureau, argued against automatic concessions on trade issues.

[22] Interview with very senior MITI official, 10/16/97.

happier when the GATT panel ruled in Japan's favor.[23] From this point on, more and more officials realized that such panels might indeed judge cases based only on the merits.

The WTO fundamentalists were also practical enough to realize that the existing international trade organizations and rules were not yet strong enough to effectively deter US unilateralism. This group therefore became consistent proponents of strengthening and expanding multilateral trade mechanisms. With the founding of the WTO in late 1993, the fundamentalists argued that, as a matter of principle, Japan needed to rely solely on multilateral mechanisms in dealing with trade pressures. This group now contended that there should be no further bilateral negotiations. Although the Japanese government in the 1990s did not follow this recommendation, and continued to deal bilaterally, the influence of this group meant that concessions in bilateral talks were no longer a certainty.

The other significant role of this group was that it allowed the two central ministries, MITI and MOFA, to cooperate to a degree rarely seen before. The two had historically been divided by an intense rivalry and struggle over resources and roles, so genuine cooperation was always difficult. However, because the WTO fundamentalists were in place in both ministries, officials were able to form a cross-ministerial alliance. Two senior officials were later crucial in this regard, one each from MITI and MOFA. Okamatsu Sozaburo, who was MITI's Director General for International Trade Policy during the Uruguay Round, and later MITI's lead negotiator in the Framework, was the key high-level MITI official who helped to hold the Japanese government to a firm line. A senior MOFA official, Hayashi Sadayuki, who had spent half of his career working on multilateral issues, became another strong voice within this group. Hayashi was crucial in that he was well respected even by MITI, and because he and MITI's Okamatsu were able to form a close working relationship. As described in the next chapter, these two often cooperated in preventing their 'less principled' colleagues from making last-minute concessions. As one senior MITI official put it later, MITI was 'lucky to have someone like Hayashi' inside the MOFA, since he understood multilateral principles and was willing to hold his colleagues to them.[24]

---

[23] Interview with senior MITI official, 10/7/97.

[24] Material in this section was first drafted in 1997 and appears also in Uriu 1999. Another key senior WTO fundamentalist in MITI was Hatakeyama Noboru, described by one official as Japan's 'first high-level WTO fundamentalist.' Toyoda Masakazu, described below, was also involved in the Uruguay Round negotiations (as well as being involved as a junior MITI official in the semiconductor negotiations). Furthermore, under these officials were a group of more

* * *

By the end of the 1980s, then, Japan's attitudes toward trade pressures had stiffened visibly. In this context, America's growing fascination with revisionist assumptions was especially alarming, and soon became the focal point of Japanese attitudes toward America. Now, American criticisms of Japan were increasingly portrayed as mere whining about Japan's success, with Japan becoming the scapegoat for America's own problems. Rather than getting its own house in order, the US was calling on Japan to bear the costs of adjustment. Even after Japan had continued to cooperate, the US was adopting an ever more strident and critical tone. Popular attitudes were now being described in terms of *kenbei*, literally a 'dislike' or 'disdain for America.'

The Japanese government increasingly began to step up its rhetoric, contesting American arguments and counterattacking with criticisms of its own. For instance, officials became vocal critics of the US government, both in private and in public, and tried to shift the blame for the trade problem onto the US. The decision to make the SII negotiations a 'two-way street,' dealing with economic problems in both countries, provided a green light to point out the many shortcomings in the US economy.[25] And in an attempt to counteract America's unfair trade reports, Japan in 1992 began to issue its own 'unfair trade report' that highlighted US protectionism. Although few in the US (or anywhere) took these reports seriously, they did demonstrate that Japanese officials were becoming

junior people who also had developed their commitment to multilateral principles through their experience in the Uruguay Round negotiations. Within MITI, WTO fundamentalists were strongest in the International Trade Policy Bureau, while in MOFA these officials were more likely to be found in the Treaties Bureau and the Economic Bureau, organizations in charge of multilateral negotiations and overall economic policy, respectively. Two junior fundamentalists in MOFA also formed an effective team: Haraguchi of the Economic Bureau and Nishimiya in the 2nd North American Division.

It should be noted that the ideological commitment to multilateralism did not conform neatly to generational lines, as some of the most important proponents of the position, including Okamatsu and Hayashi, were older bureaucrats who happened to be central figures in the Uruguay Round negotiations. And many, if not most, of the younger generation of bureaucrats who were not associated with this group were uncomfortable with the zealous nature of the later almost religious commitment to principles. In this sense, the basis of the WTO fundamentalist school was more experiential than generational. While Schoppa's argument that the generational change in the Japanese bureaucracy was one of the enabling factors that allowed Japan to construct a more defiant position on trade is correct in general terms, attitudinal differences did not conform so neatly to generational lines. That is, some of the most adamant critics of constantly saying yes to the US were in fact senior bureaucrats who had their training during the US Occupation (and thus should have been more interested in cooperation, according to Schoppa). And a great number of younger generation bureaucrats still defined Japanese interests in more cooperationist terms.

[25] Kuroda 1990; and Hatakeyama 1996.

more adept at using the media to respond rapidly whenever new criticisms or demands were raised.

As revisionist ideas gained in resonance in the US, the Japanese government focused its energies on refuting this new way of thinking. Increasingly, Japan began to counterattack, trying to discredit and delegitimize revisionist assumptions one by one—for every charge or claim that was put up, Japan now more vocally responded with their own versions and interpretations. To some extent these efforts were part of an intentional and coordinated strategy. MITI's Toyoda Masakazu, who has been credited by many as the key architect of Japan's response, has said that he tried to 'think as an American would think, wearing American shoes' when deciding how Japan should respond. The end result was essentially a PR effort that took the form of an aggressive counter-information campaign, designed to counteract the revisionist version of the trade problem; MITI was now no longer willing to let the US have the final word.

Although Japanese officials have always denied it, it seemed that a conscious part of this strategy was to discredit not only revisionist ideas, but also the revisionists themselves. Revisionists quickly became *persona non grata*, tagged with the insinuation that the harshness of their attacks meant that they were inherently biased. At the extreme, revisionists were unfairly portrayed as racist, motivated not by scholarly thought but by base attitudes. Whether these personal attacks were part of the official Japanese information campaign is not clear but, as discussed in the next chapter, American revisionists certainly perceived them as such.

It is extraordinarily difficult, perhaps impossible, to say definitively where true beliefs end and mere tactics begin; there is a gray area in between that is difficult to define. Japan's attack on the revisionists is one example of this. Some officials did view the revisionists as biased and perhaps even racist, and thus deserving to be attacked; but others did not believe this, and furthermore recognized some truth in the revisionist interpretation of Japan. These officials, however, also realized that the implications of allowing revisionist ideas to go unchallenged were great. Accepting the revisionist version would only open it up to increasing pressures and demands; if Japan were portrayed as an outlier that was not even playing the same game, then the US would feel justified in taking more extreme measures—something that Japan wanted to avoid at all costs.

Whatever the combination—whether revisionist arguments were seen as wrong and dangerous, or as correct but inconvenient—the Japanese government by the early 1990s was focusing its attention on discrediting revisionist assumptions. In this atmosphere of heightened rhetoric, bilateral interactions were steadily becoming a battle over the legitimacy of assumptions, and at times over the legitimacy of the proponents of those assumptions.

Up until the Framework talks, however, Japan's rejectionist bureaucrats were not yet able to control the policy making process. Rather, cooperationist ideas remained the dominant mode of thinking at the highest levels of government and continued to shape policy responses. Cooperationist thinking was still quite strong within MOFA, which tended to take a more comprehensive view of the relationship relative to MITI's focus on economics. This was certainly true among those bureaucrats who had developed expertise in dealing with the US; these officials felt a great deal of discomfort in flatly rejecting US demands. However, it was within the LDP that cooperationist thinking was the strongest, particularly at the top levels of the party and among the relatively small number of politicians who had an active interest in foreign policy. As before, the top politicians continued to intervene to force the economic bureaucrats to back away from their preferred approach.

The rejectionists were thus very unhappy with the politicians for brokering deals in the two controversial negotiations at the end of the Bush administration, described in Chapter 3. In 1991 the Japanese government agreed to extend the 1986 Semiconductor Agreement for another five years; this time, however, the agreement made explicit the 20 per cent foreign market share target that had been mentioned only in the secret side letter in the 1986 pact. Although MITI bureaucrats fought hard against the inclusion of the market share numbers, they were overruled by the party politicians. MITI was able to make it clear, however, that the 20 per cent target was a purely private sector commitment, not a government one, and so believed that Japan would not be subject to sanctions if the target was not reached.[26]

Rejectionist officials were also unhappy with the outcome of the Bush–Miyazawa summit meeting in January 1992. Bush's decision to bring along the executives of the Big Three, they felt, put the auto and auto parts issue too high on the summit agenda. Given this, combined with

---

[26] MITI's opposition to the 1991 extension may have been muted because the foreign share of the domestic market was indeed rising at the time, giving some hope that the goal would actually be reached. This was due more to changes in the market (especially the shift in demand to microprocessors and the overall growth of the Japanese market), and also in part due to the tie-ups between US and Japanese firms. I thank Hugh Patrick for these points. So MITI's opposition was essentially on the issue of *principle*: Japan should not make agreements that could even conceivably lead to sanctions.

the Japanese government's desire to have a successful summit, there was simply no way that it could completely reject all of Bush's demands. But MITI again insisted that any numerical target for auto parts be completely private in nature. MITI agreed, reluctantly, to have the Japanese auto firms announce their future plans to expand their purchases of US auto parts, and these private pledges were then totaled and included in the final agreement.[27] However, MITI tried to make it absolutely clear that these commitments were made by private sector firms, and thus that the government could not legally be held responsible for their fulfillment.

* * *

On the eve of the US 1992 presidential elections the Japanese government thus provides a mirror image to the policy shifts going on inside the US government. Japan's rejectionist officials were clamoring for a harsher approach and criticizing cooperationist-oriented officials and politicians for too easily caving in to the demands of the other side. Those advocating a harsher line were making concrete headway over time, as their views spread from the economic agencies to those concerned with overall political relations. With the end of the Cold War, rejectionists also saw the new era as a chance to reassess national interests in the relationship: officials could now argue that the country did not have to feel the same urgency in insulating the security relationship from economic tensions, and thus could contemplate a fuller range of national interests. Rather, the priority of putting a halt to America's incessant trade demands needed to be elevated.

In another mirror image of what was happening in Washington, however, the rejectionist approach was constrained and frustrated by the more cooperationist-oriented part of the government, which still saw national interests as best served by preserving the status quo of a stable and close relationship. In spite of rising economic conflicts and the end of the Cold War, cooperationists clung to the belief that political accommodation had to take precedence over confronting economic tensions. For the time being, the prevailing assumption at the top levels of MOFA and among the LDP leadership was that Japan still could not afford to say no or in any way risk a break in the relationship.

As Clinton took office, therefore, it was not yet clear whether cooperationists or rejectionists would prevail in Japan. Although the end of the

[27] MITI had discussed these purchasing plans with the Japanese auto makers the previous fall, in preparation for the November 1991 summit, which was cancelled by George Bush. MITI requested that the firms increase the amount of their purchases in time to announce them at the January 1992 summit.

Cold War and shifts in relative economic power made a clash over economic issues more likely, significant policy change was far from preordained. To return to the counterfactual exercise with which I ended Chapter 3, had the Bush administration been re-elected and had not followed a strong results approach, I believe that the Japanese probably would have continued with their cooperationist approach to bilateral relations. The harsher line adopted by Japan during the Framework, and the subsequent rupture in relations, was by no means inevitable.

Reading Clinton's Policy: Japan Tries to Say No

In the remainder of this chapter, I go back over the events leading up to the Framework that I discussed in Part II, only this time from the Japanese perspective. I portray a stark contrast with what the US side said and did, and what the US believed the Japanese to be saying. In this account one can see the origins of many of the disputes that led to the near-derailment of the relationship in the Framework talks.

Japanese government officials had watched the 1992 presidential campaign with enormous interest, with special attention paid to the debate over trade issues. Japanese officials were thus relieved that the protectionist-oriented candidates were making little headway, and that the traditionalist-leaning Bush seemed to have a good chance to win re-election. Like many observers, Japanese officials were surprised at Bill Clinton's recovery from the brink of disaster in early 1992 and his subsequent upsurge in popularity leading up to the election.[28] In the aftermath of Clinton's November victory, Japanese officials scrambled to read the President-elect's attitudes.

Japanese officials were initially unsure what to make of Clinton. He did not seem to be a trade hawk or particularly harsh in his attitudes toward Japan. Furthermore, Clinton had said very little about Japan during the campaign, and his pronouncements on international trade did not sound like a typical (protectionist) Democrat; but little else was known about the new President. Immediately after the election a handful of Japanese businessmen who had had some dealings with Clinton as Arkansas governor

---

[28] It was a little guarded secret that the Japanese government preferred dealing with a Republican administration. Despite the growing tensions of the past decade, the Japanese assumed that a Democrat in the White House would be even harsher toward Japan, and probably more protectionist as well. Besides, Japanese officials had established stable working relations with Republicans administration officials.

became overnight celebrities of sorts. Most prominent was Iue Satoshi, president of Sanyo Electric, who had met Clinton in 1978 during the latter's visit to Japan. Iue described Clinton as a 'decent and nice young man' with whom he once sang karaoke until 2 a.m. Further, 'when he came to Osaka...we played molehill games [whack-a-mole] together in a game center, shouting for joy when we successfully used our hammers to beat the mole springing up from one of 20 holes.' Other executives described Clinton, somewhat hopefully, as 'pro-Japanese' and as someone 'who has more knowledge about Japan than any other US president in history.'[29]

In the early months of the new administration, officials scrutinized every statement and rumor coming out of Washington for some indication of upcoming US trade policy directions. Japanese officials, however, now found that they had very few points of contact with the new Democratic administration, especially compared to the regular channels of communications they had enjoyed with the Republicans. Japan discovered that most of the members of Clinton's policy team were not Japan experts—like the American revisionists, Japanese officials also complained that they had never heard of Bo Cutter.[30] Now, a great number of officials in Tokyo, Washington, and New York had to rely on scouring administration testimony and statements, press and trade journal reports, and whatever rumors were in the air.

Over time, as the new administration's results-oriented approach took shape, the Japanese government's relief at not being the focus of the campaign turned to concern. Japan was discovering that although Clinton was indeed a 'New Democrat' and thus not likely to try to close the US market, he was also highly committed to expanding international trade. Inevitably, 'opening markets abroad' was being defined as 'opening the Japanese market.'[31]

[29] *Japan Times* 11/5/92, Nikkei Needs Database <http://www.nikkeieu.com/needs/>; and *Yomiuri Shimbun* 11/5/92, Nikkei Needs Database <http://www.nikkeieu.com/needs/>. Robert Orr (1993:2) reported that ten days after the election he found 50 books on Clinton in Japanese bookstores, and counted at least 30 *kenkyūkai*, or study groups, devoted to the new President or his possible policies.

[30] Japanese contacts with American line officials were also not of much help in this period. Normally, line officials in the two governments are quite communicative with each other, providing regular briefings and exchanges of information, in both directions. This is not surprising since we are, after all, allies. But now, even veteran US bureaucrats had little sense where the Clinton political appointees were heading.

[31] The priority that Clinton placed on market opening was especially evident during the discussions at Clinton's economic summit in Little Rock in December 1992.

What was most alarming, however, was the evident impact of revisionist thinking on the new Clinton team. Japanese officials watched with concern as top officials, including the President himself, warmly received groups such as ACTPN. Japanese officials had also done their homework on the new Clinton trade team, and in particular Laura Tyson, who was a well-known advocate of managed trade with Japan.[32] Officials also paid close attention to informal comments by US officials, as for instance in the much-publicized conference at the Economic Strategy Institute in February 1993. As described in Chapter 5, during that conference Tyson and a number of other Clinton officials spoke openly in favor of a results-oriented approach, including market share targets.[33]

Given the resonance of revisionist assumptions in the US, many Japanese officials now assumed that Clinton's approach would be revisionist in orientation, which would inevitably lead to demands for results and numerical targets. Japan's worst fears were gradually confirmed as officials listened to Clinton's new political appointees disavow the Bush administration's process-oriented approach. Although all expected a new administration to distance itself from its predecessor, they were surprised at the across-the-board rejection of the Reagan/Bush approach to negotiations. Now the Clinton people offered a constant stream of criticisms of all past agreements for their failure to produce *any* positive outcomes.

Instead, in public and private statements US officials were endorsing the need for results, then numbers, and finally sanctionable numbers. By March, Japanese officials had become convinced that the administration was moving toward numerical targets and managed trade—almost before the administration had in fact made any sort of policy decisions—and were gearing themselves up for a fight.

The next concern was whether the US was going to seek actual numerical targets, something that the deterrence bureaucrats and the WTO fundamentalists agreed was unacceptable. Japanese officials were thus alarmed with Clinton's endorsement of the Semiconductor Agreement, with its inclusion of market share numbers, as the only successful agreement. The March 1993 announcement that the foreign share of the domestic chip market had risen above the 20 per cent market came at

---

[32] Another figure that received attention was Treasury Secretary Lloyd Bentson, who had been known as a harsh critic of Japan in the 1980s.

[33] See Chapter 5 for details on the ESI conference. Administration officials included Laura Tyson, Derek Shearer, and John Rollwagen; campaign advisors included Mike Mochizuki and Clyde Prestowitz.

absolutely the worst time for Japan, as it gave further momentum to the Clinton administration's interest in a numbers-oriented approach.[34]

The final issue was whether any such targets would be sanctionable under US trade law, another demand that all in the Japanese government agreed had to be rejected. This question was settled in late March by the Kantor-Brown letter, discussed in Chapter 5, which demanded to know exactly what the Japanese government intended to do to honor the 'pledge' it had made to President Bush in January 1992 to increase purchases of American auto parts.

The impact of the Kantor-Brown letter on the Japanese government cannot be overstated. It came at a crucial moment, right as Tokyo was deciding if it could compromise with Clinton's likely trade demands, and helped shift the parameters of the debate toward the rejectionist position. The letter confirmed Japan's worst fears, providing the first solid evidence that the US was interested not only in 'results,'as in some sort of market share target, but also "results plus"—the achievement of market outcomes on the threat of sanctions. The letter weakened the cooperationists, who were still arguing that Japan could make concessions so long as the demands were not so concrete as to involve hard targets and sanctions. Now, America's insistence on sanctionable numbers indicated an unacceptable escalation in demands.

From this point on, even many cooperationists stopped arguing that the benefits of accommodation were still worth the costs. More importantly, the letter solidified the conviction that Japan simply had to reject US demands *now*. If Japan did not say no to sanctionable numbers, where could it possibly say no in the future? It thus was the impetus that drove deterrence school officials and WTO fundamentalists to join forces behind a common, rejectionist position. In essence, the Kantor-Brown letter had the effect of unifying the contending schools of thought within the Japanese government in a way not deemed possible before, sowing the seeds for what was to become the MITI–MOFA alliance.

The Kantor-Brown letter, and its less than diplomatic tone, also brought to the forefront the issue of trust, a nebulous concept that nevertheless played an important role here.[35] Japanese officials were reading between

---

[34] There is some question as to whether MITI was responsible for engineering this result. Given MITI's growing abhorrence with numerical targets, this does not make sense. Why would MITI try to show results when it was fighting so hard to avoid exactly this sort of trade agreement? Rather, the economists' explanation makes more sense to me: that is, that the rise of US sales was due more to market forces such as the growing demand for American-made microprocessors. Again, I thank Hugh Patrick for this point.

[35] Schoppa 1999: 323–5.

the lines, looking at the tone adopted by the US for clues to American attitudes. What they saw was not reassuring: the harshness of the administration's rhetoric, so similar to the revisionist rhetoric of the past few years, raised hackles among Japanese officials, and more than subtly affected how they reacted. This deterioration of trust further damaged the position of the cooperationists, who in the past had argued that 'good faith efforts' to negotiate with the US would be rewarded by some reciprocal restraint.

More concretely, the Kantor-Brown letter reinforced the suspicion that the new administration could not be trusted to honor the agreements its predecessors had made. It was bad enough that the Clinton people were repudiating past agreements as being worthless and yielding no benefits, it was now trying to unilaterally change the interpretation of those agreements. From MITI's point of view the letter was alarming because it contradicted the clear understanding that the 1992 agreement on auto parts was a purely private sector affair that the government was not liable to enforce. It should be noted that this was an interpretation held not only by the Japanese government, but also by veteran US officials. In fact, Kantor's USTR staff had made sure to take the word 'commitment' out of the letter, knowing that this would alarm the Japanese, but was unable to delete the term 'pledge,' or to stop Kantor from verbally mentioning the Japanese government's commitment to fulfill the auto parts purchasing plans. This is what the Commerce official meant when he commented that 'we knew MITI would go nuts' once it saw the letter.

That, in effect, was exactly what MITI did. From this point on, Japanese officials were reluctant to agree to discuss anything that even resembled numbers, as the US might later try to reinterpret any such numbers as a formal government commitment. Now, the contention of rejectionists was easy for all to grasp: the US simply could not be trusted with numbers.[36]

It may be hard to believe that a single letter could have had such an impact, but this is the contention of numerous Japanese officials to whom I have spoken. Not only did it tip the balance toward the rejectionist position in Japan, it also turned out to be an indiscretion that came back to haunt US negotiators all through the Framework talks. At a number of crucial points in the negotiations, when the US side would claim that it was not seeking numbers or sanctionable numbers, the Japanese side

[36] Hatakeyama 1996: 72–7.

would invariably bring up the Kantor-Brown letter. At one point the top Japanese negotiator even brought a hard copy of the letter, pointedly handing it to the US team: 'if we even discuss anything resembling a hard number, how do we know this won't be turned into a "commitment" later on?'[37] During the Japanese government's ensuing public relations campaign, it was able to use this letter as 'proof' of America's desire for managed trade. One veteran US Commerce official put it more bluntly: 'that letter was a complete disaster... [it] poisoned our ability to ever get any agreement on numbers, permanently and forever. It has haunted us ever since.'[38]

* * *

By March 1993 rejectionists in the Japanese government were already hard at work getting ready to say no—even before the US had put forward its formal demands. Now, officials in both MITI and MOFA agreed that they needed to maintain a unified, position if they were ever going to neutralize cooperationist voices elsewhere in the government. Even if the rejectionists could hold their own ministries steady, they also needed to ensure that the other ministries were on the same page. Japan's bureaucracy had had a history of sectionalism and disunity, and this meant that it was constantly being 'divided and conquered' by the US, which was always wringing concessions out of cooperationists in one ministry, and then using those concessions to pressure the other ministries.[39] The problem for the rejectionists was that bureaucratic disarray allowed the party politicians to play a mediating role, with the result usually being some undesirable concession. The rejectionists needed to make sure that the party politicians were neutralized and thus prevented from yielding to their compromising natures.

To overcome these obstacles the MITI–MOFA leadership took the extraordinary step of convening an informal, cross-ministry forum to serve as a high-level policy coordinating body. This forum, known as the 'three by three meetings,' brought together the top three officials of the three main ministries, MITI, MOFA, and MOF, and became the key

---

[37] Interview with very senior MITI official, 10/16/97.

[38] Interview with veteran US Commerce Department official, 4/14/97.

[39] This is another mirror image of revisionist frustrations in the US, where it seemed that it was *Japan* that was always coherent and the US the one that was being picked apart. As Jervis has argued, one perceptual constant is the tendency to see the other side as coherent and unified, while recognizing one's own government as being hopelessly divided Jervis (1970). In addition, it appeared to Japanese officials that the US team was even more unified than in the past, and was indeed 'speaking with one voice,' making the need for effective coordination even greater.

locus of policy making in this period.[40] Like the deliberations then going on in the US government, the three by three participants found that they were essentially on the same page—all of the participating officials agreed that Japan simply had to say no to any demands for sanctionable numerical targets. The quick agreement on this basic position was made possible because all six of the MITI and MOFA officials included in it were members of either the deterrence or WTO fundamentalist school.[41]

The only question was over tactics and strategy. One issue was whether to use the multilateral realm to deflect US pressures, as advocated by the WTO fundamentalists. The consensus of the group, however, was that Japan would have to say no directly to the US, basically because officials were not confident that multilateral arrangements were strong enough. But the three by three officials did see the arguments and rhetoric of the WTO fundamentalists to be potentially useful. Up to then, whenever rejectionists had argued that Japan needed to say no on pragmatic grounds, they were often overruled by those who made equally pragmatic arguments that Japan had to compromise. Now, couching the refusal to compromise in the language of principles, norms, fairness, and legitimacy, would bolster Japan's position by allowing it to claim the moral high ground.[42]

In order to stake out and hold a rejectionist position, three by three officials realized that they needed to maintain a unified front, both within the bureaucracy and with the LDP politicians. The MITI participants were thus gratified that MOFA's top officials had clearly joined the rejectionist camp. However, convincing other more cooperation-oriented MOFA bureaucrats of the wisdom of saying no was still a problem. The three by three

[40] Informal, cross-ministerial fora like the three by three meetings are a relatively rare phenomenon. A version of the three by three had been used during the SII, since those talks also cut across ministry lines. In the case of the SII, however, the three by three was largely symbolic and used as a coordinating mechanism. The three by three in 1993 was a much more substantive body. The 1993 meetings were usually held over breakfast, and lasted between one and two hours. These meetings were considered to be so sensitive that they were always held at a neutral site—usually one of the major Tokyo hotels—and were always held in secret. The decision to use local hotels was in part to avoid unwanted press coverage.

[41] These officials were Matsuura, Ogura, and Sasae from MOFA; and Hatakeyama, Okamatsu, and Toyoda from MITI. Matsuura was considered to be the weakest link in the group, although he initially supported a rejectionist approach.

[42] In addition, the WTO fundamentalists, who were in a weaker institutional position, realized that teaming up with those who wanted to deter the US was the only way that their principled position could become policy. There was thus a confluence of principles and pragmatism, which helped to strengthen both.

officials realized that the only way to solve this problem was to present an unassailable and unyielding argument in favor of a hard line.[43]

MOF officials also agreed that Japan had to take a tough stance, another welcome development for the rejectionists. In the past, MOF had been criticized for being too independent, in part because its main issues— macroeconomic policy, financial deregulation, and the like—were normally handled separately from trade issues. Also, its relationship with its US counterpart, the Treasury Department, was less contentious than on the trade side. Although MOF certainly did not favor numerical targets or sanctions, it could not always be counted on to back MITI's hard-line on sectoral issues. What brought MOF on board this time were US pressures for a numerical target for reducing the overall current account surplus, which fell directly on MOF. Especially after its experience with the SII talks, MOF was not willing to make broad numerical commitments. Reportedly, MOF's hard-line stance gave MOFA officials further confidence that they were doing the right thing in holding to a hard line.[44]

In order to ensure that the rest of the bureaucracy stayed in line, the three by three also carried out consultations with two key ministries involved in the upcoming negotiations, Transportation, and Health and Welfare. In addition, consultations were held with the ministries of Construction and agriculture, both of which were involved in negotiations handled outside the Framework. As these ministries had their own, more protectionist reasons to want to deflect trade pressures, it did not take much to persuade them to fall in line. Besides, all were considered to be junior ministries, and so a united front of MITI, MOF, and MOFA officials should be enough to ensure bureaucratic discipline.

Dealing with the politicians was a much more difficult problem, since the top LDP leaders were still highly cooperationist and thus willing to offer whatever concession was needed to avoid a confrontation. However, three by three officials were now more confident that their case was a compelling one, and furthermore that bureaucratic unity would prevent unwarranted political compromises. After numerous briefings of the party politicians, three by three officials believed that they had persuaded the top LDP politicians, including Prime Minister Miyazawa, to finally stand up to the US.

---

[43] In addition, top officials made sure that drafting responsibility during future negotiations be given to the 2nd North American division (which was responsible for economic issues and which took a harder line than the 1st North American division).

[44] Interview with MOFA official, 9/25/97.

The final task was the most difficult of all: effectively communicating Japan's new resolve to the United States. In early 1993 a series of high-level officials delivered the message that Japan would not accept numerical targets or any other form of managed trade. In February MOFA Minister Watanabe Michio had communicated a request for a new round of bilateral talks, which obviously would not be based on any sort of numerical target. MITI Minister Mori Yoshio had also strongly rejected the claims made in the Kantor-Brown letter, reiterating the position that the 1992 plans of the auto firms were private commitments, and that it would not again agree to numerical targets.[45]

Finally, officials thought that Prime Minister Miyazawa had communicated the rejectionist position directly to President Clinton during the April summit in Washington, during both formal and informal discussions. Miyazawa's public message was that resolving the trade imbalance 'cannot be realized by managed trade or under the threat of unilateralism.'[46] In addition, according to a high-level MITI official, Miyazawa elaborated on this during private talks with the President, explicitly rejecting the use of any form of managed trade. Miyazawa argued that since both countries were trying to convince the rest of the world to liberalize their markets, the two should stick with free market solutions as well. Miyazawa, according to his advisors, felt that he had made his position completely clear in these private talks with the President: no more numbers.[47]

At least one senior Miyazawa aide, however, in listening to Clinton's statements at the subsequent press conference, felt that the President had heard Miyazawa's words, but was not taking them seriously enough.[48] This view was confirmed when the US offered its initial negotiating position, as laid out in the May proposal for the 'basic bargain' in the Framework. This proposal made it clear that the US was pushing forward with a results-oriented approach, including the call for a 'highly significant' decrease in the current account surplus (implying a reduction to 1–2 per cent of GDP within three years), and sectoral negotiations that would include 'objective criteria, either qualitative or quantitative, or both' to measure sectoral results (read as 'numerical targets' by Japanese officials).

Rejectionist bureaucrats now blamed the party politicians for not delivering the message strongly enough, and thus set out to further harden Japan's opposition to numbers and sanctions. During the remainder of

---

[45] *Inside US Trade* 4/2/93: 9–10, 4/9/93: 7, 4/16/93: 7–8, and 4/23/93: 7.
[46] Office of the Federal Register 1993: 441.
[47] Interview with very senior MITI official, 10/16/97.
[48] Interview with LDP official, 10/15/97.

May the three by three officials hammered out a set of principles that set Japan's parameters for the upcoming negotiations, which were then communicated to the US government.[49] The key principle was the last one, entitled 'no managed trade,' which read in part:

'consultations...will be premised on adhering to the principles of free trade and market economy...Accordingly, measures amounting to managed trade will not be taken by either the United States or Japan as a result of these consultations. In this connection, there will be no discussion of establishing numerical targets.'

Other principles also reflected the thinking of the WTO fundamentalists. One principle, 'no unilateralism,' stated explicitly that 'consultations under the Framework will be outside the scope of Article 301 of the US Trade Law.' In the principle entitled 'multilateral dispute settlement,' Japan specified that 'in the event that either country puts into effect unilateral measures, discussions under this framework can be halted during the time that the propriety of these measures is being evaluated according to international rules, such as under the GATT.'[50]

Entering the June 1993 talks to initiate the Framework, the three by three officials were confident that these new principles would be strong and clear enough to at least convince the Japanese government to maintain its unity, if not to completely deter the US. This confidence seemed to be warranted as bilateral talks through the end of June seemed to be going nowhere, as described in the last chapter. The main stumbling block was over how to assess sectoral openness. While the US did agree to avoid the phrase 'numerical targets,' it seemed to be searching for some other phrase that would amount to the same thing, such as 'objective criteria' or 'quantitative criteria.' The two sides also could not agree on whether to specifically mention the automotive industry as a part of the negotiations, and if so, whether to mention Japanese efforts to 'increase purchases' of autos and auto parts. Although Miyazawa had urged the bureaucrats to reach some sort of compromise, MITI negotiators stuck to their intransigent line.

With the US negotiating team heading back to the United States on June 28, it seemed that the two sides were going to miss the July 9 deadline. The three by three officials welcomed this prospect, even if it meant that

[49] The principles were announced at the end of May. They appear in *Inside US Trade* 6/4/93: 9.
[50] Furthermore, the new principles argued that the object of sectoral negotiations should be limited to those 'within government reach,' which hard-liners hoped would eliminate private sector industries such as autos and auto parts. The final two principles were entitled 'Two-Way Approach,' and 'Third Countries and Benefits,' which stipulated that third countries should also benefit equally from any agreement.

the summit would be deemed a failure—it looked like the battle was being won. Now, finally, it seemed that the Japanese government had reached a consensus against accepting any numbers-oriented agreement; if the US would not drop these demands, Japan would have no choice but to reject them.

This feeling of determination was cut short by the last-minute intervention by Miyazawa, who now took a much more active and direct role in the negotiations than had been the norm for Prime Ministers. In part, this was due to his own precarious political position: due to the LDP's deep involvement in scandals, and because of an internal split in the party, Miyazawa had lost a vote of no-confidence in the Diet on June 18. Yet despite his 'lame duck' status, Miyazawa was determined not to let the talks collapse, evidently hoping that a breakthrough in negotiations would bolster his political credibility and that of the LDP—or, failing that, would be a final legacy for his administration. On June 29, after the Clinton team had returned to the US, Miyazawa instructed MOFA's Matsuura to contact Cutter to try to reopen negotiations. A day later Miyazawa bypassed his bureaucracy completely in sending a personal letter to President Clinton that was aimed at coming to some compromise. Significantly, Miyazawa did not go through the usual process of gaining consensus with the permanent bureaucrats. As one MITI official put it later, 'we did not think it wise to reinitiate talks ... But he finally prevailed because we couldn't stop him from sending a letter.'[51]

It should be noted that Miyazawa did not feel that he was making major concessions in re-opening the talks. Miyazawa's letter indicated a willingness to take steps to reduce the trade surplus, but did not specify an explicit target or timetable. Although he wrote that he was willing to include some 'illustrative set of criteria' in the sectoral negotiations, he also reiterated Japan's position that it would not agree to the idea of setting any sort of numerical targets.

Japanese negotiators thus continued to hold to their previous line even after the US had returned to Tokyo and resumed the negotiations. In the talks that began on July 6, the bureaucrats continued to insist that the 'illustrative set of criteria' referred to by the Prime Minister should be used only as a gauge to measure progress, not as a government-endorsed target or

---

[51] *Asian Wall Street Journal* 7/12/93: 22; see also *JEI Report* 7/16/93: 6. On July 1 Miyazawa also asked outgoing US Ambassador Armacost to convey his desire to reach some compromise. Certainly Ambassador Kuriyama and other cooperationists pushed Miyazawa to send this letter (see Kuriyama 1997: 178), but the decision also surely reflected Miyazawa's experiences and proclivities.

commitment. With the US still holding out for a more concrete government commitment to enforce any new agreement, talks again broke down on the eve of the summit. It was at that point that Miyazawa intervened again by asking that the talks be raised to the political level, and then instructing his lead negotiator, MOFA's Owada Hisashi, to close some sort of deal. Owada made some progress with the US negotiators during discussions on July 8 and 9, but the final arrangements were not finalized until the Miyazawa–Clinton 'sushi summit' on July 9.

The three by three officials were furious when they learned that Owada had compromised on the remaining sticking points: the agreement to aim for a 'highly significant decrease in the current account surplus,' and to negotiate 'sets of objective criteria, either qualitative or quantitative or both as appropriate.' MITI officials were also angry at the inclusion of the automotive sector as one of the baskets, but more so over the mention of 'expanded purchases' of auto parts. MITI officials had become resigned to including the auto sector, but had hoped to kill the issue of expanded purchases now rather than during later negotiations. It was this issue that led to the shoving match between MITI Vice Minister Okamatsu and fellow three by three official Matsuura in the Okura lobby. While perhaps not significant in itself, the 'Okura incident' demonstrated to the Japanese rejectionists that they were not as unified as they had thought.

Japan's Rejectionists Coalesce

Although the three by three officials were frustrated with some aspects of the agreement, they also felt that Japan had not yet made any significant concessions. Japanese officials understood more clearly than their US counterparts that what had been decided was only the parameters of the upcoming negotiations, not the final agreement itself. Japanese rejectionists realized that the most difficult part of the negotiations—agreeing on the final details—was yet to come, so they still had the time to stiffen Japan's resolve. Officials further believed that they had prevailed on some important issues. Japan was able to remove any mention of a specific numerical reduction in the current account surplus, as the US had originally desired, substituting instead the vague phrase of a 'highly significant decrease.' Although autos and auto parts were to be included in the Framework talks and 'expanded purchases' was mentioned, Japan had stuck to its position that it would not negotiate numerical targets or any sort of managed trade, and furthermore that any agreement would not be subject to sanctions.

It also turned out that the rejectionist coalition in the three by three was not as shaken as it appeared on the surface, and as the US now firmly believed. Whatever the exact cause of the Okamatsu-Matsuura shoving match, the core of the alliance between the deterrence school and the WTO fundamentalists remained intact. Furthermore, because these schools of thought cut across ministry lines, rejectionist officials in both MITI and MOFA were now working on ways to isolate the remaining cooperationists inside MOFA. The three by three officials clearly realized that the concessions that had been made were more *political* in origin, rather than the result of bureaucratic disagreements. Now the clear task was to somehow keep the LDP from undermining this bureaucratic position in the future.

The rejectionists' efforts were given a boost by the post-agreement statements of the Clinton administration. Especially given Japan's interpretation of what it had actually agreed to, Japanese officials—both rejectionist and cooperationist—listened to the interpretations of the Clinton officials with growing consternation, then with a degree of anger. In particular, these officials were shocked as the Clinton people described nearly an opposite understanding of three contentious Framework issues: the macroeconomic target, the interpretation of 'objective criteria,' and the question of enforcablility.

In contrast to US officials, who hinted that Japan had agreed that a 'highly significant reduction' in the current account meant that it would reduce its surplus to below 1.5–2 per cent of GDP within four years, the Japanese side claimed that it had not committed itself to any such number or time frame, and that the US figures were a completely unilateral interpretation. Charlene Barshefsky's statements on the 'objective criteria' to measure market access were worse still. As mentioned in the last chapter, Barshefsky made it clear that if the two could not agree on specific indicators, then the US would define these unilaterally. Again, this interpretation was one that was not at all shared by Japan. In statements after the Framework agreement, Japanese politicians and bureaucrats claimed victory in that Japan had avoided any mention of numerical targets.

Furthermore, Clinton officials stated that the Framework agreements were to be fully enforceable under US trade law, including Section 301. Both Kantor and Barshefsky argued that the US 'reserved the right to enforce Japan's compliance,' and that it was not reluctant to do so.[52] The Japanese

[52] The Kantor letter and Japan's response appear in *Inside US Trade* (7/16/93: 10).

government for its part argued that the phrasing of the Framework did not commit it to enforcing the agreements, much less making it liable to sanctions. Miyazawa, for instance, stated in a TV interview that failure to achieve results would not lead to sanctions. The Japanese government had earlier sent Kantor a letter stating that it 'reserves the right, however, to withdraw from any particular structural or sectoral issue...in the event formal procedures (such as a 301 action) are initiated.'[53]

While Japanese officials were already beginning to learn that 'spin' was one of the Clinton administration's favorite tactics, the unilateral nature of these statements still came as a shock. The administration's statements further confirmed the Japanese belief that they could not trust the Clinton people, and that any concession would be unilaterally reinterpreted in the future. If anyone still had any doubts, they were fast disappearing now: Japan could not let the US prevail on numbers.

Now the three by three officials redoubled their efforts to forge a rejectionist position. The mounting evidence that Japan could not afford to make results-oriented concessions had finally silenced the cooperationist bureaucrats; but only a completely unified bureaucratic front would convince the party politicians to stick to a rejectionist line.[54]

The break the rejectionists needed came in July, just weeks after the Clinton–Miyazawa summit, when one of the LDP's larger factions splintered and then defected from the party. In the subsequent elections for the Lower House, held on July 18, the LDP was unable to regain the majority and thus lost hold of power for the first time in more than 40 years of uninterrupted rule. As the various opposition parties jockeyed to see what sort of coalition would emerge, the political world was essentially in upheaval, with little attention to substantive policy making. The bureaucrats thus had an essentially free had during the summer of 1993.

The coalition that emerged, inaugurated on August 6 under the leadership of Hosokawa Morihiro, head of the Japan New Party, was initially concerned mostly with its main domestic agenda, electoral reform. The influence of the bureaucrats was also higher in this period because the new ruling coalition had had little experience dealing with the bureaucracy. Also, because it was not clear how long it would remain in power, the

---

[53] *Inside US Trade* 7/16/93: 10.

[54] The Ministry of Finance was initially a member of this group because initial US demands included the possibility for a numerical target for Japan's overall current account surplus, which fell under MOF's jurisdiction. When the two sides agreed to aim for a 'highly significant' decrease in the current account, MOF's opposition to numerical targets weakened. From that point on the informal coordinating group centered on MITI and MOFA.

coalition found it difficult to overrule the bureaucrats on foreign policy issues. Finally, interference from the politicians was less of a concern because Hosokawa himself was determined to change old ways of doing things, and this included making the bilateral relationship a more equal one. In this sense the vacuum in domestic politics was instrumental in allowing new thinking to come to dominate Japan's negotiating position.

By the time the actual Framework talks commenced, in September 1993, the Japanese government had thus been able to develop a coherent rejectionist strategy that proved to be effective, and which it sustained through the 1995 Geneva auto talks and beyond. Throughout this period the government repeated an unwavering message that it was opposed to managed trade, and that it would not agree to a government commitment to use quantitative indicators to increase imports.

The strength and steadfastness of Japan's new position seems clear in hindsight, since we know that Japan eventually did say no. At the time, however, the Clinton people were assuming just the opposite.[55] American officials believed that the hardest part of the negotiations, getting the Japanese to agree on the Framework principles, was already over. Furthermore, the US was confident that it had maintained its own unity while the Japanese side crumbled. Japan had always made last-second concessions, the most recent being July 1993, and so probably would continue to do so. US officials thus might be forgiven for holding to these expectations. After all, many of Japan's bureaucratic rejectionists still worried that their own politicians would continue to cave in at the last moment. Unknown to the US, however, was that these bureaucrats had been hard at work to make sure that this was not going to happen this time around. In the fall of 1993, American officials were thus blithely unaware of the sea changes that had taken place inside the Japanese government, and thus unprepared for the brick wall they were about to encounter.

---

[55] I have seen no evidence that US government officials knew of the three by three meetings; indeed, many in the *Japanese* government were not aware of the group at the time. Unlike past administrations, the Clinton team had cut its informal ties with Japanese officials, or never truly developed them. Thus, 'back channel' communications were not an option. Furthermore, the US spy agencies had evidently not been yet used to eavesdrop on internal Japanese government deliberations, at least that I know of. That would (allegedly) come later.

7

Negotiating the Framework

Doomed from the Start?

In the summer of 1993, during the run-up to the opening of the Framework talks in September, the US soon discovered that its belief that it was more unified than Japan was only an illusion. In fact, the US soon discovered that it was unable to overcome the internal division between the moderate group that was willing to compromise on the issue of concrete numbers and sanctions, and the hard-liners who still insisted on achieving both. Its inability to come to an internal consensus put it at a disadvantage all through the Framework negotiations. Furthermore, this division was skillfully exploited by the Japanese side, which used an informational and diplomatic campaign that managed to outgun and outflank the US position. To their frustration, American officials found that their own position was being defined by everyone but themselves—by outside critics, by the media in both countries, and especially by the Japanese government.

As the US withered under this sustained assault, its position became increasingly divided, resulting in policy behavior that was both confused and confusing. Hard-liners led by Kantor had already realized that it would be difficult to achieve sanctionable targets but, behind closed doors, continued to press Japan for numbers and targets anyway. Hard-liners also sought to achieve something close to numerical targets through a semantic change: dropping the term but seeking to include enough numbers or quantitative indicators in the agreements that would amount to the same thing. Moderates, led by Cutter, were willing to offer a more substantive compromise, for instance by developing qualitative benchmarks, criteria, and the like, that could at least be used to monitor compliance, and downplaying the extent to which the Japanese government would be held legally accountable for enforcing any agreement. However, the US team was never able to completely solve its internal divisions, and this haunted it throughout the Framework discussions. It was never able to 'stay on message' precisely because it never *had* a single message.

It also turns out that the Japanese position was simultaneously becoming tougher, making any compromise nearly impossible to achieve. The Framework talks thus offered the extraordinary image of the US taking one step back only to have the Japanese take one step forward; the room for compromise always seemed to disappear as soon as it was created. This combination of American indecision and Japanese intransigence led to the failure of the Clinton–Hosokawa summit meeting of February 1994—the first and only time in postwar history that a bilateral summit meeting ended in failure. The lines drawn at that summit remained virtually unchanged through the summer of 1995, when the Geneva auto talks finally, mercifully, ended. In retrospect, then, the period leading up to February 1994 turned out to be the last chance the two had to avoid a collision.[1]

Japan's Diplomatic Offensive: The Managed Trade Mantra

As described in Chapter 5, in July 1993 many in the US government believed that the hard part of the negotiations had ended when Japan agreed to the principle that the new agreement was to be 'results oriented.' These officials did not seem concerned over their own lack of consensus as to what this phrase really meant and how it was to be operationalized. As mentioned, this lack of urgency was in part due to the belief that the Japanese side could be counted on to eventually agree to whatever position the US ended up advocating. That is, most saw no reason to expect that Japan's protestations against numerical targets would lead it to actually reject *all* US demands. The Japanese government seemed even more divided than ever, especially after the Okura incident, and Japan's cooperationists still could be counted on to make concessions at critical points. Even if its resistance was stronger than usual, it could be expected to yield if the US was willing to apply a little pressure. If pushed hard enough, Japan would revert to form.

Besides, American officials had high hopes that the new Hosokawa administration was seeking real change. Hosokawa (who became Prime

---

[1] In retrospect, analyzing the interactions of the two governments is almost like watching a Greek tragedy—the protagonists, fatally flawed, locked on a clear course toward disaster, and with no way to stop it. As Hugh Patrick has pointed out, however, no one died in this particular play, at least not in a literal sense, so perhaps the play was closer to a comedy of errors!

Minister that August) was the first non-LDP Prime Minister in nearly 40 years, and came into office with the look of a vibrant leader who was committed to change. The US assumption all along had been that the LDP was part of the problem, and so the Clinton team welcomed political change. Like many in Japan, the US saw Hosokawa as a new style of politician who might be able and willing to force a real shift in Japan's past behavior. Hosokawa further seemed to be a leader who was willing to deal forthrightly with many issues that the LDP had refused to touch, including for instance acknowledging Japan's responsibility for the Pacific War. The new Prime Minister was seen as someone the US 'could do business with.'

Most encouraging was the new government's statements about Japan's economic and bureaucratic systems, many of which confirmed the charges that American revisionists had been making for decades. In particular, new MITI Minister Kumagai Hiroshi was surprisingly blunt in his criticisms of the bureaucracy for being closed and secretive, for overly protecting industries through regulation, and thus as the source of many of the anti-competitive practices in the economy. Hosokawa also seemed bent on deregulation and reducing the power of the bureaucracy, a policy that was taken as an admission that the bureaucrats had come to over-shadow the politicians. Since he was willing to own up to the closed nature of Japan's economy and its responsibility for causing the current trade problems, he might thus be willing to take unprecedented steps to rectify them.[2] In any case, there were few signs that Hosokawa would have either the inclination or the guts to say no and to stick with it.

In retrospect, Hosokawa's desire for deregulation should have raised concerns among American hard-liners, since this goal was contrary to a results-oriented trade agreement. That is, any government-guaranteed numerical target would require *more* government intervention into and interference with the market mechanism, not less. It turns out that Hosokawa's desire for deregulation was a sincere one, and to him this meant getting the government out of the market. Furthermore, Hosokawa did want to change the nature of Japan's relationship with the US, but again in the opposite direction than the US wanted. Hosokawa himself seems to

---

[2] Barshefsky, for instance, indicated to reporters that Hosokawa represented the 'first possibility of real change in Japan' (*Inside US Trade* 10/22/93: 13). Other hard-liners, including Kantor, felt that Hosokawa would not be able to achieve any significant deregulation, and thus stuck to their pursuit of hard numbers. Top coalition members, including Foreign Minister Hata, also seemed willing to consider the US demands for current account targets.

have desired a more equal relationship with the US, and this entailed having to say no when the occasion called for it.[3]

During this period the power of the economic bureaucrats was magnified because of the political turmoil and vacuum that beset the Japanese system. Hosokawa's new and untested coalition was never able to fully control the bureaucrats, and so in this crucial period it was the bureaucracy that played the central role in designing and implementing Japan's response to US demands. As described in the last chapter, Japan's rejectionist bureaucrats were forging a clear consensus on the need to stop US demands in their tracks, and thus were less constrained by cooperationist thinking than was normally the case.

* * *

Beginning in the summer of 1993, these bureaucrats put Japan squarely on the offensive. Their response, which continued throughout the Framework period, was an unrelenting offensive designed to undermine the US revisionist position. Using a combination of an informational campaign, an appeal to multilateral norms and institutions, and a more conventional diplomatic approach, the Japanese managed to expose—and then exploit— the division of opinion inside the US government, and eventually forced it onto the retreat.

The first part of this campaign took the form of a PR attack that succeeded in shifting the parameters of the debate. In this, the Japanese took dead aim at undermining the assumptions that formed the basis of the US approach. These efforts actually were longstanding ones, dating back to the 1980s, but the Japanese government now redoubled its efforts. The government focused its attack on revisionist assumptions and now tried to link the revisionists with the push for managed trade—and then sought to discredit them both. To an unprecedented degree, Japanese officials channeled information and position papers to the media in both countries. Japan also took its case directly to American audiences; in countless speeches, interviews, and publications, officials pounded the anti-revisionist and anti-managed trade drum. The constant refrain continued to be that the revisionists were wrong in their depiction of the Japanese economy as closed and as a threat. Japan was not an outlier or an exception, but rather operated on the same terms as any other capitalist economy; there was therefore no reason to force exceptional remedies on it. As Prestowitz had earlier put it, 'spurred in part by the Ministry of Foreign Affairs and MITI,

---

[3] Curtis 1999.

Japanese analysts and commentators filled the media with analyses purporting to prove that the Japanese economy is squarely within the neoclassical framework.'[4]

More controversially, Japan's effort to undermine revisionist assumptions also involved attacks on the credibility of the revisionists themselves. This effort is one that Japanese officials still deny ever consciously making, at least openly. But it was also proving to be very effective, at least judging by the reactions of prominent revisionists. Prestowitz, for instance, pointed to the government's 'official instigation and support of the virulent attack on the revisionists.' He went on to quote a journalist:

[those who made harsh statements about Japan] were stigmatized by the Japanese Ministry of Foreign Affairs as 'revisionists.' This was because the Ministry feared that accurate knowledge among foreigners about the structure of Japanese capitalism might lead to countermeasures against Japanese business activities, and it sought through propaganda and dirty tricks to prevent this from happening.[5]

Similarly, Chalmers Johnson argued that:

some officials in Japan's Ministry of Foreign Affairs concluded that their immediate interests would be better served if my writings were not taken seriously among my fellow countrymen. They therefore began a campaign to label me a 'Japan-basher,' and this campaign was enthusiastically taken up by some of their supporters in the United States.

Johnson went on to note that this 'Japan-basher' label 'turned out to be a code for racism.'[6]

Another part of this campaign was what one US negotiator called Japan's 'managed trade mantra,' in which Japanese officials defined the American position solely in terms of its most extreme demands for market shares or numerical targets. As will become clearer in the rest of this chapter, over time Japan lumped together anything that even smacked of results, including efforts simply to monitor progress, as attempts to impose a managed trade solution. Even though the US negotiating demands were in fact more complicated and nuanced, the Japanese side latched onto the managed trade rhetoric and used this blunt instrument to bash the US negotiators over the head all through the Framework talks.

---

[4] Prestowitz 1992: 78. See also Yamaguchi 1995; and Armacost 1996: 184–5, and 196.

[5] Prestowitz 1993: 80–1. The journalist was Peter Ennis. See also *Tokyo Business Today* 1/90: 30.

[6] Johnson 1995b: 11 and 101. The Gang of Four also felt it necessary to explicitly refute criticisms of them for being 'personally vindictive or inappropriately ambitious...[or for] harboring some innate prejudice against the Japanese people and their culture, and perhaps against non-caucasians in general' (Fallows et al. 1990: 54; see also Fukushima 1991a: 43).

As mentioned in the last chapter, it is difficult to tell when these officials truly believed the arguments they were making, and when they pushed them because they were proving so effective. Many Japanese officials probably saw little distinction between results, managed trade, and numerical targets; many had become so distrustful of American officials that they assumed that one would lead to the other. However, many other Japanese officials I spoke with were well aware that the US government was not unified on the question of hard, sanctionable numbers, and that it would be possible to achieve a results-oriented agreement that did not include numbers. But, as one official put it, Japanese officials were also pragmatic enough to realize that 'managed trade' had become a 'dirty phrase' internationally, and that they could keep the US off-balance if they could make this charge stick.[7]

Although some Japanese officials continue to deny that the government ran a conscious PR campaign, others are willing to acknowledge that this was a part of a concerted strategy.[8] Some officials also acknowledge learning a lesson from how effectively the US had used the Japanese media during the SII talks. Then, the US government was able to get the message out that deregulation would help average Japanese consumers, and thus was able to shift the outcome of the negotiations.[9] Now the Japanese government made a special effort to make sure that the media stayed on its side. In addition, most officials I spoke with acknowledge that the US penchant for voicing extreme demands made their PR job a relatively easy one: 'no managed trade' was a sound bite that audiences everywhere could understand. One of these high-level MITI officials put it in stark terms: 'it helped that the US took such a stupid position!'[10]

A second part of Japan's strategy was to appeal to normative arguments to discredit the revisionist/managed trade approach. But in an interesting change from the past normative debates, which had been over the issue of fairness, the Japanese side now appealed to more principled norms—the norms of free trade and non-interference in domestic markets, and multilateralism in the international realm. Officials now repeatedly argued that America's managed trade demands contravened the principle of allowing market forces to determine market outcomes, and thus sought to portray themselves as the defenders of the free market, opposing excessive

---

[7] Interview with senior MITI official, 10/7/97.

[8] Ibid. Japanese journalist Ayako Doi, in contrast, believed that the government of Japan was simply incapable of conducting a coordinated media strategy (Economic Strategy Institute 1995: 5).

[9] Schoppa 1997.   [10] Interview with very senior MITI official, 10/22/97.

government involvement in the economy, and supporting free trade. Japan as the defender of market principles was a position that many in the US (and not few in Japan) found to be highly ironic, if not ludicrous. After all, Japan, and MITI in particular, had been one of the most interventionist in the world, and had long helped to manage competition for many of its industries.[11] As one astute observer put it,

there was no shortage of irony about the Japanese government waving the free trade banner and alleging that the United States was becoming a managed trader—this coming as it did from a country that has had perhaps the most pronounced and successful record of a heavily regulated market economy in modern economic history.[12]

The Japanese government also sought to portray America's trade demands as contrary to the international norm of multilateralism, in that the US was not even making an effort to utilize existing multilateral trade mechanisms. Complaints about American unilateralism—in which the US tried to serve as prosecutor, judge, and jury—were of course not new, but Japan now tried to make the charges stick. This appeal found considerable international resonance, as many in Europe and elsewhere had become increasingly opposed to American unilateralism in the trade arena. Many agreed that the imposition of numerical targets on a single country would represent a dangerous escalation in this trend, and thus needed to be deterred. If a powerful country like the US could disregard trade norms whenever it pleased, these norms would be weakened to meaningless. On this point as well US officials scoffed at Japan's argument. After all, they believed that it was Japan that had been the main violator of international trade norms of openness and reciprocity; America was now simply trying to level the playing field. Nevertheless, this appeal to multilateralism proved to be the more effective of Japan's normative appeals, intersecting as it did with fears throughout Europe and Asia that the US would be unconstrained in escalating its trade demands against everyone.

Japan used both normative and pragmatic appeals in a third part of its strategy: using conventional diplomacy to isolate the US. Immediately after the July summit, Japan lobbied OECD members to insert a phrase opposing managed trade into their joint communiqué. The OECD did so, over US objections. The Japanese government also lobbied individual governments directly, utilizing not only regular consultations with

---

[11] Uriu 1996. [12] Janow 1992: 77.

European officials but also numerous meetings with the European Union. Japanese officials argued not only on normative grounds, but also appealed to Europe's bottom-line interests: if the US were to achieve some sort of market share target, the real losers would be European exporters. Even if the US was always careful to say that market share agreements would increase access to Japanese markets for *all* countries, everyone recognized the political reality that it would have to be the American share of the market that would rise.[13] As one American observer put it, the Japanese appeal to the Europeans was (in effect), 'you got screwed on semiconductors; you don't want to see it happen again.'[14]

The European governments found themselves torn by these arguments. European anger at its chronic trade deficits with Japan and the closed nature of the market was if anything stronger than in the US, and revisionist assumptions were more readily accepted. To many, a results-oriented approach was a logical one—indeed, some European officials had proposed even more drastic solutions. But while many agreed that Japan deserved to be treated as an outlier, the newer, more worrisome issue was whether the US should be allowed to impose market share targets unilaterally. On this score, Europe was willing to stand with the Japanese.

Japan's diplomatic offensive was similarly effective in other Asian countries, many of which were also highly critical of the closed nature of the Japanese economy. But, like the Europeans, many of the Asian economies also opposed American unilateralism. In particular, Korea was not at all happy with being labeled an unfair trader under Section 301.[15] Now Japanese officials issued clear warnings that if Japan were forced to bow to demands for numerical targets, it would only be a matter of time before the US demanded similar agreements with the smaller and weaker Asian economies. Although the Asian countries did not always openly back Japan in the subsequent negotiations, neither were they willing to take the US side.[16]

---

[13] In the Semiconductor Agreement, for example, the market share target included all foreign chip sales, but the only number of concern to the US government was American sales. The US was always very careful to keep up the pretense that it sought multilateral benefits, even if the reality differed.

[14] Interview with DC official, 4/18/97.

[15] Interview with USTR official, 4/15/97; see also Bhagwati and Patrick 1990; and Kim 1990.

[16] Later, in key votes in the GATT and then the WTO, the Japanese were relieved to find that the Asians had taken Japan's side, or at worst had remained neutral. Japan also had its eggs lined up in Japan as well: in January, Keidanren issued a strong statement opposing numerical targets.

The US Wavers

Over the course of the Framework discussions the US team was dismayed to find that the Japanese PR offensive was working, and that support for its results-oriented approach was slipping away on all fronts.

America early on was diplomatically isolated, with Europe and many of the Asian countries taking the Japanese side of the dispute. For instance, when the US held talks with some of the Asian countries as early as the summer of 1993, Barshefsky was surprised to find that the Japanese had gotten there first. America's attempts to gain support in Asia essentially fell flat. More distressing was the attitude taken by the European Commission (EC), in part because the US expected to receive some backing there. The Europeans were also voicing their sympathy for the US approach—but only in private. In contrast, in various public statements the EC commissioner, Sir Leon Brittan, made clear his disdain for the managed trade approach. One DC participant recalled a number of times when Kantor assured the group that he had just spoken with 'Sir Leon' and had secured his support, only to see Brittain soon issuing another damaging public statement condemning managed trade. The participants would ask Kantor 'what happened?, at which point Mickey would call again, and Brittan would say it was all a misunderstanding—and then [Brittan] would go out and criticize the US position again.'[17] Kantor later commented that 'the Europeans are always delighted when they can hold our coats and we can go out and get our noses bloodied.'[18]

That the US was now finding itself alone was an ironic and stunning turnabout; given the worldwide anger and antipathy toward Japan's economic practices that had characterized the last 50 years, no one even a year earlier could have imagined Japan gaining the support of the international community. As an editorial in the *Far Eastern Economic Review* put it: 'Mr. Clinton, in his pursuit of numerical 'targets' has managed to do what no American president in recent memory has done before: give the Japanese the moral high ground on free trade.'[19]

The US had tried to define a new norm for the treatment of Japan, but now found itself isolated and beaten at its own norms game.

---

[17] Interview with DC official, 4/18/97.

[18] *Inside US Trade* 3/11/94: 4. Kantor went on to criticize the Europeans, saying that 'what we don't look for is criticism from those who sit on the sidelines and are not willing to get in the game.'

[19] *Far Eastern Economic Review* 2/10/94, Nikkei Needs Database <http://www.nikkeieu.com/needs/>.

The Japanese position also struck a responsive chord in parts of the American media and academia. The *Wall Street Journal* in particular took a strong position opposed to managed trade as the solution to the Japan problem. Other less conservative newspapers did not take such a clear stance, but the groundswell of support for targets or indicators was never as strong as US officials had hoped. The Japanese government's position got a further boost when a prominent group of economists came out in support of their arguments. In September 1993, on the eve of the first face-to-face meeting between Clinton and Hosokawa, these economists, including five Nobel Prize winners, sent a highly publicized letter to the two leaders questioning the assumptions behind the numerical targets policy and calling for an end to US pressures for targets and managed trade.[20]

The US was thus losing the PR battle even at home, to the amazement of the Clinton team, which saw only duplicity and hypocrisy in the arguments the Japanese were making. As Cutter put it, 'for the most managed economy in the developed world to level [managed trade charges] against the most open economy in the developed world is preposterous.'[21] One problem was that the US found that it was unable to mount an effective PR counterattack of its own. In part, this was because the Clinton team never seemed to feel that an effective press strategy in Japan was needed.[22] Later, even after the US realized that it had to mount a counter-PR campaign, it found that it was unable to do so. In part this reflects the success of the Japanese PR campaign, which had already been able to cast American demands as unreasonable and extreme. Another problem was that the US side remained divided on just how much it actually wanted to pursue numbers. One USTR official recalls drafting an op-ed piece arguing that it was Japan that was the managed trader, and that the US desire for indicators was only an effort to open markets, but was dismayed to find that the policy team was unable to agree even on these basic points.[23]

In sum, the US allowed Japan to turn the debate into one of Japan's defense of free markets versus America's desire for managed trade. One

[20] The letter originated from Columbia University, particularly economist Jagdish Bhagwati (Kunkel 2008: 171).

[21] *Far Eastern Economic Review* 1/20/94, Nikkei Needs Database <http://www.nikkeieu.com/needs/>.

[22] This is in stark contrast to the US approach during the SII talks, where it was the US that was able to effectively use the Japanese media, in what Schoppa (1997) calls an attempt at 'participant expansion.' No such efforts were made during the Framework. This was another consequence of the adoption of the revisionist approach, since one of its assumptions was that Japan was essentially unchangeable, and thus that the US should not expend any energy trying.

[23] Interview with USTR official, 4/4/97.

official expressed grudging admiration at how effective Japan's PR strategy was: 'We didn't see it coming, and couldn't figure out how to counter it. The Japanese had us for lunch.'[24]

* * *

As the official Framework negotiations began in September 1993, the fact that the US side still had not figured out exactly what it wanted to achieve, and how it was going to achieve it, now came back to haunt it. As Ed Lincoln later put it, even though the US was adamant in demanding some Japanese commitment to objective criteria, 'nobody [in the US government] knew what it meant . . . [and in the] fall of 1993 they were still trying to figure it out.'[25] Furthermore, the ground had already shifted, with Japan gradually having eroded support for the US position in Europe, Asia, the multilateral institutions, and even domestically in the US. In some ways, the battle was already being lost, although the US side was blithely unaware of this.

Now, within the DC as well, the balance between hard-liners and moderates was shifting. The original hard-line consensus was gradually eroding, as some high-profile advocates for numbers or targets were switching to the moderate camp. The two most crucial were the group's academics, Tyson and Summers. Both had been early advocates of numbers, Tyson in particular, and had played an important role in the crafting of the initial Framework approach. Their conversion to a lukewarm attitude toward numerical targets thus came as a sharp disappointment to the hard-line camp. As one official later put it, 'Summers and Tyson made a formidable team.'[26]

Growing support for the moderate position also reflected a partial questioning of the revisionist thesis, in that some were becoming skeptical of the argument that the Japanese economy posed an imminent threat to the US economy. The recession in Japan had by then lasted nearly four years, and it was not clear when or how strongly its economy would rebound. In addition, many saw mounting evidence that some Japanese industries were not as competitive as had once been feared. Cutter, for instance, found that as he learned more about Japan, he realized that its economic system was not the perfect machine that it had been built up to be, causing

[24] Interview with Commerce official, 4/9/97.   [25] Cited in Kunkel 2003: 171.
[26] Interview with State Department official, 4/24/97. The moderates were still led by the NEC's Cutter. It is important to remember that the moderates agreed on the need for some sort of indicators, and also that the US needed to deal forcefully with Japan, but were less adamant about hard numbers and question of sanctionability.

him to re-evaluate the nature of the Japanese threat.[27] In addition, the US economy was doing much better by the fall of 1993, with unemployment falling and growth continuing to rise. Now, as the sense of crisis declined, so too did the urgency in dealing decisively with the Japan problem. Not only was some sort of drastic policy response less necessary, it was also more difficult to justify in terms of its cost effectiveness. That is, because Japan was putting up a real fight on numbers, moderates now began to wonder if the outcomes the US sought would be worth the costs of a bitter negotiation. If the Japanese economy was not such an extreme threat, did the US really need to pursue such extreme remedies?

Other factors went into the shift toward the moderate's position, according to direct observers of the process. Some officials were uncomfortable being labeled 'managed traders,' especially because they believed that this label misrepresented their position. In this, Japan's attempt to label anything even remotely resembling targets or results as managed trade appears to have been effective.[28] Other participants insist that Summers was also strongly affected by the economists' letter opposing managed trade since he, after all, was a professional economist himself and thus highly sensitive to this constituency.[29] In the case of Tyson, colleagues believe that she was constrained in part by the nature of her appointment as the head of the CEA, traditionally a position that has been associated with free trade. Tyson, however, was also finding that proposing a numerical approach was easier than achieving it. Tyson, one official said, 'found that the reality of negotiations was more difficult than simply writing a book about it.'[30]

Still, the moderates never abandoned the other parts of the revisionist thesis: that Japan was structurally closed and needed to be dealt with as such. As one senior moderate put it, from start to finish, 'I never once stopped believing that Japan is closed.'[31] Moderates therefore continued to feel that a results orientation was still needed in order to rectify the trade problem. And, in their heart of hearts, most still seemed to prefer numerical targets: that is, if the Japanese government would have

[27] Interview with very senior DC official, 4/29/97.
[28] Interview with USTR official, 4/15/97; and very senior DC official, 4/29/97.
[29] Interview with DC official, 4/18/97; and USTR official, 4/23/97. In addition, Summer's father-in-law, Nobel Prize winner Paul Samuelson, had also signed this letter. Aides to Summers maintain that he was never an advocate of numerical targets on the sectoral level, and only vaguely in favor of hard macroeconomic targets. In any case, once the latter issue was resolved in the July negotiations, Summers now spoke against numerical targets for specific sectoral markets.
[30] Interview with NSC official, 4/14/97.
[31] Interview with very senior DC official, 4/29/97.

willingly agreed, these officials would have welcomed a numbers-oriented agreement. But because the Japanese were most certainly not agreeing, the moderates were now convinced that the most that could be achieved was the use of quantitative indicators that could be used to verify that imports were increasing and that progress toward results was being made. A results orientation was still the only way to achieve real market access, but this could be achieved without the diplomatic costs of forcing hard numbers down Japan's throat.

Already by the fall of 1993, then, it was the hard-liners who were losing control over the DC. But this group, still led by the USTR's Kantor and Barshefsky and Commerce's Brown, never deviated from the conclusion they had derived from the revisionist thesis that explicit import targets, subject to sanctions, were the only solution to the Japan problem. The hard-liners were thus angry and frustrated as the early consensus on numerical targets began to weaken. The hard-liners were especially chagrined as they watched the Japanese informational campaign, which they saw as hypocritical and dishonest, also prove to be remarkably effective. The hard-liners were further angered by what they saw as weakness and lack of resolve among the moderates, who seemed willing to back off at the slightest resistance from the Japanese.

The hard-line camp was realistic enough to understand that getting an agreement that included hard numerical targets even as concrete as the 1986 Semiconductor Agreement was becoming difficult, if not impossible.[32] Not only was Japan taking a very strong line, moderates in the US government were no longer on board either. However, the hard-liners were by no means giving up on their goal of meaningful, enforceable numbers. Quite to the contrary, some hard-line extremists, dismayed by their inability to achieve a consensus on numbers, were now also willing to fight what one official described as a 'guerilla war' in order to get some sort of numbers-oriented agreement. The enemies in that war were those officials who seemed willing to consider a less hard-line approach—or, as this revisionist hard-liner put it, 'those without religion.'[33]

---

[32] Thus, revisionist assumptions were increasingly enmeshed with international political realities. Hall has argued that for ideas to be implemented, they must be viable economically, politically, and in terms of administrative acceptance; to this must be added *international* viability as well. Hall 1989. That is, unless a country is powerful enough to implement them unilaterally, ideas must be acceptable to the targets of those ideas. The revisionist thesis had seemed to have passed the domestic test in the early part of the administration, but was now withering under international pressures. Indeed, now that the US government found itself under attack from all quarters, revisionist ideas were even beginning to lose a degree of domestic viability.

[33] Interview with USTR official, 4/23/97.

One strategy was to try to convince the Japanese side, behind closed doors, to agree to the equivalent of numerical targets, as discussed later in this chapter. Another tactic was to achieve numerical targets without actually calling them numerical targets. As one official commented, the USTR nearly tied itself into knots 'trying to figure out how to get targets without asking for targets.'[34] A USTR staff member recalls writing over 65 memos trying to redefine some basic terms—benchmark, objective criteria, qualitative versus quantitative indicators, significant versus substantial, and the like—all with the aim of sneaking in some sort of 'directional feel.'[35] In the fall, for instance, Barshefsky argued that one useful 'benchmark' would be the average level of imports of the other OECD countries, which was much higher than Japan's. The US could insist that Japan increase its imports to this level, but could avoid having to ask for 'targets.' Barshefsky reportedly felt that this should be acceptable to Japan since it did not represent a hard, concrete number.[36] A Commerce official put it bluntly: 'Charlene became a theologian on numerical targets, calling for targets, but not targets—it was very confusing, even to us.'[37]

If administration insiders were confused so too was everyone else. Take, for example, this extraordinary exchange between Barshefsky and Representative Christopher Cox (R-California) during Congressional hearings in 1994:

Mr. COX. But what is the quantity we're measuring, then?
Ms. BARSHEFSKY. We would be looking at a trend, basically at a trend of continual access based on the expected outcome from deregulation.
Mr. COX. An access as measured by?
Ms. BARSHEFSKY. Value. Value, typically.
Mr. COX. Value of what compared to what?
Ms. BARSHEFSKY. Well, one could look at volume of sales or value of total procurements.
Mr. COX. Volume of sales by whom?
Ms. BARSHEFSKY. Foreign producers in total.
Mr. COX. As a percentage of?
Ms. BARSHEFSKY. It could be as a percentage of the market in an absolute sense.
Mr. COX. All right. If it's as a percentage of the market, isn't that called market share?
Ms. BARSHEFSKY. We are not saying you would never not look at market share.
Mr. COX. OK. The reason I asked this is that—
Ms. BARSHEFSKY. That's a legitimate factor, but what I'm saying is—

---

[34] Interview with State Department official, 3/24/97.
[35] Interview with USTR official, 4/23/97.   [36] Interview with US Embassy official, 4/7/97.
[37] Interview with Commerce official, 4/9/97.

Mr. COX. What I would like to ask for the record... if in negotiating with foreign countries we are not quite clear, then the opportunities for language, cultural differences, and so on to expand our differences itself expands. If we have trouble as Members of Congress understanding what you're saying in English, I can't imagine how it translates into Japanese.[38]

Linguistics and semantic confusion, however, was the least part of the difficulty for the Clinton team. The core of the problem was that the moderates were never able to effectively rein in the hard-liners, and never able to fully stop their guerilla tactics. The US side thus sent too many mixed signals that were then open to reinterpretation by the Japanese side. Even if the official US position never called for market shares or numerical targets, there were enough in the DC who remained fully committed to targets, and continued to try to make sure their position prevailed, through whatever means necessary.

Thus, while the Japanese had used the summer of 1993 to hammer out a unified position, the US found itself increasingly divided. The Clinton team was unable to effectively communicate its policy objectives because it could never agree on what those objectives really were. In the process, it let its position be defined by the Japanese government, which latched onto the more extreme American rhetoric and behavior as proof that the US was indeed interested only in numbers. Now the US was not only incapable of 'speaking with one voice,' it was also sending contradictory and confusing signals, with some officials trying to publicly back away from numbers even as others pushed even harder for them in secret. One participant summed it all up very simply: 'We couldn't say we weren't managed traders because some of us wanted to *be* managed traders!'[39]

America Retreats, Japan Advances

The Framework talks were marked from the beginning by tense relations among the negotiators.[40] While US–Japan negotiations have always been tough and intense, past negotiators were often able to establish some sort of positive personal relations. Not so in the Framework, with

---

[38] US House 1994: 179. The exchange actually was a post-mortem on the failed Hosokawa Summit of February 1994.

[39] Interview with DC official, 4/18/97.

[40] The first round was held September 19–22, in Hawaii, followed by subsequent rounds from October 12–22, in Tokyo, November 9–12 in Washington, and December 6–7 in Tokyo. The fifth round was held in Washington from January 4 to 14, 1994.

few exceptions.[41] American negotiators 'made little effort to conceal their disregard for their [Japanese] bureaucratic counterparts.'[42] And Japanese officials did not try to hide their disdain and even dislike for many top American officials, especially the hard-liners, Barshefsky and Kantor. At one point a Japanese official told an American counterpart, 'I wish Carla Hills was here!'—an ironic statement given how much criticism Japan had levied at what they saw as the former trade representative's heavy-handed approach.

However, these personal antagonisms only exacerbated the real problem: the simple incompatibility of positions, and particularly what meaning would be attached to the quantitative indicators that were to be included in the agreement. Both sides recognized a clear distinction between the two government procurement baskets (medical equipment and telecommunications equipment) and the two private sector negotiations, on insurance and the automotive sector. The US felt fully confident in demanding 'results,' including quantitative indicators, in the negotiations over Japanese government procurement practices. After all, it was the Japanese *government* that was making most of these procurement decisions, so it could hardly make the argument that this was 'beyond the government's reach.' Barshefsky, for instance, was quoted by one participant in a January 25 negotiating session as calling for a 'prompt, substantial, and continuous increase in foreign sales,' and that the US wanted a 'substantial increase in foreign sales over the medium-term toward the G-7 range.'[43]

Japanese officials also recognized the distinctive nature of the government procurement basket, and were willing to be a bit flexible on the use of indicators. Still, they stuck to their desire to use indicators only as ways to measure the improvement of the *process* of procurement, not in terms of a commitment to any sort of market *outcome*. According to the same participant in that meeting, Matsuura rejected the Barshefsky argument by pointing out that:

[the] foreign share of the US medical technologies is 15%. In Japan it is 25%. So should the US government make a commitment to increase its foreign share to the Japanese level? We're not proposing that—it is just a hypothetical question. Of course your answer would be 'no.'

Furthermore, Japanese negotiators did their best to avoid any mention of targets and official commitments that could later be subject to sanctions.

---

[41] Interview with veteran Commerce official, 4/14/97. [42] Armacost 1996: 184.
[43] Interview with State Department official, 6/15/97.

Japanese rejectionists also wanted to avoid setting any precedent for the auto talks, fearing that any arrangement that included numbers could be used as leverage by the US: if it would agree to numbers on medical equipment, for instance, why couldn't it do the same on autos?

It was in the private sector baskets, notably autos and auto parts, that the Japanese staked out their strongest position against any form of managed trade. As described in Chapter 6, Japanese officials felt that including numbers in any private sector agreement would open the gates for the US to push for similar agreements in many other industries, and for this reason MITI had been adamantly opposed to including autos in the Framework discussions in the first place. As Okamatsu put it, 'if we compromise with the US and pledge any import targets, we have to provide the same to all other trade partners . . . that's something that we could never do.'[44]

As the auto negotiations opened in October 1993, Japanese officials were still unsure what the US bottom-line position really was (not surprising since the US team had still not come to closure on its final position).[45] Japanese officials thus debated amongst themselves exactly which of the mixed signals they were getting was the genuine one. Japanese cooperationists pointed out that the US officially was only asking for 'results' rather than targets. Furthermore, the moderates in the US government were privately reassuring them that they would use indicators only to monitor progress, rather than as the basis for sanctions—there would be no expectations built into the agreement that Japan had to achieve a certain increase in imports. So long as the US was willing to back off from sanctionable numbers, Japan could live with some vaguely worded language involving 'results.' Indeed, cooperationists believed that Japan needed to agree to some sort of a results oriented agreement, not only because this is what it had promised to do, but also because to refuse to compromise at all would unnecessarily worsen relations.

Rejectionist Japanese officials still insisted that Japan needed to squelch any agreement that included numbers, even if these were purely private sector commitments. As discussed earlier, these officials felt that the

---

[44] *The Nikkei Weekly* 1/10/94, Nikkei Needs Database <http://www.nikkeieu.com/needs/>. Significantly, Okamatsu was one of the MITI officials most directly involved in the 1986 Semiconductor Agreement, which let to the retaliatory sanctions against Japan. As Toyoda Masakazu later put it, 'Japan's agreement to (numerical targets) in the semiconductor agreement—Okamatsu is the responsible person for agreeing to that.' From an unpublished transcript of a University of California, San Diego talk, 'The Future of US–Japan Relations,' 11/30/95.

[45] Lincoln 1999: 7.

inclusion of any number could later be construed by the US as an official Japanese government commitment that would then be subject to sanctions.

This rejectionist position was bolstered early in the negotiations when it became clear that the US was tacitly pushing for numbers, even if the official rhetoric and statements claimed that they were not. One high-level Japanese participant described an early low-level meeting on auto parts in which Jeffrey Garten, the US negotiator from Commerce, was clearly asking for specific numbers, but was smart enough not to put this request on paper. Instead, Garten used a white board where he would outline the areas of agreement and disagreement, pointedly drawing a blank box where the numbers on auto parts would have gone, and indicating that a numerical target was all that was needed to wrap up a deal. The US side was careful to erase the white board as soon as the meeting concluded.[46]

Given their growing distrust of American officials, rejectionists were inclined to interpret this sort of mixed signal coming out of Washington in the worst possible light. Furthermore, even if some in the US government did not insist on hard numbers, and even if they were sincere in what they were saying, it was not clear that their position would carry the day. Rejectionists in Japan could also point to the many private statements by other US officials that hinted at numbers and sanctions. As a senior trade official put it, 'if it walks like a duck, talks like a duck and smells like a duck, it probably is a duck.'[47] Given these uncertainties, it was best to avoid numbers altogether.

An unofficial proposal put forward by the US effectively resolved this debate in favor of the rejectionists in Japan. This proposal, which was presented by Garten on October 19, 1993 called for Japan to 'agree to specific targets for future purchases of US auto parts and vehicles,' including a series of quantitative criteria to achieve 'a prompt, substantial, and sustained increase' in sales of autos and parts. Furthermore, the US demanded that the Japanese government issue 'guidance' to its firms to increase their purchases of US-made auto parts. The proposal also stated that 'regarding the above quantitative indicators, specific expectations

---

[46] Interview with very senior MITI official, 10/16/97. Another Japanese official insists that the US had delivered to Okamatsu a document months earlier, in September, that specified numerical targets for auto parts, but this was not reported in the media (interview with MITI official, 9/24/97).

[47] *The Nikkei Weekly* 2/7/94, Nikkei Needs Database <http://www.nikkeieu.com/needs/>.

shall be included in the Arrangement.'[48] As *Inside US Trade* noted, this phrase was significant because 'the specific expectations language was used in the US–Japan semiconductor arrangement.'[49]

This unofficial proposal very quickly found its way into the press, leaked there by the Japanese side to *Inside US Trade*, which published it at the end of the month. One US participant later said that they could not figure out how the proposal got into the press so quickly. And a top Japanese official, somewhat disingenuously, said that he could not believe how transparent and leaky the White House was, since even its unofficial proposals wound up so quickly in the press![50]

There is still some confusion as to what the Garten proposal was all about, and what the US officially asked for on autos and auto parts. Some still insist that the US never officially demanded numbers or targets, and thus that the Garten proposal was an unofficial one that did not fully reflect policy. In fact, had it not appeared in the press, the US side could easily deny that it had ever been made. Others are willing to admit that the US was more forthright in asking for numbers behind closed doors, but that this was merely an extreme negotiating position, a trial balloon that could be quickly retracted if it met with stiff opposition. If the Japanese were amenable, fine, but if they were absolutely opposed, Washington was prepared to back away from the position.[51] Still others, however, see the Garten proposal as one of the guerilla tactics of the hard-liners, designed to inject some sort of concrete numbers into the negotiations.[52] If so, this tactic heartened some in the US but also puzzled many others: one of the US moderates expressed surprise at seeing the Garten proposal in the press, since 'up to then, I really thought that we were *not* going for numbers.'[53]

Regardless of these interpretations of what the US side thought it was doing, once the Garten proposal hit the trade press, it was immediately forced to disavow it.[54] *Inside US Trade* in December paraphrased Garten as saying that 'it is a misinterpretation of the US position to say the Administration wants targets and emphasized that it was never the intention of the US to try to force the Japanese private sector to make a commitment to

---

[48] *Inside US Trade*, 'Special Report,' 11/1/93.

[49] *Inside US Trade* 1/7/94: 4. The US also asked for numbers on the insurance market.

[50] Interview with very senior MITI official, 10/16/97.

[51] Interview with veteran Commerce official, 4/14/97. These interpretations also reflect a degree of hindsight, in that the US failed to achieve numbers; it is not unusual for officials to later walk away from failed objectives, or to argue that these were never really the objective in the first place.

[52] Interview with USTR official, 4/23/97.   [53] Interview with Treasury official, 5/14/97.

[54] Lincoln 1999; interview with very senior DC official, 4/29/97; and US Embassy official, 4/7/97.

any specific number of sales.' Spero similarly stated that 'we want to have benchmarks, we're not setting them as actionable targets.'[55] Privately, as well, the administration was going out of its way to assure the Japanese side that numerical targets were not at all what the US was seeking. The Japanese press reported that in late December 'a top-level official at the US Embassy in Tokyo informed the Japanese government [that] the US would not pursue numerical targets in upcoming Framework trade negotiations.'[56]

After the Garten debacle, the US was forced to make a significant retreat, at least in public: from this point on, hope of achieving an agreement with hard numbers or targets was effectively dashed. The maximum US position was now that the agreements should include numbers and indicators that would be used only to verify that imports were in fact going up, and that the market was actually opening. US officials thus sought 'the establishment of numerical indicators that could measure increases in foreign access' as a way to achieve some form of results.[57] As Garten put it, 'we want to see certain trends and be able to measure them.' The trade press reported that Garten, in January 1994, had 'begun to make specific requests on the levels of Japanese purchases it will seek under a new agreement'; specifically, the US was now hoping for 'a roughly 20 per cent annual increase in Japanese auto parts purchases.'[58]

Some analysts in hindsight maintain that the US never *officially* asked for 'numerical targets,' which is both true and almost beside the point.[59] The real impact of the Garten proposal was in Japan, where Garten's strong hint at numerical targets settled things in favor of Japan's rejectionists. The proposal undercut the position of those who believed America's official disavowal of targets, and who had argued on that basis. At the same time, it underscored the rejectionist argument that the Clinton people were not to be trusted with numbers. Here was another example of US spin tactics—asking for numbers in private while completely denying it in public. Even as some in the US were saying that numbers would not be

---

[55] *Inside US Trade* 12/24/93: 12.

[56] *Mainichi Daily News* 12/20/93, Nikkei Needs Database <http://www.nikkeieu.com/needs/>.

[57] *Inside US Trade* 12/24/93: 1.

[58] *Inside US Trade* 12/24/93: 12, and 1/21/94: 19. Behind closed doors, however, there is some evidence that hard numbers were still being pushed by the US; in the same January 25 meeting cited earlier, Garten is quoted as asking as 'preconditions': 'a very substantial increase in sales of US-made parts to Japanese auto companies . . . [and a] substantial increase in dual dealerships in Japan—that's quantifiable.' He also added that 'the political and substantive reality is [that] there is no flexibility' (interview with State Department official, 6/15/97).

[59] Lincoln 1999: 146–7.

the goal, here was direct evidence to the contrary: now, no one could maintain that the US was seeking only vague results. If Japan were to yield even an inch on numbers, the end result would inevitably be numerical targets and sanctions.

The rejectionist position in Japan thus prevailed, and in fact in the months leading up to the summit failure in February 1994 actually became even more intransigent. Market share targets were already out of the question, as was any explicit commitment on the part of the Japanese government to increase imports. Japan now resisted any sort of number at all, whether government-sanctioned or not, that even implied an *expectation* of future increases in imports. That is, Tokyo now took a harsher attitude toward even such concepts as 'future trends' or 'extending past trend-lines' into the future, as these implied that imports should be going up. The rejectionists felt that these future expectations would be open to unilateral interpretation by the US; at some point in the future, even if imports were up, the US might announce that it was not satisfied because imports were not up enough. Furthermore, Japan was now willing to consider only indicators that could be used only to assess progress on market opening. If any indicators were to be included, they could be used only to measure what was happening in terms of import trends, but should be totally neutral in terms of the expected direction of these trends. In effect, these indicators could be used only to describe what was happening, not to assess whether the agreement was being implemented faithfully or not.

Japan's counterproposal on autos reflected its now harsher attitude toward US demands. In what Tokyo termed its 'cooperation approach,' quantitative indicators would be used only to measure past efforts at improving market access, with no mention at all of future trends.[60] Japan also parried other American attempts to achieve 'targets, without targets.' In response to the argument that it should increase its imports to the OECD average, negotiators countered that this number was not a useful benchmark. Okamatsu argued, for instance, that if one factored out trade inside the European Union, and US trade with its NAFTA partners, then Japan's import levels were not so exceptional. Furthermore, using any sort of average really had no meaning: some countries would be above this level and some would be below, so why should Japan be at the average?[61]

---

[60] *Japan Times* 2/4/94, Nikkei Needs Database <http://www.nikkeieu.com/needs/>.
[61] Interview with very senior MITI official, 10/16/97; and US Embassy official, 4/7/97.

Japan's more forceful rejectionist line was communicated clearly and at length in a high-level letter sent by senior negotiator Okamatsu to Garten on December 28, in which Okamatsu argued that Japan had already been burned once in agreeing to 'benchmarks,' even private ones, as it had in the Semiconductor Agreement. Okamatsu wrote that:

the US Government [then] emphasized that the 20% figure was merely a bench-mark to assess progress and not a guarantee or a commitment... However, the 20% figure had a life of its own which left a painful lesson for us. No matter how the US side explains its intention, and no matter how the language is carefully drafted, once [the] number relating to the future is referred to, the nature of the number will be subject to distortion. The explanation by the US side... reminded me of the similar explanation the US side had provided to us during the semiconductor negotiations.[62]

Furthermore, Japan would not again agree to include even private firm pledges on increased purchases, as it had done on auto parts in 1992. Okamatsu argued that in 1992:

the Government of Japan only aggregated the numbers announced by each company. However, the aggregated number was eventually characterized as a 'pledge' by the US Government... This experience left us with another lesson that [a] private sector announcement can be easily turned into a commitment of the Japanese Government.

Finally, Okamatsu expressed to Garten his distrust of American officials when they assured Japan that numbers would now be used only to assess progress, not as sanctionable targets:

While you stressed the differences between your proposal of setting standards or trend-lines and numerical target setting, the two appear to be no different from our point of view. You did not fully answer my following questions concerning this issue: What will be [the] effect if the standard or the trend-line is not reached? Will the Japanese Government be held responsible for that?... Is there any possibility that unilateral actions may be taken against Japan when standards or trend-lines are not attained or reached?[63]

The impact of the Garten proposal was thus far greater than some have recognized. It, like the Kantor-Brown letter before it, not only helped tip the balance in Japan toward the rejectionist position, it also turned out to

---

[62] *Inside US Trade* 1/14/94: 14.

[63] Okamatsu's letter is reprinted in *Inside US Trade* (1/14/94: 14–15). Okamatsu ended his long and harshly worded letter on an incongruous note: 'I am looking forward to seeing you soon. Happy New Year!'

be the final element that cemented the decision to stand firm until the bitter end. It thus became another 'smoking gun' that haunted the US throughout the remainder of the Framework negotiations.[64] Even after the US had denied that the proposal was an official one—or even that it was ever made—Japanese officials constantly referred to it in later negotiations as evidence that what the US really wanted was numerical targets. 'Here was another mistake,' noted one US official. Another later described it as 'a stupid initial proposal, written by people who did not know what they were doing.'[65]

In this period one can see a rising level of frustration among American officials, of all orientations. Most hard-liners felt that they had already made a meaningful concession by backing off from explicit numerical targets, and thus felt that it was time to force Japan to make some sort of compromise. At the very least, Japan needed to agree to some way to ensure future increases in imports; without this sort of commitment, no agreement could be considered results oriented. Moderates in the US who sincerely wanted a mutually acceptable compromise were also frustrated, as their best efforts to make the US position more reasonable were still being rejected out of hand by the Japanese. These officials were dismayed to see each US softening being matched by a hardening of Japan's position. The Japanese position was a moving target that the US never seemed able to catch.

Now US officials, both moderates and hard-liners, were becoming exasperated. Clearly, Japan was following a conscious strategy of simply being rejectionist. Spero felt that 'the Japanese are totally resisting any serious dialogue. They don't want to talk about measurement even though we agreed very clearly... that we will discuss these indicators.'[66] Another official summed it up later: Japan was 'reciting a mantra, not negotiating.'[67]

American officials were also angry at having their positions misrepresented by Japan. Moderate Cutter told reporters just before Christmas 1993:

In not one of the proposals that we currently have on the table have we requested a market share agreement... What we have had thrown at us, rather than efforts to negotiate in good faith and try to find a creative way to solve what are clear

---

[64] Interview with US Embassy official, 4/7/97.
[65] Interview with Commerce official, 4/9/97; and US Embassy official, 4/7/97.
[66] *Far Eastern Economic Review* 1/20/94, Nikkei Needs Database <http://www.nikkeieu.com/needs/>.
[67] Interview with US Embassy official, 6/15/97.

economic problems between the two countries, is an ideological dispute that on the face of it is absurd. It's time to drop it.[68]

Hard-liners were even angrier, seeing in Japan's position hypocrisy and outright dishonesty. How could Japan dare to stand on the principle of non-interference in the market, when its government had been one of the most interventionist in history? How could it label the US as 'managed traders' when Japan had practiced just that for decades? In December, Kantor wrote a letter in which he castigated Japan for its own managed trade practices at home, including its use of regulation and administrative guidance to tolerate or create anti-competitive practices. Kantor went on to write, 'As to those who charge that we are "managed traders," I am reminded of the chief of police in the movie *Casablanca* who was "shocked, SHOCKED" to discover gambling in Rick's Place, just as he pockets his own winnings.' The Japanese did not seem to appreciate Kantor's attempt at cinematic humor; when pressed later about the tone of the letter, Kantor commented that 'he was "having a bad day" when writing it.'[69]

The Hosokawa Summit Fails

Given the complete and growing intractability of the two sides, the failure of the Hosokawa–Clinton summit, set for February 11, 1994, seemed inevitable. While there had been some progress on the government procurement talks, there had been almost none on autos and auto parts. The administration thus faced the possibility of having a summit fail for the first time in the postwar period. In order to avoid damage to the relationship, the administration also considered whether to seek agreement on the procurement baskets, but leave the auto agreement for a latter date, as Hosokawa was then urgently requesting.[70] This position, which Ambassador to Japan Walter Mondale was reported to have backed, reflected a concern for Hosokawa's political future, since the US did not want to undermine the one leader they believed was the best hope for reform.[71] Alternatively, the US could agree to a deal on autos that did not include

---

[68] *Inside US Trade* 1/7/94: 4. This was technically true, since the Garten proposal was never officially 'on the table.' But Garten himself seems not to have disavowed anything, telling the press in late January that the US 'definitely did not take this proposal off the table' and in fact had added proposals to it (*Inside US Trade* 1/21/94: 19).

[69] Ibid. 12/24/93: 4.   [70] Interview with LDP official, 10/15/97.

[71] *Inside US Trade*, 'Special Report' 2/11/94: 7; Ibid. 1/14/94: 4; and *Far Eastern Economic Review* 1/20/94, Nikkei Needs Database <http://www.nikkeieu.com/needs/>.

quantitative indicators if these at least implied a future increase in imports.

Strong voices inside and outside the US government argued for the first course of action: stick with the numbers oriented approach even if that meant a failure of the summit. The catch phrase at the time was that 'no agreement was better than a bad agreement,' an explicit warning against allowing concern for the health of bilateral relations to trump specific trade concerns. This phrase was repeated widely by a number of industry officials, members of Congress, and administration officials.[72]

Representatives from the automotive industries were naturally quite vocal, arguing that the US should be taking an even tougher approach. The head of the AAMA, Andrew Card, argued that the US should seek a sales target of 100,000 foreign vehicles per year within three years, up from the 1992 level of 40,000 units. Card called this a 'reasonable target' that was necessary before the industry could justify the re-tooling costs it would have to pay to enter the Japanese market. As Card put it, 'You tell us we can come in, and you give us the market share, and we will meet the demand.' A numbers approach was necessary, Card argued, since 'we have found numbers have worked in the past.'[73]

Congress was also vocal in urging the administration to hold to a tough line. On January 25, more than 30 House members sent a letter to Garten in which they charged that past auto talks with Japan 'have been characterized by endless unfulfilled promises,' and warned that 'the outcome of these trade negotiations will have a great impact on future trade legislation.'[74] Two bills then under consideration were more explicit. Joint legislation sponsored by representative Dick Gephardt and Senator Jay Rockefeller 'would require the Administration to set and enforce those targets unilaterally' if the framework talks fail. *Inside US Trade* reported that the bills 'would require the Commerce Department . . . [to] estimate what percentage of the Japanese market would be captured by US firms if

---

[72] The insurance industry, for instance, argued that 'No agreement would be better than a bad agreement' *Nihon Keizai Shimbun* 1/26/94, Nikkei Needs Database <http://www.nikkeieu.com/needs/>. Treasury Secretary Lloyd Bentsen opined that 'no agreement would be better than weak agreements' *Inside US Trade* 1/28/94: S-2; and Michigan Senator Carl Levin said that 'the worst thing we could do is have another fuzzed-over agreement and pretend it's progress' (*Inside US Trade* 2/4/94: 11).

[73] *Inside US Trade* 2/21/94: 11. JAMA president Kume Yutaka reacted sarcastically: 'it will be all right for US automakers to set their own plan to sell 100,000 autos in Japan,' but that target should be met through market forces, not government fiat. (*Japan Times* 1/27/94, Nikkei Needs Database <http://www.nikkeieu.com/needs/>).

[74] *Inside US Trade* 1/28/94: S2–S3.

the market were as open as that in other developed countries.'[75] Other Congressional voices urged the President to revive the Super 301 provision by executive order, since this would be quicker than the passage of explicit legislation.[76]

Outside advisors also advocated maintaining a tough stance. A much publicized memo written by former USTR official Glen Fukushima was eventually shown to the President, who then circulated it to his top trade officials with a hand written note: 'worth reading and often accurate. Should discuss.'[77] Copies of this hard-line memo, complete with Clinton's handwritten notes endorsing Fukushima's key arguments, were later passed widely among Japanese media and government officials. Although this memo was not the source of the US position, it at least bolstered what many hard-liners in the administration were already thinking; it is also interesting in that it provides a fleeting glimpse into how the President was thinking at the time.[78]

In the end, the US decided to go ahead with the original Framework timetable, which required that all agreements be finished by the February 11 summit. In addition, the administration continued to pursue results in the automotive sectors. Now, the success or failure of the summit depended on these contentious negotiations.

The US side, on the eve of the February summit, was still internally divided. Kantor, the leader of the hard-liners, had re-engaged more fully on Japan policy after the completion of the WTO negotiations in mid-December, and had turned his attention to the Japan question two weeks before the Hosokawa summit.[79] Kantor in this period was intimately involved, on a daily basis, and was clearly interested in maintaining a tough position. Cutter, the leader of the moderates, was nominally in charge, but realized that the USTR and Kantor would be taking the lead in the upcoming auto issue.[80]

---

[75] *Inside US Trade* 1/21/94: 3. The bills were drafted by Representative Dick Gephardt (D-Missouri) and Senator Jay Rockefeller (D-West Virginia).

[76] *Inside US Trade* 2/11/94: 8. This was suggested by Senator Max Baucus (D-Montana), chair of the Senate Finance trade subcommittee.

[77] *Tokyo Business Today* 5/94: 30.

[78] Fukushima later wrote that he did not write the memo for Clinton, but that it had been passed to the White House by his friend, Derek Shearer, the revisionist professor who had advised Clinton during the campaign. Fukushima also does not feel that his memo 'had much to do with the outcome' of the summit (*Tokyo Business Today* 5/94: 56).

[79] Interview with US Embassy official, 4/7/97.

[80] Interviews with DC official, 4/18/97; US Embassy official, 4/7/97; and very senior DC official, 4/29/97.

At this point Cutter evidently hoped to make some sort of deal with Japan while there was still time to avert a failure of the summit, and at the last moment made one final attempt to strike a bargain. According to press and other reports, Cutter had a series of one-on-one meetings with his Japanese counterpart, MOFA's Matsuura Koichiro, on the evening of February 9, in what one participant described later as 'a sincere attempt to move away from quantitative targets.'[81] The exact content of Cutter's proposal is in some dispute, but it seems that he basically offered to back away from using indicators to measure future increases in market shares. Rather, Cutter suggested an index of indicators that would be used to assess progress, but without specifying what sort of progress was needed for success—that is, how much or even the direction that these numbers needed to move. Cutter's idea was that the two sides could sit down later to discuss and analyze what had happened, since a lack of progress could be due to factors other than Japan's lack of cooperation.[82] In other words, prior expectations would be removed from the negotiations.

This represented a significant retreat from the official US position, which then called for at least an 'increase above current trend lines,' and was actually very close to what the Japanese side was proposing at the time. However, as an aside, before one criticizes Cutter for beating too hasty a retreat, it should be noted that, in terms of quantitative indicators, his proposal was better than what the US ended up achieving at the end of the auto talks in Geneva, after a year and a half of bitter negotiations.[83]

Matsuura immediately faxed an outline of Cutter's proposal to the Japanese negotiating team, then en route to Washington. One Japanese participant describes officials crowding around the fax machine on the plane as Matsuura's communication came through. Cooperationists in the group reacted with a sense of relief. One official remembers thinking, 'not bad,' and that 'this is an offer we can accept.'[84] Rejectionists, however, were suspicious, and refused to agree to a quick, positive response. After all, the US had been deceptive in the past, offering one thing in private and then spinning it 180 degrees after Japan had taken the bait. Besides,

---

[81] Interview with DC official, 4/18/97. Details of Cutter's proposal appear in Ennis 1994a; and Karube 1996: 389–93.

[82] Interview with DC official, 4/18/97. Cutter's index included such things as the percentage of imports to total sales, sales efforts by US firms, and others. Cutter also said that the US would drop its numerical demands on insurance, and would consider postponing the auto agreements past the upcoming summit.

[83] Interview with DC official, 4/18/97. Destler (1996: 39) concurs with this assessment.

[84] Interview with MOFA official, 5/9/97.

Cutter's proposal was the first time that the US was indicating an official willingness to back away from using numbers to ensure increased imports, and it was not clear if this back-channel approach represented a true change in the US position. Rejectionists argued that Japan should wait and see if the US team was indeed firmly behind Cutter.[85]

Japanese officials, led by Foreign Minister Hata Tsutomu, arrived for the final round of discussions on February 10 fully prepared to agree to the Cutter proposal, and had even prepared new draft agreements incorporating these changes.[86] What they got instead was Mickey Kantor presenting the old US position seeking numerical indicators to measure increases in imports. There was no trace of the Cutter phantom proposal; instead, Kantor 'blew Hata out of the water' with an unmodified hard-line position.[87]

It is not clear exactly what happened with the Cutter proposal, whether 'Cutter acted on his own, and did not have enough time to consult with his colleagues . . . [or whether] Kantor knew about the initiative, but withdrew it in the hope that [Japan] might compromise first.'[88] Another official saw this exchange as just another 'failure to communicate' in that Cutter 'likes to talk in hypotheticals. But to Matsuura, a hypothetical is a proposal, so what Cutter thought he was saying was probably very different from what Matsuura thought he was saying.'[89] In any case, hard-liners in the US had torpedoed the Cutter initiative, and had taken control of the negotiations. The suspicions of Japan's rejectionists were confirmed.

Although any meaningful chance of compromise was essentially dead from this point on, cooperationists in the Japanese government persisted in arguing that it should not let the summit fail, an unprecedented occurrence that might truly jeopardize the overall relationship. MOFA's Kuriyama was the most outspoken on this point. Foreign Minister Hata had earlier argued that 'given the scale of US–Japan economic relations, there can be no possibility of a rupture.'[90] Even after Hata met with Hosokawa at Blair House on the morning of February 11, just two hours before the meeting with Clinton was to begin, cooperationists were urging Hosokawa to strike some sort of deal.

---

[85] Interview with very senior MITI official, 10/16/97.   [86] Ennis 1994a: 35.

[87] *Mainichi Daily News* 2/18/94, Nikkei Needs Database <http://www.nikkeieu.com/needs/>; interview with NSC official, 5/15/97.

[88] Ennis 1994a: 35.   [89] Ibid.: 37.

[90] *The Daily Yomiuri* 2/11/94, Nikkei Needs Database <http://www.nikkeieu.com/needs/>.

Until the very end, MITI bureaucrats were nervous that Hosokawa might still be persuaded to make a last-minute compromise. As one put it, 'Hosokawa is so caught up in other activities that he has no time to think about trade problems, so our negotiators are quite negative about shaking hands on any deal with the Americans.'[91] At another point MITI officials took the unusual step of calling in fellow rejectionists from MOFA to meet with Hosokawa and to demonstrate that the bureaucracy was unified and adamant that the time had come to say no. Hosokawa sided with this MITI–MOFA alliance.

The final negotiating session took place in the USTR building late on the night of February 10, and included only Kantor, Cutter, Hata, and Matsuura. With the US side now insisting that any agreement 'make specific reference to an expectation that the past trends would continue into the future,' there was little hope for a last-minute deal. At one point in this meeting, Matsuura is reported to have said, 'we just do not trust you with numbers,' to which Cutter replied, 'and we don't trust you without numbers.'[92]

The three-hour summit meeting between Hosokawa and Clinton ended where it began, with neither side backing away from its position. But in perhaps the most bizarre twist in this entire story, aides to the two leaders later reported that the talking points Clinton presented during this meeting were actually very close to the Cutter compromise rather than the Kantor hard line. Essentially, the President's talking points had been prepared by the NEC and NSC staff, as is usual, and this included Cutter and his aides. The initial talking points had reflected Cutter's back-channel proposal and, for whatever reason, these were never changed to reflect Kantor's reassertion of the hard line.

During the summit meeting, then, Clinton basically presented the Cutter proposal. However, Hosokawa's staff had prepped him that the US had hardened its position and that he should just say no, and so he did. Aides on both sides—sitting at the back of the room—stared at each other across the table, dumbfounded, unable to intervene. Here Clinton, following his script, had just offered a proposal that Japan should have found acceptable, but Hosokawa, following *his* script, had just flatly rejected it.[93]

In any case, as the meeting came to an end, both sides recognized that the summit had failed. Clinton later argued that although the two 'could have disguised our differences with cosmetic agreements... it is better to

[91] Ennis 1994a: 31.
[92] Ibid.: 34. Ennis quotes Cutter here, but this was clearly a Kantor talking point.
[93] Interview with senior NSC official, 4/14/97.

have reached no agreement than to have reached an empty agreement.' Hosokawa called the summit failure 'a necessary readjustment in bringing forth a more mature US–Japan relationship.'

The immediate reaction of trade officials in both countries—relief in Japan and elation in the US—speaks volumes about how far the relationship had moved away from earlier assumptions. Even though MITI officials had been confident that they had killed any last minute compromises, they still worried that Hosokawa would agree to some final, face-saving deal in his one-on-one meeting with Clinton. Rejectionists were thus relieved once they heard that the summit had ended without any damaging compromises. Now that Japan had finally said no, at the highest level, it would be only a matter of time before the US would have to back off from its demands.

USTR officials were openly elated. These officials had gathered that morning in the USTR's Winder building, across the street from the White House complex, to listen to the press conference. Many also expected to hear that the Prime Minister and President had somehow 'solved' their disagreements. USTR officials had grown weary of doing the hard negotiating work, only to see the politicians undo everything through last moment, political-level compromises. This had been the pattern for what seemed to be forever. So, when the President announced that the summit had failed, some actually stood to clap, cheer, and high five; one later described the mood there as 'euphoric.'[94] The feeling was that because the President was finally willing to stand firm, the US would eventually be able to pressure the Japanese to come to an acceptable agreement. Now that the US was sticking to its guns, it would be only a matter of time before the US could use its leverage to force Japan to back down.

These USTR officials were right that the battle was almost over, but were wrong about who was winning. These officials did not yet know it, but the final outcome of the auto talks, even after a year and a half of contentious negotiations and the threat of significant sanctions against Japan, was to come very close to the Japanese position.

[94] Interview with USTR official, 4/15/97.

8

The Auto End Game

From Potential Blowup to Anticlimax

The abrupt failure of the Hosokawa summit ushered in a period of great uncertainty in US–Japan relations. At the extreme, it caused considerable consternation among observers of the relationship, some of who now worried about the very future of the bilateral tie. Most others were less alarmed, recognizing that both countries still shared so many common interests. But no one was quite sure what direction the relationship would now take.

As before, the US government remained internally divided in its views of Japan. As a result of the unprecedented breakdown in relations, some were questioning the revisionist assumptions that underlay the current app-roach, and were increasingly doubtful that Japan represented a true eco-nomic threat. Furthermore, pol-mil officials were returning to their traditionalist view of Japan as an important ally whose cooperation was essential. On the opposite extreme, hard-liners in the USTR, led by Mickey Kantor, continued to argue that the US needed to stick to its guns and get as close to a results oriented agreement as possible. This division was to last all the way through the conclusion of the automobile talks in Geneva in June 1995, with the economic hard-liners leading the negotiations, while behind the scenes those on the pol-mil side were trying to bring the relationship back into balance.

The Re-emergence of Traditionalist Voices

As mentioned in the last chapter, doubts about Japan as an economic threat had been growing ever since the collapse of its stock market at the beginning of 1990. As the Japanese economy entered its fifth straight year of slow growth, it was becoming clear that it in fact suffered from some deep and inherent flaws. To moderates such as Cutter, what had once seemed such a compelling view of Japan now seemed out of step with reality as new information about the economic situation came to light. Now the unique features of that system, which had once seemed so superior, were beginning to look more like sources of weakness. At the same time, the rapid recovery of the US economy in this period also relieved many of America's underlying anxieties. America's economic growth had resumed at the end of 1992 and continued to pick up speed in the subsequent years. US exports to Japan continued to grow in this period, and at a faster rate than Japanese exports to the US; as a result, the bilateral trade deficit reversed course and began to decline in 1994. Furthermore, many of the previously embattled industries, including advanced semiconductors, were seemingly on the road to recovery.

This re-evaluation of the threat posed by the Japanese economy also called into some question the accuracy of the revisionist approach in general. Some officials were gradually realizing that the stark revisionist version of Japan might have been exaggerated and overblown. If the revisionists had exaggerated the superiority of their economic system and the threat that it represented, what else had they been wrong about? As one White House official put it later, many were now beginning to 'revise the revisionists.'[1]

It should be repeated here that this redefinition of revisionism was confined to the view of the Japanese economy as an imminent threat; the views of Japan as uniquely structured and inherently closed seem not to have changed. However, without this feeling of threat, the need to solve the Japan problem so immediately and decisively was receding. Conversely, the costs of forcing it to accept some form of specific reciprocity were becoming more salient. In any case, this reassessment of the revisionist thesis was leading some officials to question the wisdom of the hard-line approach.

In addition, some in the administration had by now grown tired of battering their heads against the Japanese wall, all to seemingly no good purpose. The past year and a half of sparring over trivial semantics, being criticized as 'managed traders' seeking numerical targets (and having those charges stick), and seeing a string of concessions matched only by an even more rejectionist line from Japan, had all begun to take their toll. As one

---

[1] Interview with Clinton campaign advisor and NSC official, 5/12/97.

Congressional critic put it later that summer, the administration 'had lost its zeal' for the framework; instead, 'They want to claim victory and get out of it.'[2]

An even more significant change was the gradual reemergence of traditionalist voices on the pol-mil side of the government. As discussed in Part II, the pol-mil community at the beginning of the Clinton administration was of two minds on the revisionist approach on trade. Some truly saw the Japanese economic threat as a national security problem that demanded immediate attention, and thus supported the early push for results. Others felt that Japan did not threaten America's national security, but worried that economic frictions could poison an otherwise stable security relationship. These officials felt that fixing the economic leg of the stool would make for a healthier overall tie. Almost all of the pol-mil community, however, had supported the initial approach on the condition that the cost of fixing the economic problem would not be so high as to damage the overall relationship. Now, in the aftermath of the summit breakdown, the diplomatic costs of the initial approach were becoming clearer.[3]

Furthermore, as the Japanese recession continued to deepen, many of the formerly revisionist-leaning officials were also becoming convinced that Japan did not pose such a threat to American high technology industries or national defense. Like the moderates on the economic side, these officials began to question whether the diplomatic costs of the heavy-handed trade approach were worth the economic gain. If Japan was not an imminent economic threat, did it make sense to imperil the relationship for the sake of fixing the trade problem? Perhaps the traditionalist view was right, after all.[4]

At the same time, security developments in the East Asian region also helped revive traditionalist thinking and assumptions about the importance of Japan. The most alarming at the time was the possibility that North Korea was attempting to develop an independent nuclear capability. Back in March 1993, even before the first Clinton–Miyazawa summit, the North Koreans had announced their intention to withdraw

[2] *Inside US Trade* 6/17/94: 3.
[3] Interview with ex-CIA official, 5/7/97. Most Defense officials were not so worried, since none feared that economic frictions would actually ruin the relationship. Still, these officials did desire a more balanced, stable approach.
[4] As a result, revisionist-oriented officials who stressed the technology threat argument became more isolated, less vocal and less involved in setting policy priorities. Interview with Defense official, 4/1/97. Changes were also underway inside the NSC, where the new head of the Asian Affairs office, Stanley Roth, recognized that the US had let its Asian priorities drift in the wrong directions.

from the Nuclear Non-Proliferation Treaty (NPT), which most took as a clear sign that it intended to develop a nuclear capability. The Clinton administration thus engaged in a series of talks with the North trying to persuade it to stick with its NPT commitments. But by May 1994 the North was again threatening to move ahead with its nuclear program, thus initiating a new level of regional crisis. The US now moved toward the imposition of sanctions to bring the North back into the NPT.

In this context, the pol-mil community understood that Japan was an important player in solving the North Korean crisis. It was a crucial source of foreign exchange for North Korea, most notably the private currency transfers from Korean residents of Japan. Tokyo's cooperation would be needed if this flow was to be cut off. In addition, the agreement that was eventually worked out with North Korea—helping it to build nuclear facilities that could only be used for peaceful purposes—would require a great deal of money. In this, the likeliest sources would be South Korea along with Japan.

The irony of the situation was not lost on many observers: here the US was seeking to punish Japan on the trade side, while asking for its help on the security side.[5] Later, when the US was threatening to impose sanctions during the Geneva auto talks, the US was in the awkward position of threatening sanctions against both its biggest ally and most dangerous potential foe in East Asia. One Japanese official noted with irony that the US had chosen the more mild-mannered and diplomatic Robert Gallucci to be its chief negotiator with North Korea, while using the more hard-nosed and obstreperous Mickey Kantor to deal with Japan; given that one was an ally and the other was not, these appointments should have been reversed.[6]

A visible turning point inside the US government was the so-called 'malaise memo' written in April 1994 by Winston Lord, State's Assistant Secretary for East Asian Affairs. Lord argued that the US had created negative relations with the two most crucial Asian nations. Relations with China had gotten off to a bad start, especially as Clinton followed through on his campaign pledge to bring human rights concerns to the top of the agenda with China, leading to a predictably harsh response. In terms of relations with Japan, Lord argued that the focus on economic

---

[5] Interview with State Department official, 3/24/97.
[6] Interview with MOFA official, 9/25/97.

frictions was becoming counterproductive, and that the US needed to reassess the costs of this approach.[7]

The most fundamental change, however, came inside the Defense Department, where the origins of what became known as the 'Nye initiative' were beginning to take shape. The initial process was actually the idea of CIA official Ezra Vogel, the Harvard professor and well-known Japanologist who most certainly was in the traditionalist camp when it came to the political and security relationship. Vogel now began to hold a series of informal meetings of like-minded officials on a monthly and sometimes weekly basis, in an effort to shift policy back to a more balanced approach.[8] In the summer of 1994 these officials began to draft a series of memos that argued that the US needed to strengthen high-level contacts with the Japanese pol-mil community and explore other ways to rebalance the relationship. These officials also noted that the Japanese seemed to be drifting away, citing recent Japanese government documents in which the US alliance had been downgraded in terms of Japan's top priorities.

In Japan, as well, cooperationist voices were becoming more assertive. Especially officials in the First North American division of MOFA argued more vocally that the bilateral relationship was the bottom line that needed to be maintained. Defending against instability on the Korean peninsula or anywhere in the region required cooperation with the US. This relationship was not unbreakable, and could not withstand many more diplomatic blowups such as the February summit. Besides, Japan had already deterred the most egregious of America's trade demands, and in particular its original push for explicit quantitative targets. These officials argued that the time had come to rebalance the relationship.

All of these growing doubts, however, were taking place behind the scenes, and thus did not have an immediate impact on the conduct of the Framework talks. Through the end of the Geneva negotiations in June 1995, US–Japan relations thus proceeded on dual and divided tracks, with pol-mil voices in both governments talking about how to improve relations, while economic hard-liners moved the relationship closer to confrontation. However, this shift in thinking on the pol-mil side was to play

---

[7] Some traditionalists grumbled that Lord was himself partially responsible for some of the failed policies he was now criticizing. But the memo clearly strengthened the hand of the traditionalists. Interview with former NSC official, 4/24/97. Excerpts from the Lord 'malaise memo' appear in Ennis (1994b: 39).

[8] Up to this point, Defense officials working on Japan had complained that their ideas were not being passed up the chain of command. Now, these officials felt that they could go through Vogel to reach Assistant Secretary Nye. Interview with Defense Department official, 4/1/97; and veteran Defense Department official, 5/12/97.

a crucial role once the auto talks concluded in the summer of 1995, when American traditionalists and Japanese cooperationists once again took control of the agenda.

The US After the Summit: Moderates Versus Hard-liners

In the spring of 1994, during the 'cooling off' period following the summit breakdown, traditionalist voices in the US first began to reassert themselves. In a crucial April 5 Deputies Committee meeting to consider next steps, State Department officials spoke up about their deepening worries over the tone and direction of the relationship. *Inside US Trade* paraphrased one State Department official's concerns that the economic stand-off could 'spill over into the political and security relationship at a time the US needs Japanese help on other Asian issues, such as the threat posed by North Korea.' According to this official, the approach therefore should be to 'get agreements whenever possible,' even if this meant 'ratcheting down our objectives.'[9]

Other moderates also called for a toning down of American rhetoric, which some felt had only unified the Japanese bureaucrats in a way that had not seemed possible before. In addition, some recognized that the administration's initial rhetoric had also raised expectations too high, especially in Congress and the auto industry. Because the US had already given up on its initial hopes for hard, actionable targets, the initial, overly optimistic rhetoric about achieving results needed to be deflated. One Commerce official later commented that, beginning in this period, many officials began to draw the conclusion that 'we may have oversold the framework as a panacea for all of our economic problems with Japan.'[10]

Finally, some in the administration felt that the conduct of the negotiations had led to a dead end, and that a true results orientation was already out of reach. *Inside US Trade* paraphrased an outside observer's criticisms of the administration for making the results oriented approach 'the subject of an academic debate about principles from which Japan emerged as a champion of free trade.' This observer also commented that 'there is a recognition among several senior players that the framework was a mistake

[9] *Inside US Trade* 5/20/94: 19. The DC debate is also covered in ibid. 4/8/94: 1 and 21–2; 4/22/94: 5; and 5/20/94: 19.
[10] Ibid. 12/9/94; the official was Marjory Searing, the director of Commerce's Japan office.

that dug the US into a hole which the Japanese government filled with garbage.'[11]

On the other hand, the administration's hard-liners, especially Kantor and Barshefsky, were still in a defiant mood. In a DC meeting after the Hosokawa summit, for instance, one participant recalls: 'At the end Kantor got up, shook his fist, and said, "We're going to kick their asses."'[12] Kantor's bravado seemed out of place, however, given that the hard-liners were fighting to salvage their goal of a results-oriented agreement, and to prevent further softening of the administration's position. Since the early days of the administration they had seen their original hopes for actionable targets gradually eroded by Japan's counteroffensive and what they saw as the faintheartedness of the moderates in the US government. As a result, the US had backed away from an overall macro target, had dropped language pertaining to market shares and numerical targets, and had decided not to even push Japan to increase its imports to the OECD average.

Now Japan was resisting the discussion of numbers that even mentioned a future increase in imports. The hard-liners argued that Japan's new position was unacceptable. The US needed to insist that the agreements had to at least include 'forward-looking indicators' that could be used to measure whether imports were actually rising—that is, they must specify that the direction of change was expected to be upward. One official described this as:

[a] 'quasi-numerical' approach, in which the US would insist that rather than measuring 'change' in sales and market share, the criteria would require a 'substantial increase' in sales and share...The US is [also] insisting that the idea of increased sales, not merely change, be contained in the criteria themselves, not merely in the [generic, introductory] language.[13]

Thus, by the spring of 1994, what the hard-liners had originally meant by a 'results-orientation' had already been substantially gutted, and now the issue was whether they could salvage what one USTR official described as 'a numerical feel, a directional feel' to the agreement. The hard-liners now felt that they needed 'some numbers, any numbers.'[14]

After the summit breakdown the hard-liners were adamant that it was up to Japan to make the first concession. During the subsequent cooling

---

[11] *Inside US Trade* 4/8/94: 22.

[12] Quoted in Destler 1996: 39. Destler makes clear that Kantor was 'talking of his *foreign*, not domestic, adversaries.'

[13] *Inside US Trade* 7/29/94: 28.   [14] Interview with USTR official, 4/23/97.

off period the hard-liners insisted that no one in the US government should engage in economic discussions until the Japanese came forward with a new proposal.[15] Ironically, the hard-liners decided to use this cooling off period to 'turn up the heat.' Hard-liners remained convinced that Japan would never make concessions unless it faced imminent retaliation, and then only when a clear deadline was looming. Conversely, it was felt that if such pressures were applied, then some form of concessions would be forthcoming. President Clinton on March 3 thus issued an executive order reviving the controversial Super 301 provision of the 1988 Trade Act, which had been allowed to lapse in 1993, a move that the trade press believed was 'aimed primarily at ratcheting up pressure on Japan following the Feb. 11 breakdown of trade talks.'[16]

Some signs of movement came almost immediately. In early March, progress on the long-stalled talks to expand Motorola's access to Japan's cellular phone market suddenly materialized. Progress seems to have been initiated by the intervention of Ozawa Ichiro, then the Vice-Chief Cabinet Secretary in the Hosokawa government.[17] In addition, the US had earlier threatened sanctions on Japan, totaling US$300 million, which was announced on the day after the February summit failure.[18] The resulting cellular telephone agreement also included some explicit numbers, for instance the number of new cell sites and voice channels that foreign firms could access. Although these numbers were more on the technical side of things rather than as targets or market shares, hard-liners took Japan's willingness to include numbers as a hopeful sign. As Kantor put it in testimony to Congress on March 15, the agreement 'validates the results-oriented approach we are pursuing under the framework.'[19]

In the middle of March it was also becoming clear that Ozawa was putting pressure on the bureaucrats to prepare a new set of 'external economic measures' including something constructive on the auto parts issue.[20] Although this package, announced on March 29, was not deemed

---

[15] Moderates in the US government, however, broke this 'moratorium' and continued to make unofficial contacts with their counterparts in Japan, which infuriated Kantor and led him to increase his control over the policy process (interview with ex-USTR official, 4/4/97).

[16] *Inside US Trade* 3/4/94: 1.

[17] These negotiations were not officially a part of the Framework agreement. The deal was completed just ten days after Ozawa intervened (interview with State Department official, 4/4/97).

[18] See Kunkel 2003: 174 for details.

[19] *Inside US Trade* 3/18/94: 13. Interviews with State Department official, 3/24/97; and USTR official, 4/23/97.

[20] Interview with MITI official, 9/24/97.

sufficient to restart the talks, the US saw some indications that Japanese political leaders were at least trying to be more forthcoming.

In the end, it took another change of government in Japan to get the talks going again. On April 8, 1994, Hosokawa stepped down over accusations that he had been involved in the Sagawa Kyubin bribery scandal. A week later, on the April 15, Kantor met with Foreign Minister Hata Tsutomu for two hours in Marrakesh, Morocco, just before the signing of the Uruguay round. Although the two spoke only in general terms, they at least expressed a willingness to talk again; this willingness was confirmed during Clinton's May 9 phone call to congratulate Hata on his selection as the new Prime Minister.[21]

In the discussions leading up to the restart of the official talks, the only concessions of note were made by the US. In a two-page agreement completed on May 23, the US stated unequivocally that the criteria to be negotiated 'do not constitute numerical targets, but rather are to be used for the purpose of evaluating progress.' As one official put it, the US had long since dropped numerical targets 'thought of as single-point quotas or single-point commitments on the part of the Japanese government,' but now it was hoped that this more explicit disclaimer would be enough to reassure the Japanese side of US intentions.[22]

When the Framework talks resumed on May 24, however, the Clinton negotiators discovered that the summit failure and the cooling off period had done nothing to convince Japan to be more forthcoming. The two sides continued to make almost no progress on the private sector auto talks, but were also stalemated on the government procurement baskets, which had seemed close to completion before the February summit. As before, the negotiators were stalemated over seemingly small semantic differences. The US continued to insist that the agreements should include objective criteria that would lead to significant increases in foreign goods. The US now proposed that the Japanese government commit itself to making 'annual progress in value and share' of government purchases of foreign made medical and telecommunication products.[23] Japan's

---

[21] *Inside US Trade* 4/22/94: 5–6. During the interim, on April 30, the US decided to delay for two months the naming of Japan for discrimination in the government procurement of telecommunications and medical equipment. The US deferred this decision again on June 30, for one month.

[22] Ibid. 5/27/94: 1–2. The US did make another concession, dropping its insistence that the remaining baskets be wrapped up as a 'package deal,' which US hard-liners had earlier insisted on. US moderates felt that making some progress on the less contentious government procurement baskets could provide some momentum to the more difficult talks on autos and auto parts. (ibid. 4/22/94: 5–6, and 5/27/94: 1).

[23] Ibid. 9/30/94: 21.

position was that any criteria included in the agreement would only be used to evaluate progress, and that these could not be 'forward looking.' At least one moderate US official understood that the Japanese feared that 'if they agree to very specific language and then make their best efforts and don't succeed, they will get nailed.'[24]

With the negotiations at a standstill at the end of July, the US decided to threaten sanctions in both the telecommunications and medical equipment industries, by citing Japan under Title VII of the 1988 Trade Act. This step set in motion a 60-day 'consultation period,' which made September 30 the effective final deadline.

True to past form, the two governments reached an agreement in these two fields at the last moment—and this time it was literally at the last moment, with the agreement finalized after midnight on September 30.[25] The results of the final agreement were ambiguous, with both sides able to claim a partial victory. The US argued that it had reached results-oriented agreements, since both included ten quantitative and qualitative indicators that could be used to assess progress on market opening. Most importantly, the US had overcome Japanese reluctance to include the 'annual progress' phrasing.[26] However, Japan claimed that it had avoided any mention of a numerical target, pointing to the language of the agreement that made it clear that 'These criteria do not constitute numerical targets, but rather are to be used for the purpose of evaluating progress toward the goals of the framework.'[27]

* * *

The US negotiators were certainly heartened by what they saw as a partial victory, and hoped that the Japanese side would be so forthcoming on the final remaining contentious negotiation, on autos and auto parts. As before, the two sides remained deadlocked, with the US continuing to push for 'forward-looking indicators' while the Japanese continued to insist that indicators could measure only change in imports, not the *direction* of that change.[28] The Japanese side, however, had drawn a clear

---

[24] *Inside US Trade* 7/29/94: 27–8.   [25] Lincoln 1999: 130.

[26] ACCJ 1997: 33–6 and 47–50. The key phrasing in the Quantitative Criteria section was: 'Annual evaluation of progress in the value and share of procurements of foreign telecommunications products and services . . . to achieve, over the medium term, a significant increase in access and sales of competitive foreign telecommunications products and services.' The agreement also called for an annual review which would keep the focus on forward movement.

[27] At the same time, however, MITI rejectionists were unhappy that Japan had agreed even to evaluate 'progress,' but because both agreements referred to *government* procurement, it was felt that the maximum rejectionist stance would not be appropriate.

[28] *Inside US Trade* 9/30/94: 21. The auto end game is also covered in detail in Bhagwati 1996: 272–5; Maswood 1997; Lincoln 1999: 131–4; and Kunkel 2003: 179–84.

distinction between the government procurement baskets, which after all were within the scope of government control, and the private sector talks. Japan's willingness to give ground on government procurement simply did not apply to the automotive industries.

The two sides were still unable to resolve the three issues that had derailed the Hosokawa summit. First was the sale of finished foreign cars in Japan, which critics had for years been arguing were discriminated against. Even though the US industry would have welcomed a specific market share, the US government seems never to have asked for a numerical target on finished autos. Instead, the focus was on alleged barriers to the distribution of autos, and in particular the structure of Japan's network of auto dealerships. Specifically, the US argued that the Japanese automakers had effectively captured the domestic dealer networks, and could thus force dealers to carry only Japanese-made autos. Dealers who tried to carry foreign-made cars could be subject to having their relations with the Japanese car firms severed. Here the US demanded that the Japanese government more strongly apply its anti-trust laws to prevent such restraints on trade, but also wanted to nego-tiate an expansion in the number of dealers that handled foreign autos. Although the US was not asking for specific numbers, it was still seeking a quantitative indicator that could verify that this number was in fact increasing.[29]

A second issue was the sale of replacement auto parts in Japan, also known as the aftermarket for parts. One of the core problems here was that Japan's car inspection (*shaken*) system, in which the government required that all cars periodically undergo rigorous safety inspections, was biased 'toward use of the original manufacturers' parts.'[30] According to the US, the car inspection stations had also been captured by the Japanese firms, which made it virtually impossible for foreign parts manu-facturers to compete fairly. Here the US was interested in improving antitrust enforcement procedures and clarifying regulations, none of which were adamantly opposed by the Japanese government. At the same time, the US also hinted that it wanted Japanese inspection stations 'to carry US made parts.'[31] In an effort to put more pressure on Japanese negotiators, the Clinton administration in October 1994 self-initiated an

---

[29] Outside voices were more explicit. In March, for instance, the AAMA called for an agreement that would increase access to 1,200 high-volume dealers (*Inside US Trade* 4/21/95: 16).

[30] Lincoln 1999: 131.   [31] Bhagwati 1996: 273.

investigation of the aftermarket for auto parts under Section 301 of the 1974 Trade Act.[32]

The third remaining issue was the most contentious: the level of sales of auto parts for new cars, both in Japan and in their North American plants. Here the focus continued to be on close-knit *keiretsu* relationships between the automakers and their parts suppliers in Japan, which implied that outsider firms were discriminated against. It was here that the US demands were more bottom-line and results oriented: pressuring the Japanese car firms to expand their plans to purchase foreign auto parts, both in their plants in Japan as well as in the US, and to include these plans as part of the Framework. It was this issue that hamstrung negotiations through the end of the auto talks in June 1995.

Earlier, in March 1994, the major car firms had all announced their new forecasts for their purchases of foreign auto parts, extending the business plans they had issued back in January 1992. Although the firms used different reporting dates, 'deliberately designed to avoid any efforts by the US to turn them into firm targets,' the Commerce Department used its own methodology to calculate that these plans would translate into a total of US$21.3 billion in sales by the end of FY 1996.[33] If this estimate was correct, Japanese purchases would barely be above the US$19 billion mark it had reached in 1994, and far short of the 20–30 per cent annual increases the US was still clearly hoping for.[34] Kantor immediately criticized these plans as inadequate, first because it was 'not as large as we might have expected,' and furthermore because 'we are concerned that the government of Japan is not involved in these so-called voluntary efforts.'[35]

The US now asked that these forecasts be revised upwards. As reported in the trade press, Kantor told Hashimoto 'in meetings Sept. 27 and 28 that the US must have commitments by Japanese auto companies for a more rapid increase in future purchases of auto parts.' Although Kantor did not mention specific numbers, earlier, 'Undersecretary of Commerce Jeff Garten has told Japan the US wants an increase in foreign parts purchases from an anticipated $19 billion at the end of FY-1994 to $40 billion by the end of 1998,' or approximately a 20 per cent annual expansion.[36]

In an effort to entice the Japanese government into a deal, Kantor now also offered to move these purchasing plans 'outside of the government to government framework talks'—that is, into an appendix to the agreement.

---

[32] *Inside US Trade* 10/7/94: 15–16. The US decided not to immediately designate Japan as an unfair trader under Super 301, as this would not have 'appropriate' at the time.
[33] Ibid. 4/1/94: S-4.   [34] Ibid. 3/24/95: 17.   [35] Ibid. 4/1/94: S-4.
[36] Ibid. 9/30/94: 1 and 19.

In doing so, however, Kantor never meant to dismiss *any* Japanese government involvement in this issue. As he later put it in a confidential letter to Japan, in March 1995:

the Government of Japan played an important role in working with the auto companies to bring about a successful result (after the January 1992 Bush Auto Summit), and frankly, the situation should not be different at this time. You need to understand our view that the 1992 voluntary plans resulted in important progress, and that the issuance of new voluntary plans is an essential part of successfully resolving the automotive issues between us.[37]

The US now hoped for at least the same treatment that the Bush administration had received—but was again to come up short.

Japan After the Summit: The Rejectionists Remain in Control

In Japan, there was still a strong consensus that the final auto agreement could not include any form of numerical targets or quantitative indicators that implied a government commitment to increase imports; as before, the position was that indicators could be used only to assess progress without any endorsement of trends or direction. But now the question was whether Japan should once again take an even harder line, by refusing to pressure the auto companies to revise their plans, and by opposing even the inclusion of these plans in the final agreement.

As mentioned earlier, some cooperationist voices had been urging a more moderate approach ever since the Hosokawa summit breakdown. In April 1994, Ambassador to the US Kuriyama Takakazu, for instance, argued that if President Clinton would 'categorically assure' Japan that he would not apply sanctions, then it should be flexible on the inclusion of numerical indicators.[38] Now even some officials in the deterrence school had begun to get the feeling that the US had so lowered its demands on true managed trade that the war had already been won. America's official demands now looked similar to what the Japanese had been asking for at the Hosokawa summit. Asking for more would only be rubbing it in. Besides, the outline of a deal was already clear, and easily attainable: all that was needed was some vague and minimal revision of the industry's auto parts plans, and to attach them as an appendix to the agreement. This would help the US save face, and would not be an official commitment

---

[37] Ibid. 3/24/95: 17.   [38] Ibid. 4/8/94: 6.

that could be enforced later on. Japan should include the revised purchasing plans, declare victory, and walk away—and thus avoid any further damage to the relationship.

The Japanese auto firms also took this position. On the one hand, they had an interest in deterring future trade demands, and were not happy with the Clinton administration's earlier attempt to treat their 1992 forecasts as some sort of official, government-sanctioned 'commitment.' However, these firms, acutely conscious of their image among American consumers, were becoming increasingly uncomfortable as the auto talks dragged on. All of the Japanese firms were deeply dependent on the US market, and thus could not afford to alienate the American public. Many had made significant direct investments in the US, in effect tying their own future to what happened in the overall US–Japan relationship. These firms now argued quietly that so long as the voluntary nature of these announcements was made clear, they would be willing to include them in the agreement. The firms were going to announce these plans regardless of what happened in the negotiations, anyway, and furthermore understood that neither government would actually enforce them. If this concession was all that stood in the way of an agreement, then the auto firms were willing to offer it.[39]

Japan's rejectionist stance was also being questioned elsewhere in Japan. Although Hosokawa's approval ratings had increased immediately after the summit breakdown, over time, the media began to criticize him for not having an alternative to move the relationship forward—it was not enough just to say no. Some voices in the private sector also began to argue that Japan had perhaps overplayed its hand, and that the bilateral relationship was being put in jeopardy.[40]

It was at this point, however, that the WTO fundamentalists in MITI and MOFA were able to convince the rest of the bureaucracy to hold to the maximum rejectionist line. This is a case, I believe, where a commitment to core principles pushed these officials to take an even tougher line than a rationalist calculation would have called for. Specifically, even the WTO fundamentalists by now recognized that Japan had achieved its 'no managed trade' goals, and that continued obstructionism risked real damage to the overall relationship. The feeling was, however, that there were principles involved, most notably equal treatment and non-government interference in the market, and that defending these principles was of overriding importance. Japan could—and should—cooperate in deregulating

---

[39] Interview with JAMA official, 10/28/97.   [40] Interview with MITI official, 10/8/97.

objectionable standards and procedures, but anything that smacked of government interference had to be rejected.[41]

The fundamentalists argued that the automotive issue was a purely private sector matter that the government should not even be negotiating over at all. Any discussions of the parts purchasing plans were thus especially troubling, since this implied government involvement in influencing the behavior of an industry. Now that the US government was demanding that these companies increase their purchasing plans, the Japanese government simply had to wash its hands completely—even if the companies were to step forward on their own, it would now *appear* that the Japanese government had pressured them in this direction. The WTO fundamentalists thus argued that it would be best if the talks were to focus only on areas strictly 'within the scope and responsibility of government'—in other words, that the negotiations should only be about deregulation, and that the purchasing plans should be removed entirely.

Finally, the WTO fundamentalists raised again the issue of trust, appealing to the underlying fear that the Clinton team would take advantage of any Japanese concession. This argument was bolstered when the US initiated its Section 301 investigation of the replacement auto parts market. With sanctions once again pending, voices in Japan calling for non-cooperation were strengthened. Japan decided to adopt the maximum rejectionist position espoused by the WTO fundamentalists.

This approach was not overruled by the party politicians even though most believed that the existing terms of the deal were good enough. But Japan's deepening political turmoil now played directly into the hands of the WTO fundamentalists. In late June, after the Hata government was forced to step down after only two months in office, the political world was stunned when the long-time rivals, the LDP and the Japan Socialist Party, joined hands to form a new coalition. On June 29 Murayama Tomiichi was selected as the first socialist Prime Minister since the early postwar period. Even though the LDP was back in power, there was still a large political vacuum at the top of the political system. In essence, this meant that the bureaucracy, and especially the WTO fundamentalists,

---

[41] Interview with senior MITI official, 10/7/97. Schoppa (1997: 272) is undoubtedly correct that part of Clinton's overall failure in the Framework was the lack of domestic support in Japan—as he points out, there was almost no voices supporting Clinton's demands, in contrast to what happened during the SII talks. But at some point this became more of a story of *bureaucratic intransigence*, in that the Japanese governments' rejectionist stance was even harsher than domestic actors, including the auto industry, were comfortable with.

remained in charge for the remainder of the auto talks, and thus did not have to worry about any political pressures to 'preserve the US–Japan relationship.'

Japan's rejectionists also considered themselves fortunate that Hashimoto Ryutaro was named the new MITI Minister by Murayama.[42] Hashimoto has been viewed by outsiders as a rejectionist, willing to stand up to American pressures. However, Japanese bureaucrats saw him in a very different light: as a great role player willing to follow his bureaucratic script. One argued that Hashimoto liked to appear in control, but that the reality was nearly the opposite.[43] In either case, MITI bureaucrats later acknowledged that they would not have been able to maintain, let alone strengthen, their intransigent stance without a minister who, like Hashimoto, was willing to play his part.

Hashimoto now communicated Japan's more rejectionist line in a series of statements. Hashimoto first jumped on Kantor's offer to downgrade the official nature of the auto parts plans. In early October 1994, he insisted that the US had accepted the Japanese position that the parts purchasing plans were outside the scope of the talks. Hashimoto contended that 'our two countries reached a common understanding that it is a matter of managerial judgment in the private sector, and government should not interfere.'[44] Japan would discuss deregulation but nothing else. After this attempt to dismiss the issue was ignored by Kantor, Hashimoto took a strong position opposed to any government efforts to encourage the auto firms to revise their purchasing plans. Furthermore, Hashimoto criticized the US government after some Clinton officials had made contact directly with the Japanese firms.

Finally, the Japanese government returned to its old language criticizing numerical targets, even though it was by now clear to all that the US had backed away from any meaningful targets. In a November letter to Ron Brown, Hashimoto wrote that 'the expansion and revision of the voluntary plans and the future number of dealerships are in effect numerical targets, and are beyond the scope and the responsibility of government as well.'[45] This position was reinforced by MITI auto negotiator Sakamoto Yoshihiro, who in late April argued that the US 'is still insisting on a numerical targeting approach...if the US side will not insist upon a numerical target approach, then we on our side think that we will be

---

[42] Interview with MITI official, 9/24/97.
[43] According to this official, this was also true when Hashimoto was the Minister of MOF and the Ministry of Health and Welfare (interview with MOFA official, 5/9/97).
[44] *Inside US Trade* 10/7/94: 15.   [45] Ibid. 11/25/94: 6.

able to arrive at an agreement very quickly. But if the US will insist on the numerical approach, there will be no agreements.'[46]

The Auto End Game: The Sanctions Decision

By May of 1995 the Clinton administration had finally had enough of Japan's completely unyielding position. By now even the moderates agreed that the Clinton team could not retreat again: they had clearly lowered their demands and had offered compromises, while the Japanese had given no ground at all. If they were going to salvage anything on the auto issue, they were going to have to take some firm action.

The decision to go the sanctions route was premised on the still unshaken assumption that Japan would make concessions if and only if it was threatened with punishment. Even if Japan had become more stubborn and uncooperative than ever before, the threat of sanctions would at least force them to make *some* concession. Furthermore, many were growing weary of the long, drawn-out negotiations, and felt that a sanctions threat followed by some concession, followed by some sort of deal, would be the only way to salvage something out of the talks.

Another factor was that, given the political importance of the automobile industry, the US could not come away completely empty handed. Indeed, the original decision to include autos in the Framework in the first place was not made according to strategic trade logic; as described in Part II, the DC members understood that, politically, the Framework was not going to happen without autos. Mickey Kantor, for instance, seems to have been constantly attuned to the electoral implications of the auto talks. One colleague remembers a Fall 1994 meeting in which Kantor rattled off details on all of the electoral races in the key auto-related states.[47] Furthermore, I. M. Destler reports that around this time, 'Dick Morris, the president's old/new political guru . . . saw attacking Tokyo as a domestic political winner.'[48] Clearly, the administration could not conclude these talks without some sort of results to show for their efforts.

Mostly, however, the decision to threaten sanctions reflected the anger and frustration that many in the administration had come to feel. Here even the moderates had grown angry at what they saw as Japan's conscious

[46] *Inside US Trade* 4/21/95: 25.
[47] Interview with senior NSC official, 4/18/97. The official remembers thinking at the time, 'we all knew the debate was over.'
[48] Destler 1996: 46.

twisting of the American position, complete intransigence and unwilling-ness to listen to reason, and for 'moving the goalposts' whenever the US made some sort of compromise. In addition, US officials still seethed over the hypocrisy of the Japanese negotiators who were standing on the principle of 'non-governmental interference' while at the same time quietly instructing the Japanese auto firms *not* to be more forthcoming on their parts purchasing plans. Anger, resentment, and even a degree of enmity were by now seeping into American calculations. Kantor, in par-ticular, was fed up. As President Clinton later put it, 'Mickey Kantor had reached the limits of his patience.' Another colleague remembered that Kantor 'just wanted to nail [the Japanese] to the wall, make them bleed, and *then* sanction them.'[49]

For all of these reasons the internal debate to proceed on sanctions was not as contentious as one might have expected. The USTR's Kantor and Barshefsky of course took the lead, backed by the Department of Com-merce. Destler reports that Laura Tyson, who had just replaced Rubin as NEC head, countered Kantor's pro-sanctions memo with her own that discussed the costs and risks of the move. But actual opposition to sanc-tions was not strong, even from the traditionalist agencies. State, for instance, while not completely comfortable supporting sanctions, did not actively oppose them. In part, State's position reflected the view that Japan's complete intransigence had finally forced the US hand. This was a position taken by Ambassador to Japan Mondale, who was one of the strongest supporters of sanctions as the only way to bring the auto talks to an end.[50]

However, Kantor was not leaving anything to chance, out of fear that the moderates might once again 'wimp out.'[51] Destler reports that the sanctions decision had in effect been made a week earlier, the result of another of Kantor's guerilla tactics to circumvent the moderates. Evi-dently, Kantor in late April had 'sent a memo to the president directly, through the White House staff secretary, urging an explicit decision to impose trade sanctions.' Even though this out-of-channels memo was a slap to Tyson's new authority, it also seemed to have worked. On May 4, one day before the DC had made its final recommendation, the President

---

[49] Interview with senior NSC official, 4/18/97. The Clinton quote appears in Clinton (2004: 657). It was during this period that Kantor expressed his frustration that things weren't working out as planned: 'We're the US, damn it' (interview with senior NSC official, 4/18/97).

[50] Interview with State Department official, 4/4/97. Actually, it had been the Embassy that was the first to recommend sanctions, in February 1995.

[51] Interview with Commerce Department official, 4/14/97.

had already stated publicly that he was 'personally committed to proposing formal sanctions if the Japanese do not make sufficient concessions.' He went on to say, 'I support the line that Ambassador Kantor has taken. It is my line; it is my conviction.'[52] The sanctions recommendation, finalized on May 6, was now a foregone conclusion.

It turned out that in the end the Deputies Committee actually raised the level of proposed sanctions, a surprise since most felt that agencies like OMB and CEA would fight to minimize the impact on the US economy. This lack of opposition was in part due to the choice of Japanese luxury car imports as the main target of sanctions. One official called the sanction list 'the dream list,' since very few strong business interests would lobby against it, unlike the case of the semiconductors sanctions in the late 1980s.[53] But the overall economic domestic impact would be small, and concentrated on a group that could not make much of a political fuss. As one Commerce official put it, around the country 'there was not much sympathy for Lexus buyers.'[54]

The unveiling of the sanctions decision on May 17 also included the surprise announcement that the US was filing a pre-emptive challenge in the WTO, charging that Japan's discriminatory practices in auto parts had 'nullified and impaired the benefits accruing to the US and other member countries under the WTO.' Japan had been threatening to bring a complaint to the WTO if the US ever threatened sanctions; now, it seemed that the US had beaten it to the punch.[55] The real centerpiece of the announcement, however, was the 100 per cent tariffs that would be levied on the import of 13 Japanese luxury car models, worth an estimated US$5.9 billion. Kantor announced that the sanctions would be finalized on June 28 unless there was a successful conclusion to the talks.[56]

The Clinton team was well aware that they were taking a risky step, but perhaps were surprised at how little support they received, internationally as well as domestically. To the Europeans and other Asian nations, the US

[52] Destler 1996: 54. The quotes appeared in a *Detroit Free Press* article on May 4.

[53] Interview with veteran Commerce Department official, 4/14/97. The only business group that opposed the sanctions were those firms that were involved in importing and selling these cars, a very small constituent. It turned out that US auto dealers acted as a constructive go-between during the final negotiations.

[54] Interview with Commerce Department official, 4/9/97.

[55] *Inside US Trade* 5/12/95: 15. Bhagwati (1996: 276) sees this action as a typical lawyer's tactic, of bringing a 'countersuit' merely to increase bargaining leverage.

[56] The sanctions were to hit all five major Japanese companies: Honda (two models of the Acura); Toyota (five models of the Lexus); Nissan (three models of the Infiniti); the Mazda 929 and Millenium; and the Mitsubishi Diamante. Kantor further argued that the sanctions were consistent with the WTO rules because they concerned regulatory practices that were not covered by the WTO (*Inside US Trade* 5/17/95: 1–2).

threat of sanctions was the final 'game changer' in that now the major concern was clearly the dangers of American unilateralism. The Europeans had earlier publicly warned against any 'illegal retaliation measures' against Japan, and now, in the wake of the sanctions threat, the EU immediately denounced this as American unilateralism and a threat to the new WTO. In June the Europeans even asked to participate as a third party in the counter suit Japan had brought to the WTO.[57] Kantor's reaction was characteristic in that he 'proclaimed that his [European] critics could "scream like pigs stuck on a gate" for all he cared.'[58] Still, America's diplomatic isolation was now complete.

Even support within the US was nowhere near what the administration hoped for, or expected. Now some in the Congress balked at the sanctions threat, a major disappointment to the hard-liners since congress up to then had been remarkably unified in its support of the framework. This earlier unity was a testament to how strong feelings about the Japan problem still were, as this was perhaps the only issue in this intensely bipartisan period on which most Republicans stood behind Clinton. Just a week before the sanctions announcement the Senate had passed a resolution supporting this action by an 88–8 vote, and Republican House majority leader Newt Gingrich had written to Clinton in early May expressing his support for the administration's market-opening efforts.[59] With the sanction threat now actually on the table, Gingrich reversed course and criticized the administration for moving to unilateral sanctions without first utilizing the WTO.[60]

Elsewhere in the US, a variety of voices that the administration assumed would be in favor of sanctions were less than enthusiastic. Many major newspapers had strongly supported putting pressures on Japan, but now stopped short of endorsing the threat of sanctions. Alan Wolff, now at the law firm of Dewey Ballantine, predicted that Japan would easily win its

---

[57] *Inside US Trade* 4/7/95: 13. Garten at the time admitted that the failure to brief these trading partners at the very beginning of the Framework, in July 1993, 'was a mistake we do not want to repeat' (see also Pekkanen 1991: 23).

Australia similarly asked to be included on Japan's side in the WTO suit (*Inside US Trade* 6/12/95: 1 and 20, and 6/9/95: 1 and 23).

[58] Bhagwati 1996: 267.

[59] *Inside US Trade* 5/12/95: 23 And even though 28 House Republicans had earlier advocated a shift away from a results-oriented approach to a 'deregulation-oriented policy,' most still supported the President on pressuring Japan.

[60] Ibid. 5/26/95: 1 and 20–1. Gingrich, however, also continued to stand by the President, commenting that 'the Japanese need to understand this: whether individual members of Congress agree or disagree with the tactics of the Clinton Administration, the Administration will not be undercut in Congress.' One can't but feel that this was just another instance of Gingrich playing partisan politics with the Administration.

WTO challenge against Section 301—what he termed a 'slam dunk' victory.[61] Perhaps most surprising of all, ACTPN in early June 'decided not to endorse a statement explicitly backing the Administration's actions in the auto fight with Japan.' If the administration could not count even on ACTPN, one of the earliest and strongest supporters of the results oriented approach, who could it count on?[62]

* * *

The sanction threat was not having the intended effect in Japan, either. Rather than making Japanese negotiators more flexible, this move only strengthened the hand of those who argued that Japan needed to hold out to the bitter end. The WTO fundamentalists again took center stage, arguing that Japan simply could not negotiate under the threat of sanctions. Furthermore, now that the new WTO represented a viable legal option, Japan should take advantage of this route. Fundamentalists also felt confident that the WTO would side with them, and were eager to bring a legal challenge against the controversial 301 provision. Japan on May 17 thus requested 'urgent consultations' under WTO auspices on its challenge to America's use of Section 301 as well as the sanctions list.[63]

Cooperationists inside the Japanese government, however, were now arguing that things had gone far enough, and that Japan had nothing to gain from a major blowup. The Hosokawa summit breakdown had been bad enough, but now a failure to strike a deal risked touching off a true trade war; Japan had to give *some* ground. This was also the position taken by the auto firms, who were now clearly worried that the sanctions would not only hurt their profits, but more importantly would be a real blow to their image in the US. The auto firms now put pressure on MITI to strike a deal.[64]

---

[61] Ibid. 5/19/95: 22.

[62] Chrysler had suggested this endorsement. The only active backers of the sanctions appear to have been, predictably, the auto and auto parts industries (Ibid. 6/9/95: 5–10 and 24).

[63] Ibid. 5/19/95: 21–3. Japan also insisted that these consultations should focus only on the substance of its legal challenge, not to restart the stalled auto talks.
The US was also quite aware that it stood a good chance of losing such a challenge, and thus was reluctant to see things come to this (Lincoln 1999: 133).

[64] According to the press, US officials were well aware of these efforts at the time. As was reported in the *New York Times*, the CIA and National Security Agency had for years redirected a part of their intelligence-gathering efforts toward 'economic espionage,' and this now included MITI Minister Hashimoto's discussions with his negotiating team and the Japanese auto firms. As a result, according to the *Times*, Kantor received daily briefings during this period, including 'descriptions of conversations among Japanese bureaucrats and auto executives from Toyota and Nissan who were pressing for a settlement' 10/15/95 *New York Times* <http://nytimes.com/>; see also 10/22/95; and 10/28/95. Thus there was considerable disappointment that the US did not hold out for more concessions (interview with State Department official, 4/4/97).

Unlike in past negotiations, however, Japan's concessions this time were minimal. The auto firms did announce revised business plans on June 28, but this time they referred only to their general plans to expand their production of cars in their US plants. There was no new announcement on their intended purchases of auto parts, which remained as forecast back in March 1994.[65] These plans were not included in the agreement, but were simply referred to in the joint announcement, in which the two governments expressed their 'welcome' of the new production plans. In an unprecedented move, however, the two governments agreed to disagree on what these new plans meant. In the US portion of the joint announcement Kantor inserted estimates as to the value of these parts purchases, while in the following paragraph the Japanese side pointedly stated that 'Minister Hashimoto said that the Government of Japan has had no involvement in this calculation because it is beyond the scope and responsibility of government. He said that USTR's estimates are solely its own.'[66]

In the end, then, it was the US that accepted its minimal negotiating objectives, dropping all references to numbers or quantitative indicators that would be used even to measure increases in imports or purchases, either in terms of the number of dealerships or the level of auto parts purchases. Instead, the US settled for a vague statement on the goal of the agreement that remarkably was the word-for-word language used in the initial Framework document, back in July 1993:

the objective of achieving significantly expanded sales opportunities to result in a significant expansion of purchases of foreign parts by Japanese firms in Japan and through their transplants, as well as removing problems which affect market access, and encouraging imports of foreign autos and auto parts in Japan.

In the immediate aftermath of the agreement both sides predictably tried to claim victory. The President, for instance, stated clearly that 'this agreement is specific. It is measurable. It will achieve real, concrete results.'[67] These claims, however, were quickly undercut by the inadvertent release of an internal USTR document that, in the words of *Inside US Trade*, admitted that 'the US fell short of achieving its demands in a number of

---

[65] Furthermore, the Japanese firms refused to mention any commitment to increasing the level of domestic content, something the Japanese government had opposed as 'even worse' than the overall purchasing goals (*Inside US Trade* 6/30/95: 8).

[66] 'Joint Announcement by Ryutaro Hashimoto, Minister of International Trade and Industry of Japan, and Michael Kantor, United States Trade Representative, Regarding the Japanese Auto Companies' Plans' (reprinted in MITI 1997: 178). Similar wording appeared in a second attachment pertaining to the dealerships in Japan (ibid.: 183; see also Latham 1996: 12).

[67] Office of the Federal Register, 1995: 963.

key areas of negotiations, in particular regarding the voluntary plans of the Japanese auto companies.' The memo itself acknowledged that the plans were 'difficult-to-aggregate,' contained only a 'limited parts purchases commitment,' and were 'limited in quantifiable detail.'[68]

The US thus had failed to achieve any of its oft scaled-back demands. In fact, from the US perspective, the final agreement was even less concrete than the deal that Bo Cutter had proposed in February 1994, which would at least have included a series of specific quantitative indicators to assess how much progress was actually being made. As described in Chapter 7, hard-liners at the time saw that proposal as an unacceptable capitulation, and effectively scuttled it. Remarkably, the final auto results were not even as concrete as those that the Bush administration had achieved in January 1992, which at least contained the phrase 'expectations of future increases in sales.'

The fact that the final agreement was no more specific in results compared to the initial boilerplate language of the 1993 Framework proposal prompted one senior Japanese official to remark that 'we could have had the same agreement [in 1993], maybe two months after the start of the negotiations.'[69] Former Deputy USTR Michael Smith later put it even more bluntly: 'Mickey Kantor took the trading world to the brink of disaster and came back with absolutely nothing.'[70]

---

[68] The text of the assessment appears in *Inside US Trade* (6/30/95: 15–16). The USTR evidently faxed this confidential assessment 'along with everything else by mistake.'

[69] *Inside US Trade*: 6/30/95: 15.

[70] Speech by former Deputy USTR Michael Smith, Columbia University, December 1997.

9

The Return to Balance

The signing of the Framework in the Fall of 1995 marked the end of an era in US–Japan relations, although few knew it at the time. The magnitude of Japan's 'victory' over US trade demands is clear especially in hindsight—it was evident by a decade later that the Framework marked the high water mark of American demands for access to the Japanese market, and also marked a complete end to calls for anything smacking of 'managed trade' or 'specific reciprocity.' From that point on, the US even largely refrained from raising bilateral trade issues at all.

Assessing the Framework: A Post-mortem

In the immediate aftermath of the Framework talks pundits on all sides jumped in, mostly to criticize the Clinton administration for having 'lost' the negotiations. Key revisionists were especially critical, and were at the same time careful not to acknowledge any shortcomings in the revisionist approach itself.

Chalmers Johnson was typically the most scathing, dismissing the administration's entire approach as incoherent and ineffectual. Not only did the administration appoint people without real experience or knowledge of Japan, the approach lacked any sort of integrated strategy. Rather, 'there was no coordination among its various policies, no coherence to any individual policy, and no long term vision . . . there was only the illusion of policy.'[1] Johnson thus argued that revisionism did not fail in the sense that the Clinton team never truly adopted it in the first place.

---

[1] Johnson 1995b.

Clyde Prestowitz later argued that the administration did indeed adopt revisionism, but that the approach failed due to poor execution. As he put it:

I have to say I was very disappointed. [The Clinton people] adopted my ideas, but executed poorly. If I had been trade rep . . . [The problem is that the US approach] got transformed into crude market share targets that were easy to attack. I felt that if I could sit down with Japanese officials and talk open kimono, as they say, they could be persuaded that they have a stake in achieving more foreign participation in their economy. But we took the typical US approach of pounding the table or threatening 301.[2]

Analysts also weighed in to assess the claims of both governments to have prevailed in the negotiations. On this score, most scholars and journalists came to the consensus that it was indeed the US that had lost, in the sense that it had failed to achieve its core objectives.[3]

One of the few who defended the administration's handling of the negotiations was Edward Lincoln, who was named as economic counselor in the US Embassy in Tokyo in the summer of 1994. Lincoln, in his book *Troubled Times*, argued that the popular perception that the US was seeking numerical targets and managed trade was a false one; rather, he points out that the Clinton administration never officially asked for hard, actionable targets, and instead simply wanted to include indicators that could be used to assess market opening—which he argues it ultimately achieved. Furthermore, Lincoln notes that a part of negotiating is putting forward proposals that one knows will be shot down, and then retreating to a fallback position if these demands are not met. He thus dismisses America's unofficial proposals and other hints at a more ambitious use of numbers or indicators, and essentially argues that since these were never the official position, they should not be the standard by which to judge the administration.[4]

Lincoln's book is valuable in that it gives an accurate sense of one side of the internal debates going on in the Clinton administration, and does an especially good job in conveying the real frustration that US government officials were feeling at the time. Moderates like Lincoln were especially exasperated, as they sincerely felt that the DC had backed away from its maximum demands, and that it had become less committed to a true

---

[2] Prestowitz 2002.

[3] Schoppa (1997: 267) and Kunkel (2003: 176–7) both argue that the US did not achieve anything resembling numerical targets or market share agreements (see also Bhagwati 1996 and Zoellick 1995).

[4] Lincoln 1999: 154–5.

version of managed trade than the Japanese and other critics made it out to be. They were thus frustrated by the negotiating position taken by Japan, which never seemed willing to meet the US anywhere in the middle. Lincoln's book is also revealing in that he is forced to make careful and lawyer-like distinctions between benchmarks rather than targets, and indicators rather than numbers, and so on. This analysis illustrates the difficult negotiating task the administration faced in trying to maintain subtle semantic distinctions, while Japan was able to simply intone its 'no managed trade' mantra.

Still, there are two problems with these assessments. First, while it may be that the US never officially or publicly asked for hard, numerical targets, there is ample evidence that this is exactly what the Clinton team *initially* wanted. If one goes back to the early signals coming out of the administration, the US was aiming at a complete reorientation of its trade approach—in a revisionist direction. Because the administration was explicitly adopting revisionist assumptions, it also adopted the language and tone of revisionism, and thereby created the *expectation* that it was market share targets that were their ultimate goal. Although Lincoln is technically correct that the US was later more circumspect in its actual negotiating demands, its public airing of its results-oriented desires indicated that it was seeking a radically new policy.[5]

Second, although it is also true that negotiations often involve extreme initial positions followed by tactical retreats, the fact is that from start to finish it was the US that was constantly on the retreat. As seen in Table 9.1, at each stage of the negotiations the US had repeatedly backed away from its initial goals, while the Japanese position was progressively hardening, matching each US retreat with an advance of its own. Recall that the US team initially hoped to strengthen both the front and back ends of any trade agreement—on the front end, by including specific numbers in the form of numerical targets that the Japanese government would recognize, and on the back end, the inclusion of specific sanctions if Japan did not fulfill its commitments.

The administration's early desire for some sort of market share or numerical target was not acceptable to Japan, so the Clinton team sought instead results-oriented agreements that would be actionable under US

---

[5] It is thus important to note that by the time Lincoln reached the Embassy, well after the failed 1994 summit, the US had indeed backed away from its earlier goals. But Lincoln was not directly involved in the earlier DC policy process, which I argue came closer to the revisionist trade prescription.

Table 9.1 A scorecard: Clinton's 'results-oriented' goals, and outcomes

US stated and implicit goals	Japan's stated and implicit goals	Concessions and retreats
I. Pre-Framework goals (February–March 1993)		
– Maximum: Market shares, numerical targets (as indicated by Clinton and Tyson endorsement of SCA) – Minimum: Results orientation, including quantitative indicators and a GOJ commitment to increase imports – Agreement to be sanctionable under US trade law (as indicated by numerous statements, including Kantor-Brown letter)	– 'No managed trade' – No market share agreements or numerical targets – Agreements should not be sanctionable under US trade law	– US: Drops reference to 'numerical targets' and 'market shares'; refers instead to benchmarks, criteria, quantitative indicators, etc
II. Initial Framework goals (April–July 1993)		
– 'Results-oriented' trade agreements – Numerical reduction of current account surplus; increase in Japanese manufactures by 1/3 – Results orientation for sectoral talks: GOJ commitment to quantitative criteria to be used to assess increases in imports (otherwise, US will define 'appropriate indicators') – Agreements will be enforceable under US trade law (Barshefsky testimony, Kantor letter)	Same as above, plus: – Opposed to quantitative targets on macro side – Opposed to government commitment to increase imports in sectoral baskets – Opposed to inclusion of autos and auto parts in Framework	– US: Drops reference to quantitative targets on macro side – Agrees that 'consultations will be limited to matters within the scope and responsibility of government' – Japan: Agrees to include autos and auto parts in Framework talks; agreement will 'result in a significant expansion of foreign parts by Japanese firms'
III. Early Framework talks (September 1993 – February 1994)		
– Hard-liners: at maximum, still hoped for sanctionable hard numbers (Garten's unofficial proposal on autos, 'guerilla tactics,' 'targets but not targets')	Same as above, plus: – Opposed to any numbers or indicators that imply an *increase* of imports	– US: Drops all mention of quantitative indicators, sanctionable numbers (post-summit)

(cont.)

Table 9.1. (*Continued*)

US stated and implicit goals	Japan's stated and implicit goals	Concessions and retreats
– Japan should increase imports to level of OECD average; expectation that imports should 'increase beyond current trends' – Moderates: willing to use indicators to assess progress, but short of hard numbers, sanctionable commitments, or prior expectations as to direction of change (Cutter's unofficial proposal)	– Opposed to any numbers to be used to even *measure progress* on market opening or increased imports	– Japan: None

IV. Auto End Game (March 1994 – June 1995)

US stated and implicit goals	Japan's stated and implicit goals	Concessions and retreats
– 'Forward-looking indicators' to assess increases in auto parts purchases and the number of auto dealers handling foreign cars – Expanded auto parts purchasing plans should be included in agreement	Same as above, plus: – Opposed to inclusion of private sector auto parts purchasing plans, as part of agreement – Disputes should be settled in WTO, not bilaterally or unilaterally	– US: Drops all mention of numbers or indicators to measure increase in imports – Japan: Agrees to include auto purchasing plans as appendix to agreement

trade law. By the time the negotiations opened in March 1993, the US was shooting for an overall macro target, and also a Japanese government commitment to quantitative criteria to be used to assess increases in imports in the sectoral baskets. During the initial negotiation the US agreed to drop the macro target in exchange for what it saw as a clear Japanese commitment to results at the sectoral level. As discussed in Chapters 7 and 8, the negotiations featured a constant series of tactical retreats by the US to an ever softer interpretation of what 'quantitative criteria' actually meant: from a Japanese commitment to increase imports to the OECD average, to some increase beyond current trend lines, to any increase in future imports, to 'forward looking indicators.' Japan successively rejected numbers that implied market share targets, was opposed to an overt government commitment to increase imports, then to even the inclusion of numbers that implied that imports *should* be going up. By the end of the negotiations the Japanese opposed the inclusion of *any* numbers, even if they were to be used only to measure progress in terms of market access. By the end of the negotiations the Clinton people were just trying to salvage 'some directional feel' to the agreement—hardly the results orientation it began with.

When only one side is doing all of the retreating, and the final agreement comes much closer to the other side's position, at some point this adds up to a negotiating defeat.

Yet, in spite of America's constant softening of its position, even as late as June 1995 it was still being publicly criticized for its pursuit of managed trade and even numerical targets. On this point I agree with Lincoln that the US by then had retreated significantly from its original position, but was still completely unable to shake the public perception of it as a managed trader.

In part, the Clinton people were themselves to blame. One reason the DC was unable to disassociate itself from the managed trade charge was its initial wholehearted endorsement of revisionist assumptions, which clearly called for some form of specific reciprocity. In addition, the administration's public style, which from the beginning was obsessed with spin and imagery, complicated the US negotiating position by raising these expectations to unrealistic levels. From the beginning of the Framework, in July 1993, Clinton officials were making bold and boastful statements that a results-oriented agreement was already in the bag. Most notable was Barshefsky's testimony that if Japan would not agree to actionable indicators, then the US would be willing to define them unilaterally and implement them on that basis, but there were also numerous indications from other officials. Throughout the negotiations the bombastic style and tough sounding rhetoric, especially from Mickey Kantor, gave the impression that Washington was seeking much more than it actually was. Even some of Kantor's physical actions, such as the now famous photo of him holding a *kendo* sword to Hashimoto's throat (presumably playfully), conveyed the sense that the US was pushing a tough line. And the decision to threaten sanctions itself raised expectations that the US was going after substantive concessions—even as it was retreating and softening its demands.

However, the core reason that the US was never able to dispel the image that it was seeking managed trade was the fatal division between its moderates and hard-liners that beset it from start to finish. While most officials believed that the US was not asking for managed trade, there were enough officials, including lead negotiator Kantor as well as Garten and Barshefsky, who were seeking just that. Japanese negotiators insist that US officials sought targets and hard numbers behind closed doors, and there is some evidence that backs this up. Furthermore, there were a number of US demands that made it into the public realm (often leaked there by the Japanese side), most notably Garten's November 1993 proposal on autos. Although such efforts were disavowed by the administration whenever they became public, it was never able to disavow them strongly enough to dispel public perceptions. Here, again, the administration's internal divisions became evident, with some hard-liners willing to resort to guerilla tactics to achieve a stronger form of results orientation. The DC official quoted earlier summed up the essence of the problem: 'We couldn't say we weren't managed traders because some of us wanted to *be* managed traders!'[6]

The fact that the administration was not able to credibly speak with one voice, either in words or in actions, thus made it impossible to define what it was really after. In this context, the theological distinctions the US tried to make between numbers, targets, benchmarks, indicators, and the like, confused everyone involved in the process, both inside the administration and out. For the US to maintain a successful negotiating position it first needed to agree on what it wanted, then it needed to be unified and consistent in its approach, and finally needed to communicate it convincingly to the Japanese and the public. The Clinton team never got beyond the first step.

From the Japanese perspective, the division in the Clinton administration was a source of both confusion and opportunity. Some on the

---

[6] Interview with DC official, 4/18/97.

Japanese side were sincerely unsure about what the US really wanted. In particular, the Japanese cooperationists, who continued to argue that it needed to meet the US somewhere in the middle, constantly saw their position undercut by the mixed signals coming from Washington. It seemed that each assurance from the US that it was not seeking numerical targets was immediately contradicted by rhetoric or more concrete evidence to the contrary.

Most importantly, the fatal division in the US provided a golden opportunity that Japan's rejectionists used to seize control of Tokyo's policy. Rejectionists first concentrated their fire on the Clinton administration's adoption of revisionist assumptions, and sought mightily to discredit those assumptions and the prescriptions that followed from them. They were especially adept at using the most extreme US demands to discredit cooperationists in the Japanese government. By concentrating on the more extreme demands coming from the US, and making sure that the media immediately knew of these demands, Japan was able to publicly define US objectives in the worst possible light. Japan's 'informational campaign' thus succeeded in portraying the US as more oriented toward managed trade and targets than it actually had become. All of the subtle distinctions the Clinton team tried to draw were smashed to pieces by Japan's 'no managed trade' sledgehammer.

The Framework Aftermath: Revisionist Assumptions Undermined

By 1996, the Clinton administration realized that it had reached a dead end in its trade policy approach to Japan. First and foremost was the realization that Japan simply was not going to play ball by agreeing to accept any form of a true results-oriented agreement. To the contrary, the utter effectiveness of Japan's rejectionist negotiating stance undermined any hope that the US could achieve a revisionist trade prescription.

Furthermore, Japan's rejectionists once again were trying to harden their trade policy stance. In March 1996 Sakamoto Yoshihiro, now MITI's Vice-Minister, announced that 'the era of "bilateralism" is over.' From this point on, Japan would deal with trade disputes only on a multilateral basis: 'any [bilateral] frictions from now on will have to be solved in accordance with the WTO and other international rules and by following market mechanisms.' Even if this announcement represented what one US official at the time dismissed as 'MITI's wishful thinking,' it was absolutely clear that achieving a meaningful results orientation was going to be even more difficult, perhaps impossible.[7] In hindsight, Sakamoto's declaration proved to be quite prescient.

By 1996 a new element was coloring Clinton administration thinking about Japan: what many in the White House at the time referred to as 'Japan fatigue.' Simply put, the nastiness of the Framework, and Japan's complete intransigence, made any attempt at negotiations painful, fruitless, and simply not worth it. The administration had not only lost its appetite for results-oriented negotiations, many officials now wanted to have as little do with Japan as possible, in any realm. In this sense the popular phrase at the time, 'Japan passing'—the concept that America had become less interested in the relationship with Japan and more enthralled with the potential tie with China—was not a figment of Japan's imagination. Although traditionalists in the US were quick to reassure Japan that it was still a valued partner, these statements were not reflective of how most Clinton officials, and especially trade-related officials, really felt.

(Thus, Japan's absolute refusal to yield on any point during the Framework had come at a certain price—a degree of resentment, anger, and distrust of Japan, even among US traditionalists, that was not present before.[8] Although most Japanese officials later felt that they handled the Framework negotiations correctly, it must be recognized that their squashing of America's managed trade demands was not without costs, at least in the short term.)

In any case the end result was that US officials began to realize that they did not have very many good trade policy options. Officials had earlier come to recognize that managed trade was not a 'silver bullet' that could resolve the trade problem; now officials were coming to realize that the US had no useful 'bullets' at all. Because revisionist views of the Japanese economy as different and closed still prevailed, very few had any faith that traditionalist efforts to liberalize the market process would actually lead to greater imports. Similarly, the administration had no confidence that Japan's efforts at deregulation or strengthening antitrust enforcement would lead to any meaningful change, and no faith at all that imports would rise as a result. Although the administration continued to submit to the Japanese government long 'laundry lists' of items where it thought

---

[7] *Inside US Trade* 3/22/96: 3. Sakamoto's announcement came in a March 15 speech to the Foreign Correspondent's Club.

[8] As Schoppa (1999) points out, Japan had become more distrustful of the US over time; by the late 1990s, the US has increasingly returned those feelings.

deregulation was needed, it never really believed in this approach and never got behind it.[9]

Administration officials also understood the political reality that Japan's intransigence ruled out any sort of results-oriented sectoral approach. Thus, no attempt was made to continue along the Framework path. Even when the Framework was signed, in September 1995, the US had announced that it would henceforth be used only to monitor existing agreements. In a 1996 speech, Kantor argued that exports to Japan in the industries in which the administration had negotiated trade agreements had increased at a substantially higher rate than overall exports, and left it at that. In essence, the US had finally decided to 'declare victory and walk away.'[10]

It became clear that the US was moving in a different direction in the summer of 1996. In negotiations to extend the 1991 Semiconductor Agreement, which was due to expire in July, the two governments removed the provisions that had made this agreement so controversial in the past: targets, numbers, benchmarks, and the like.[11] More significantly, in June of 1996 the US decided to drop its request for government-to-government talks on the issue of film and photographic paper, as had been demanded by Kodak. Kodak had filed a 301 petition against Japan on May 18, 1995, one week after the auto sanctions had been announced, and this case thus was seen as a litmus test for how future bilateral trade tensions would be handled. However, US officials were also acutely aware of the precarious standing of its 301 provisions in terms of international law, and few were willing to risk having these provisions openly declared illegal.[12] After being strongly rebuffed by the Japanese government, the US decided to pursue its complaint in the WTO, rather than to seek bilateral talks. Japan had once again called the US bluff.

Finally, with the 1995 auto agreement due to expire at the end of 2000, the Clinton administration presented an unofficial non-paper that outlined a five-year extension of the auto agreement. As one analyst put it, though, 'The non-paper was a non-starter,' and the auto deal was allowed to expire.[13]

The negotiating dynamics through the period I cover may thus be a case of an international norm trumping a domestic assumption. That is,

[9] In November 1994, for instance, the US presented to Japan a comprehensive 'Proposal on Deregulation' that listed over 350 clauses, including such high priority items as contact lenses, lottery prizes, and race horses *Inside US Trade*, ('Special Report,' 11/18/94).

[10] Interview with veteran USTR official, 5/2/97.

[11] See Schoppa 1999: 329; and Pekkanen 2001: 727–9.

[12] Interviews with senior NSC official, 5/15/97; and State Department official, 6/15/97. See also Schoppa 1997: 288; and Kunkel 2003: 187.

[13] Lindsey 2001.

Japan's rejectionist stance and appeal to the norms embodied in the WTO—what Pekkanen calls 'aggressive legalism'—had effectively emasculated revisionism's singular trade policy prescription.[14] US trade officials in 1996 thus faced the uncomfortable reality that the results-oriented trade policy called for by revisionism was no longer achievable, even if they agreed with the revisionists that some sort of results-oriented agreement would be the best (or perhaps only) way to insure that imports would actually increase. Although few realized it at the time, the era of bilateralism was indeed ending—the two subsequently engaged in some government-to-government talks on sectoral trade disputes, but the dominant US approach is no longer bilateralism, much less unilateralism.[15] As one USTR official later put it, somewhat wistfully, 'those days are over.'[16]

* * *

Another fundamental shift in American attitudes concerned the perceived nature of the 'Japanese threat.' This shift was due mostly to the turn-around in economic fortunes in both countries. First, the rebound in the US economy in the mid-1990s took some of the edge off concern about the threat from Japan. Industries that had once seemed imperiled, including semiconductors and other high-tech sectors, now seemed to have recovered. In addition, no major new industries were raising strong complaints about market access. With growth resuming and the stock market entering a boom period, Americans in general had grown considerably more optimistic. Bilateral trade figures were also turning around, with American exports growing steadily from 1993 to 1997, while imports from Japan slowed and then declined in 1996. As a result, the trade deficit also fell, from a peak of US$65.7 billion in 1994 to US$47.6 billion two years later. The political importance of solving the Japan problem had largely disappeared.[17]

---

[14] Pekkanen 2001.

[15] One example is the dispute over port practices, in 1997. As Amy Searight (2002: 101) argues, Japan has used a policy of 'aggressive multilateralism' in international organizations such as the WTO 'to bind the United States . . . and constraining its unilateral exercise of power.'

[16] Interview with USTR official, 4/15/97. Yet another development in this period was the turnover of political appointees inside the administration. With the exception of Charlene Barshefsky, by the end of 1996 all of the top officials who had been involved in the early formulation of Japan trade policy had moved back to the private sector. And in every case their replacements held less revisionist-oriented views of the Japanese economy, at least in terms of their views of Japan as an economic threat. By 1996 no top official advocated again seeking a 'results-oriented' trade agreement.

[17] In fact, trade tensions now focused much more on China, whose trade surplus with the US was on a steady upsurge, from a little over US$ 10 billion in 1990 to US$83.8 billion in 1999, the first year in which China's trade surplus passed that of Japan's.

Even more salient were the continued struggles of the Japanese economy. These problems had been ongoing since 1990, but were initially viewed by US policy makers as a temporary phenomenon. Even in 1993 and 1994, during the Framework, officials felt that the Japanese economy was still fundamentally sound and would rebound to be stronger than ever. After decades of the revisionist drumbeat of alarm over Japan's growing economic threat, it is not surprising that old perceptions died hard. With every passing month, however, it was clearer that Japan's economic recession was deeper than anyone had ever imagined.

By the second Clinton administration, when US officials looked at the Japanese economy they saw nothing but problems and shortcomings. In fact, if Japan represented any sort of danger, it was not because its economy was too strong but because it was too weak. By 1996 the Clinton administration was becoming more worried about a potential implosion of the Japanese economy. Of special concern was the weakness of the banking industry, whose potential collapse threatened a meltdown that might bring down all of its trading partners. Thus, in less than a decade the Japan problem had been completely redefined: now, rather than needing to contain Japan's ever-expanding economic power, the problem was how to prevent it from a disastrous implosion.

By the late 1990s, then, America's understanding of the Japanese threat had come full circle.[18] The unique features that revisionism had focused on—in particular the government involvement in the economy and collusive business practices—now seemed to be sources of weakness rather than strength. In sum, it was becoming clear to most that the revisionist paradigm had badly oversold the danger that the Japanese economy represented. The Japanese threat, which only four years earlier had been a national priority, was increasingly seen to be an empty one.[19]

---

[18] According to Horvat (2000: 4), in an ABC poll taken in 1996, when asked 'Is Japan's economic strength a threat to the United States?,' 40 per cent answered yes and 56 per cent said no. In contrast, just three years earlier, in March 1993, 55 per cent had seen Japan as a threat and 40 per cent had not.

[19] If anything the perception of external economic threat after 2000 shifted almost entirely from Japan to China. In watching the development of American attitudes and rhetoric toward economic competition with China, I have an eerie sense of déjà vu, with American attitudes in the mid-1980s toward Japan as an economic bogeyman now being replayed. First is a large and growing trade deficit, with seemingly no end in sight, that has resulted in the loss of jobs and economic dislocation. There are growing populist voices not only in the American media, most clearly represented by CNN's Lou Dobbs, but also among American politicians, especially in the rust belt. And a growing chorus of voices in the US views the Chinese economy as protected and inherently closed. China is also criticized for unfair trade practices, in particular the lack of protection for intellectual property rights, and the like. In addition, the future prospects of the Chinese economy seem limitless. With growth rates exceeding 10 per cent over the past decade, many perceive China as an inevitable economic superpower of the

Japan Policy Since 1995: The Return to Traditionalism

With core elements of revisionist assumptions being called into question, the way was open for a full re-emergence of more traditionalist views of the US–Japan security relationship. This reassessment had been in process since earlier in the Framework, as described in Chapter 8. By 1995 traditionalists had already succeeded in partially shifting the focus of the relationship to more of a balance between economics and security. The January 1995 summit meeting between Clinton and Murayama, for instance, was notable for its focus on security issues and its conscious avoidance of economic frictions, even while the auto talks were heading for the final showdown.

Traditionalist voices were given even more weight by subsequent regional security developments, in particular North Korea's continuation of its nuclear development program. By 1996 officials were also alarmed that a severe famine in North Korea threatened to destabilize the already unstable Kim Jong Il government. Fears were that a 'hard landing' scenario would lead Kim to take some sort of aggressive action, thus putting US forces in Korea in jeopardy. In this changing regional context the relationship with Japan was seen as that much more important, not only because

---

future. Some have taken to drawing straight-line projections that have China becoming the dominant regional economy in the near future. With the US so reliant on Chinese money to finance its ongoing budget deficits, a growing number of Americans perceive a dangerous sense of vulnerability.

There also is a strong element of distrust of China's overall intentions, and the tacit assumption that it seeks to expand its international economic power at America's expense. China's attempts to diversify its economic security through international investments and 'economic diplomacy' are thus seen as especially threatening. Finally, it is assumed by a growing number of scholars and policy makers that China will inevitably use its economic power to enhance its military power, again at least indirectly at America's expense. These concerns are magnified because China is not an American ally, as Japan has been. Furthermore, China's sheer size makes it a larger potential threat than Japan could ever be.

There are three key elements, however, that make a simple comparison difficult. One is that China has yet to invest heavily in the US economy, as Japan did beginning in the 1980s. What little Chinese investment that has occurred has already met with a huge degree of American distrust, and these feelings would rise dramatically if China's investments were to increase. Second is that China is not yet perceived as a threat to America's *high-tech* industries. That is, up to now, concerns have been that Chinese industries can rely on relatively cheaper labor to out-compete America's labor-intensive and lately more capital-intensive industries. Third, and most importantly for this book, there is as yet no unified *theory* of China's economy that purports to explain how it is inherently different and/or better, or why it is so dangerous. That is, there is no coherent theory of Chinese exceptionalism that calls for an exceptional response, and there has thus been no major change in the working policy assumptions held by the US government. As a result, US policy has taken the old form of protectionism and adjustment assistance. If these three elements were to change in the future, then the stage may be set for a potential replay of US–Japan tensions of the 1990s.

of the bases but also because the US needed Japan's political and diplomatic support.

It was the horrendous rape of a young Okinawan school girl by three US marines in September 1995—only days after the auto agreement was officially signed—that served as a wake-up call for those who held traditionalist security assumptions. Given the understandable explosion of anti-base feelings throughout Japan, traditionalists were now truly worried over the future of the relationship. If the Japanese public turned against the bases, the US would have no choice but to leave, and the foundation of the entire relationship would change as a result. This threat now rallied traditionalist voices in State and NSC to reassert control over Japan policy. These officials had already become worried about the negative impact of trade tensions, and were not happy about the sanctions threat (as well as their meager results).[20] Now, in the context of a possible fundamental shift in the security relationship, the focus on trade tensions was deemed to be no longer acceptable. These agencies argued strongly that the relationship needed to be reset along the lines of traditionalist security assumptions.

As a result of the reemergence of these assumptions, the US sought to reaffirm and strengthen the security relationship. First, it tried to defuse the volatile situation on Okinawa by creating a Special Action Committee for Okinawa (SACO), to discuss a possible consolidation of US facilities on the island. Second, the US pushed for a reaffirmation of the mutual commitment to the security relationship, which it accomplished in the April 1996 Security Declaration signed by Clinton and new Prime Minister Hashimoto Ryutaro. In this declaration the US essentially recommitted itself to the traditionalist emphasis on Japan as a valuable political ally. Subsequently, Washington sought to redefine the US–Japan Defense Guidelines, which in effect would clarify what actions Japan would take in the event of a 'regional contingency'—by which all involved understood to mean hostilities on the Korean peninsula. If the Clinton administration had not completely returned to a traditionalist view of the security relationship, it was close.

---

[20] Yet another complication was the fallout over the *New York Times* reports that the US intelligence agencies had spied on Japanese negotiators during the auto talks, a charge that the US government would neither confirm nor deny. To the Japanese side, the issue was once again one of trust; as cooperationist ambassador Kuriyama put it, 'I am concerned about the negative impact on the US–Japan relationship of that reporting, which has given rise to the Japanese people questioning their trust in the US' (*New York Times* 10/28/95 <www.nytimes.com/>).

By the second Clinton administration, then, the prevailing policy assumptions inside the administration had already shifted visibly to a hybrid of revisionist and traditionalist assumptions. As described, economic officials still clung to revisionist views of Japan as closed and different, but were realizing that Japan's uncooperative stance made results-oriented agreements impossible. Yet dissatisfaction over economic issues was tempered by the realization of just how important Japan was as a political ally. Thus, the traditionalist view of the importance of the security relationship was once again being elevated above the desire to resolve economic disputes. In sum, Japan was now viewed less as an economic threat, and more as an indispensable political and military ally. These traditionalist trends would continue to strengthen through the end of the Clinton administration.

* * *

The complete reassertion of traditionalist assumptions about Japan was cemented in the first few months of 2001, under the new administration of George W. Bush. This reassertion was driven mostly by the emphasis that the administration placed on realist views of world politics, which in turn led to significant reversals in US relations with all of the North-East Asian countries. To the new administration, the region represented one that was defined more in terms of security threats rather than economic opportunities.

First, the new Bush team stressed China's growing power as dangerous and destabilizing, in stark contrast to the Clinton administration, which at its end had seen the Chinese relationship as a potentially positive one. Clinton's view that Chinese economic growth would make it more stable and cooperative was now replaced by Bush's view that significant Chinese growth would make it a more formidable military power. Given its distrust of Chinese intentions, the administration seemed to gird itself for a coming confrontation with China. Thus, immediately after taking power, the administration's rhetoric toward China turned cold, and in the early months of the administration the two found themselves locked in some small but nasty confrontations.[21]

---

[21] These included Bush's comments that seemed to indicate that he was ending the 'One China Policy,' and the fallout over the downing of an American spy plane in Chinese territory. Baum 2001. The period of growing confrontation was cut short by 9/11, as the US found it had other more threatening things to worry about. Also, the US was receptive to China's argument that its crackdown on the Uighurs in Western China could be seen as part of the 'global war on terror.' Overnight, what the US had been criticizing earlier as human rights violations were now justified by the need to battle 'Islamic radical extremists.'

Similarly, the administration was eager to confront the simmering threat of North Korea, one that neo-conservatives in the administration felt had been allowed to fester for too long. Even before 9/11 and the later revelation that North Korea had violated the spirit of the Agreed Framework by pursuing a small uranium enrichment program, the new administration had signaled its lack of interest in any sort of engagement policy. One of its first foreign policy actions was to back away from South Korea's so-called 'sunshine policy' of engagement with the North. American rhetoric turned nasty, and any possibility of a negotiated settlement with the North largely disappeared.

The new administration was thus determined to restore the traditionalist emphasis on US–Japan security relations. In part, this reflected the recognition that Japan was America's most important ally in the region, and that its cooperation was absolutely essential if any of the region's problems were to be resolved. It also reflected the view that the US–Japan relationship had been damaged during the Clinton years, first by the fallout from the trade frictions, then by the problems with the US bases in Okinawa, and finally because of Clinton's strategic tilt toward China. Early on, Japan was elevated, or more precisely restored, to its place as America's most important Asian partner.

The events surrounding 9/11 and the US decision to invade Iraq in 2003, served to cement traditionalist assumptions about the security relationship with Japan. In the context of new concerns over proliferation, Japanese cooperation in resolving the North Korean threat became more important. Japan early on signaled its support of America's global war on terror, for instance by quickly agreeing to share intelligence assets, participating in the Proliferation Security Initiative, and increasing its contribution to developing a theater missile defense. More importantly, Japan was one of the initial members of the 'coalition of the willing,' agreeing in 2003 to send some 900 troops to support the US occupation of Iraq.[22] Although Koizumi also saw this as an opportunity to break down further barriers to Japan playing a more activist international role, to the Bush administration, Japan's cooperation was received gratefully. Not without reason did the Bush administration label the state of the relationship as the 'best ever.'

---

[22] Here, Prime Minister Koizumi Junichiro overcame significant domestic opposition in dispatching the Japanese Self-Defense Forces (SDF). Although the site chosen was a relatively safe one, and even though the Japanese forces were physically protected by others in the coalition, Japan's decision to send armed troops to an area that was still violent, was a momentous one.

The Bush administration gave almost no attention to the trade side of the relationship, even as America's bilateral deficit with Japan continued to reach all-time highs. In part this represented the Republican administration's return to fundamental free trade assumptions. And in part it reflected the trends discussed above, namely the re-emergence of traditionalist arguments that the security side of the relationship needed to be protected from economic frictions, and that the Japanese economy simply did not represent any sort of revisionist-style threat. Furthermore, Japan itself was undergoing a transformation of sorts, heralded by the election of Koizumi in 2001, who took office on a platform of pursuing domestic economic deregulation. Although Koizumi did not succeed in drastically revamping the Japanese economy, the combination of piecemeal deregulation and the changes wrought by Japan's decade-long stagnation softened some of revisionism's core views of the economy. To a degree, the government had become less interventionist and involved in the economy, and to the extent that it is, intervention is now more likely to support industries of the past rather than industries of the future. Certain structures of the Japanese economy, notably the *keiretsu*, have been transformed, at least on paper. A case can thus be made that Japan's economy is no longer the same one that the revisionists described back in the 1980s.

* * *

In the decade following the failure of the Framework, revisionism's status as the dominant approach to understanding the Japanese economy has been badly eroded. The popular media and academics, when they cover Japan at all, have focused mostly on the question of why the Japanese economy has performed so poorly since 1990. Here, the implication many drew from revisionism that the Japanese system was not only different, but also better, has come under intense criticism.[23] Revisionism (and Japan trade policy in general) has largely been shunted aside; indeed, if revisionism is applied to Japan it is now more likely to refer to those who seek to revise the understanding of Japan's motivations before World War II.

Revisionism's standing among academic specialists on Japan is a bit more complicated. Here it is important to consider the different parts of revisionism—the view of Japan as different, closed, and as a threat—separately. On the first two parts, most professional economists who have

---

[23] Two critiques of revisionism directly related to Japan's underperformance are Lindsay and Lukas (1998) and Horvat (2000). It should be remembered that many revisionists, especially Prestowitz, had explicitly argued that Japan's system was different, but not necessarily better.

specialized on Japan still strongly believe in traditionalists assumptions that Japan can be basically understood through a neo-classical lens, and that Japan should not be seen as overly different or uniquely closed. (Many of the comments on this manuscript by economists objected to any hint that revisionism is or was at all valid; it is as if the battle lines have not changed since the 1980s). On the other hand, political economists are more likely to give credence to the view that Japan is different and closed, in that many find it difficult to teach about Japan's economy without some reference to revisionist ideas about industrial policy, its different economic structures, and the like. But there is no question that the concepts of revisionism are no longer taught the way they once were.[24]

However, it would be too facile to completely dismiss the impact of revisionist assumptions about Japan, especially in the US government. In particular, trade officials involved with Japan still hold to the core revisionist assumptions that Japan is closed and different. That is, while revisionist assumptions are no longer the driving force behind US trade policy, US trade officials still perceive Japan as very much 'not like us.' Put differently, few trade officials embrace the traditionalist view of Japan as essentially similar to capitalist economies elsewhere, or that simply removing barriers will result in increased import penetration.

It is not the case, moreover, that officials believe that trade relations with Japan no longer matter. After all, Japan is still the second largest economy in the world and America's largest overseas trading partner, and Japan's trade surplus continues to surge (even if it has since been eclipsed by China's surplus). Japan's high-tech industries are still world-class competitors, and many American industries—notably autos—are still beset by competition from their Japanese counterparts. Although domestic concerns in the US over trade deficits have been muted (especially compared to the 1980s), there is no guarantee that this will continue. There is still a perceived need to redress America's trade deficits.

What has happened in the decade following the Framework is that there has been a growing sense of resignation that the US government simply cannot do much to curb its trade problems with Japan. Policy makers

[24] The exceptions may be the revisionists themselves: as Prestowitz (2002: 2) put it, 'my view is that revisionism is the conventional wisdom.' But if some of their ideas are still current, the strength of revisionism has also been hurt by the fact that the original revisionists themselves have largely moved on to other foci or even on to other fields. Chalmers Johnson, for instance, turned his attention to the problems caused by the American bases in Okinawa, and then in a global sense. Prestowitz has focused more on international trade policies and foreign policy issues in general. Fallows and van Wolferen have not written about Japan for a number of years.

perceived that they have no good solutions or even a good clue as to how to open the Japanese economy. In essence, revisionist-style prescriptions are no longer attainable, given Japan's complete intransigence, and thus, the US is left with second best solutions such as deregulation. To put it differently, although the revisionist arguments about the Japanese economy have been neutralized, no new paradigm has emerged to take its place. With no new solutions presenting themselves, trade policy toward Japan has remained static. The lack of an activist US trade approach to Japan is thus as much about American impotence as the perceived unimportance of the Japan trade issue. If one is powerless to do anything about a problem, the tendency is not to want to talk about it, much less shout about it.

Where academics and policy makers all agree is on the third element of revisionism: clearly, all agree that that Japan is no longer much of an economic threat. This is an assumption of revisionism that has disappeared today, buried under more than a decade of poor economic performance in Japan. In fact, this may be an element of revisionism that is gone forever, never to return. That is, like the boy who cried wolf, the revisionists may have so exaggerated Japan's economic threat, and got so many in the US so riled up about Japan as an economic enemy, that when people realized that the threat was not really all that great, it undermined everything that the revisionists had been arguing—even if one believes that the revisionists were otherwise correct about the unique and closed nature of the Japanese economy.

The Impact of New Policy Assumptions: A Recap

The US government's embrace of revisionist assumptions was relatively brief, reaching a peak in the first Clinton administration and gradually disappearing since then. Some readers may be tempted to dismiss the impact of these assumptions as inconsequential or not worth studying. I believe (obviously) that this would be a mistake.

As I have argued throughout this book, revisionist assumptions had a definite and visible impact on how the US approached one of its most important bilateral relationships. Revisionism became the centerpiece of a significant shift in American trade policy toward Japan, and became the focus of one of the most contentious US–Japan trade negotiations ever. These new American assumptions were certainly taken seriously by the Japanese government at the time, which saw huge costs in allowing them to go unchallenged. If these new assumptions, which portrayed Japan as a unique outlier to which multilateral trading rules did not apply, were allowed to stand, they would have justified a policy of specific reciprocity—managed trade—that would have been copied by all of its trading partners. Their treatment as an exception to prevailing international norms was something that Japan refused to accept. The Japanese government's counteroffensive thus focused squarely on discrediting America's revisionist ideas and assumptions, and at times appeared to be trying to discredit the revisionists themselves. Finally, these assumptions mattered because their adoption by the US as the basis for its new trade policy and their utter rejection by the Japanese, represent a turning point in bilateral relations. Since 1995, the US has refrained from pursuing managed trade solutions with Japan, or anyone else, and has also eschewed bilateral and certainly unilateral means to resolve trade disputes. The creation of the WTO does explain a part of this shift towards multilateralism, but so too does America's failure to get Japan to accepts its demands back in 1995.

Put another way, if Japan had agreed (counterfactually) to US demands for an explicit market share agreement, as most at the time assumed it would, trade relations today would look very different. Had the US succeeded it most likely would have expanded this approach to other sectors in Japan. The Clinton administration initially wanted to make this approach the cornerstone of its entire trade policy with Japan, so there is no reason to assume that it would have stopped with the initial industries. The US would also most likely have extended this approach to other trading partners, most notably South Korea and later China. As these economies were described as following the Japanese model, a managed trade solution that worked with Japan would have been seen as likely to work with them as well. Politically, South Korea would have been hard pressed to say no to the US had Japan said yes—exactly the situation that Japanese diplomats warned of in 1994. Although the WTO would have constrained American behavior to a degree, the WTO itself would not be as effective today if the two largest economies had struck a political deal—a market share agreement—that lay outside the WTO framework.[25] Japan's rejection of American demands, and its subsequent insistence on relying on the WTO dispute settlement mechanism, was not at all predictable in 1993.

[25] I recall a conversation with Jhagdish Bhagwati on the eve of the auto showdown, in which he expressed his concern that if the Japanese buckled once again—as everyone expected them to—it would irreparably harm the WTO.

In other words, if these events are now 'just history,' as one commentator put it to me, then it is important history, and therefore important to understand.

It is also important for scholars to understand why some ideational factors—in this case policy assumptions—end up being rejected. Like the norms scholars described in Chapter 6, those who study ideas very often focus on those that have a lasting or transformational impact—after all, who wants to study something that 'didn't matter'? In this case, revisionist assumptions did not end up being rejected because they were not popular—at the time, these ideas dominated American thinking, and were even more strongly held in Western Europe. In 1993 most observers assumed that revisionism would be ascendant in the future, and American political economists predicted that the Western countries would be able to come to an 'intersubjective understanding' of how best to deal with the Japan problem—in brief, in a harsh, revisionist manner. What was left out of their calculations, however, was Japan itself, which refused to accept the legitimacy or applicability of these new assumptions. The story of how revisionist assumptions were eventually rejected thus comes back in part to power, resistance, and negotiations.

* * *

If one accepts that revisionist assumptions had an important impact on US–Japan negotiating dynamics, how can we be confident that it was these assumptions that caused the change of policy approach? The task of isolating the causal impact of policy assumptions is a difficult one, as there is always some overlap with more objective or structural factors. The period under investigation represents a hard case in that it featured some major external changes that can at least partially account for the policy changes and negotiating dynamics during the Framework. Most notably, this period coincided with the rise of Japanese economic power relative to that of the US, and the end of the Cold War.

There is no question that structural changes mattered, to a degree—so momentous a shift as the end of the Cold War, especially, could not but have some impact. The rise of Japan's economic power relative to the US in the 1980s is an 'objective fact' that does explain a degree of rising tensions in the relationship; as scholars pointed out at the time, this shift in realist power relations gave the US a strong incentive to respond in some fashion. The subsequent end of the Cold War weakened an important constraint, namely the traditionalist assumption that the security tie with Japan took precedence over all other aspects of the relationship; now, the US could elevate the economic leg of the 'three-legged stool' to the top of the agenda. By 1992 some sort of confrontation over trade seemed likely.

These structural causes are, however, by themselves ultimately unsatisfying. First, the timing of the end of the Cold War does not coincide with the policy shifts that occurred; that is, even with the winding down of the Cold War in the late 1980s, traditionalist assumptions about the security relationship still constrained the shift to a managed trade agenda.[26] Second, and more importantly, these structural changes do not explain the *specific* choice of the results-oriented trade policy. That is, the US could have chosen any number of responses to meet the rising Japanese threat, ranging from straight protectionism to even more aggressive unilateralism to remove barriers in the Japanese market, to adopting a full-fledged industrial policy for its own high-technology industries. Indeed, many observers at the time predicted all of these responses.

The fact is, however, that the Clinton administration chose a different course, a results orientation, that these other theories predicted only in the vaguest of terms. In this sense, then, structural changes should be considered no more than 'permissive causes'—that is, changes in these factors may have removed existing constraints, and thus opened up a political space in which new assumptions were able to flourish.[27] But in and of themselves, these external changes do not explain the specific content of policy change, and in particular the shift towards a results-oriented policy. Furthermore, the specific choice of the results orientation was a crucial one. Put another way, different US choices at key moments would have led to very different interstate dynamics; thus our theories must be able to explain the *specifics* of these important policy changes. In this particular issue, America's policy choices are understandable only when we incorporate the rise of revisionist ideas about Japan, and their subsequent acceptance as core assumptions by the US government.

Another alternative explanation is that the administration's actions can be explained simply by looking at powerful societal actors in the US, most

[26] Schoppa (1999) makes a similar point in his analysis of Japan.

[27] Another permissive factor was political change in both countries—the election of a Democratic president for the first time in 12 years in the US and the fall of the LDP in Japan after 46 years in power. In both cases policy makers were to a degree freed from long-standing constraints or procedures, and perhaps more able to pursue new policy directions. Still, on the American side, the content of these new directions stemmed directly from revisionist assumptions.

notably the automotive industries, which stood to gain directly from market share agreements with Japan. There is no doubt that many US officials were disposed to favor the demands of these industries—a clear example is Mickey Kantor ticking off the electoral races in the auto producing states in response to a suggestion that the US should back down from its hard line.[28]

I have argued, however, that this is not a story of the Clinton administration simply responding to the demands of these industries. First, as discussed in Chapter 5, the automotive industries opportunistically supported a market share approach only after it appeared that the administration had decided to move in that direction. Up until then, the industries were more focused on protecting the US market, or creating an American industrial policy to support them, and the like, and yet the Clinton people chose to reject most of these demands. Second, I have argued that the debate in the US throughout the 1980s, and then particularly among the Clinton policy makers, transcended the interests of any specific industry or group. Rather, the struggle was over much deeper competing conceptions of how the Japanese economy operated, and what this implied for the US. It was in the shaping of a new understanding of Japan—the development of revisionism—that these industries had their most important impact. This is particularly true of the semiconductor industry, which played a large role in the early 1980s in shaping what would only later be known as revisionism.

As I demonstrated in Part I, furthermore, there were many other sources of revisionist assumptions, ranging from government officials who had dealt with Japan, academics and journalists, politicians, and other high-tech industries. What gave the revisionist paradigm its power was not that it was pushed by powerful industries, but rather its seeming ability to resolve so many of the policy anomalies that bedeviled the traditionalist school of thought. The new assumptions were also attractive because they not only offered a simple way to explain America's longstanding trade problems with Japan, but because they promised a panacea, a new way to resolve those problems.

Finally, it is important to remember that the eventual adoption of revisionist assumptions was by no means a foregone conclusion. Indeed, the bulk of the narrative in this book has traced how those who espoused

---

[28] There are many other possible instances of political expediency at work, although not all are of any importance. My favorite such example is one commentator's argument that revisionist scholars such as Laura Tyson pushed the revisionist thesis so hard out of a desire to increase sales of their books.

these new policy assumptions struggled against those who stuck to a more traditionalist approach. By the end of the 1980s revisionist conceptions had coalesced into a coherent alternative, and the revisionist drumbeat was growing so loud that it was drowning out all other voices, especially among trade officials in the US government. However, until the Clinton administration, revisionist policy assumptions never completely dominated the policy process, especially at the top levels of the administration. The result was a trade policy that was largely traditionalist in orientation, stressing market liberalization and improving the market process in Japan.

It was not until the Clinton administration that, for the first time, the US government was united top to bottom behind revisionist assumptions. As described in Part II, all of Clinton's political appointees held to revisionist assumptions about the Japanese economy, at times to an even stronger degree than the career trade officials.[29] The process of policy change came down to the question of which policy assumptions about Japan would prevail, and in this the administration's direction was quickly put into place. In a matter of months, the Clinton team distanced itself from traditionalist assumptions and clearly adopted a revisionist understanding of Japan, and this led the administration to charge off in pursuit of its results-oriented trade approach. Here is a case where we can almost *see* the replacement of one set of policy assumptions with another, with a visible impact on important policy decisions.

* * *

It is always difficult to draw a pristine distinction between the impact of ideational factors such as policy assumptions and more objective factors such as materially-based interests. In the end, however, this distinction may not be necessary or useful. That is, policy assumptions certainly interacted with material factors, at times in complex or overlapping ways. Revisionist policy assumptions in part reflected developments in the political environment, and their resonance cannot be understood without reference to that environment. Yet, these new policy assumptions

[29] Some commentators have also argued that revisionism merely provided political cover for what Clinton wanted to do anyway, or that Clinton simply took advantage of an opportunity to try out a new policy approach (see, for example, Schoppa 1997: 260). As explained in Chapter 4, however, in the early stages of the administration, although Clinton had become interested in solving the 'Japan Problem,' there is no indication that he initially pushed the managed trade approach – he was not the source of the call for targets, numbers, and the like. But once his Japan policy team, the DC, adopted revisionist assumptions and based their policy recommendations on them, the push for targets and numbers logically followed. In other words, it was revisionism itself that provided the content of the Clinton approach.

themselves also helped to clarify, and in an important way to modify, America's understanding of the Japanese economy and even the meaning of the US–Japan relationship itself.

Even if one cannot completely divorce material and ideational elements, the bottom line for me is whether the focus on policy assumptions is a useful way to help understand America's major shift in policy, and all that ensued. I have argued that it is. The contest over policy assumptions became the focal point of the policy process, and provides an important and necessary part of the explanation for this significant episode of policy change. Put differently, I find it impossible to explain the Clinton administration's choice of a results-oriented trade policy, and the subsequent dynamics of US–Japan trade negotiations, without a full understanding of the development and adoption of revisionist assumptions.

References

ACCJ (The American Chamber of Commerce in Japan). 1997. *Making Trade Talks Work: Lessons From Recent History*. Tokyo, Japan: ACCJ.

ACTPN (Advisory Committee for Trade Policy and Negotiations). 1989. *Analysis of the US Japan Trade Problem*. (February). Washington, DC: ACTPN.

——1993. *Major Findings and Policy Recommendations on US–Japan Trade Policy* (January). Washington, DC: ACTPN.

Alexander, Arthur J. 1997. 'Revisionism Revisited.' *JEI Report* 29A (August 1): 1–19.

Allison, Graham T. 1971. *Essence of Decision: Explaining the Cuban Missile Crisis*. Boston, MA: Little, Brown.

Armacost, Michael H. 1996. *Friends or Rivals? The Insider's Account of US–Japan Relations*. New York: Columbia University Press.

Barrenger, Davis. 1994. 'Automotive Parts: The Gloves Are Off.' *The Journal* (May): 8–17.

Baum, Richard. 2001. 'From "Strategic Partners" to "Strategic Competitors": George W. Bush and the Politics of US China Policy,' *Journal of East Asian Studies*: 191–220.

Berger, Thomas U. 1996. 'Norms, Identity, and National Security in Germany and Japan.' In Peter J. Katzenstein, (ed.), *The Culture of National Security: Norms and Identity in World Politics*. New York: Columbia University Press, 317–56.

Bhagwati, Jagdish. 1996. 'The US–Japan Car Dispute: A Monumental Mistake.' *International Affairs* 72, 2: 261–79.

——and Patrick, Hugh T. 1990. *Aggressive Unilateralism: America's 301 Trade Policy and the World Trading System*. Ann Arbor, MI: The University of Michigan Press.

Blaker, Michael K. 1977. 'Probe, Push and Panic: The Japanese Tactical Style in International Negotiations.' In Robert A. Scalapino (ed.), *The Foreign Policy of Modern Japan*. Berkeley, CA: University of California Press.

Blinder, Alan. 1990. 'There Are Capitalists and Then There Are Japanese.' *Business Week* (October 8): 21.

Blyth, Mark M. 1997. 'Any More Bright Ideas? The Ideational Turn of Comparative Political Economy.' *Comparative Politics* 29, 2 (January): 229–50.

Boaz, David. 1989. 'Yellow Peril Reinfects America.' Cato Institute (http://www.cato.org).

References

Brock, David. 1989. 'The Theory and Practice of Japan-Bashing.' *The National Interest* 17 (Fall): 17–28.

Calder, Kent E. 1988. 'Japanese Foreign Economic Policy Formation: Explaining the Reactive State.' *World Politics* 40, 4 (July): 517–41.

Checkel, Jeffrey T. 1998. 'The Constructivist Turn in International Relations Theory.' *World Politics* 50, 2 (January): 324–48.

Choate, Pat. 1990. *Agents of Influence*. New York, NY: Alfred A. Knopf.

Clancy, Tom. 1994. *Debt of Honor*. New York: G. P. Putnam's Sons.

Clinton, William Jefferson. 2004. *My Life*. New York: Vintage Books.

Cohen, Stephen S. and Zysman, John. 1987. *Manufacturing Matters: The Myth of the Post-Industrial Economy*. New York, NY: Basic Books.

Craib, Anne B. 1994. 'The Making of Japan Trade Policy in the Clinton Administration: Institutions and Individuals.' *JEI Report* 39A (October 14): 1–12.

Crichton, Michael. 1992. *Rising Sun*. New York: Alfred A. Knopf.

Curran, Timothy. 1982. 'Politics and High Technology: The NTT Case.' In I. M. Destler and Hideo Sato (eds.), *Coping with US–Japanese Conflicts*. Lexington, MA: Lexington Books, 185–241.

Curtis, Gerald L. 1999. *The Logic of Japanese Politics: Leaders, Institutions and the Limits of Change*. New York, NY: Columbia University Press.

——2000. 'US Policy Toward Japan from Nixon to Clinton: An Assessment.' In Gerald L. Curtis (ed.), *New Perspectives on US–Japan Relations*. Tokyo: Japan Center for International Exchange, 1–38.

Dawson, George. 1992. 'Blame the Japanese.' *New York Times* (January 29): A19.

Destler, I. M. 1979. *The Textile Wrangle*. Ithaca, NY: Cornell University Press.

——1992. *American Trade Politics* (2nd edn.). Washington, DC: Institute for International Economics.

——1996. *The National Economic Council: A Work in Progress*. Washington, DC: Institute for International Economics.

——Hideo Sato, Priscilla Clapp, and Haruhiro Fukui. 1976. *Managing an Alliance: The Politics of US–Japan Relations*. Washington, DC: The Brookings Institution.

Dore, Ronald. 1986. *Flexible Rigidities: Industrial Policy and Structural Adjustment in the Japanese Economy, 1970–1980*. Stanford, CA: Stanford University Press.

Drucker, Peter F. 1989. *The New Realities: In Government and Politics, in Economy and Business*. New York, NY: Harper & Row.

Dryden, Steve. 1995. *Trade Warriors: USTR and the American Crusade for Free Trade*. New York, NY: Oxford University Press.

Economic Strategy Institute. 1993. *Toward a New Trade Consensus: Highlights of an ESI/PBEC Conference*. Washington, DC: Economic Strategy Institute.

——1995. *The US and Japan: Déjà vu All Over Again?* Washington, DC: Economic Strategy Institute.

Encarnation, Dennis J. 1992. *Rivals Beyond Trade: America Versus Japan in Global Competition*. Ithaca, NY: Cornell University Press.

Ennis, Peter. 1993a. 'Trade Issues Take the Lead: Inside Clinton's Japan Team.' *Tokyo Business Today* 61, 7 (July): 6–11.

—— 1993b. 'US and Japan Reverse Roles in Economic Framework Negotiations.' *Tokyo Business Today* 61, 10 (October): 56–7.

—— 1994a. 'Inside the Clinton-Hosokawa Summit.' *Tokyo Business Today* 62, 5 (May): 34–8.

—— 1994b. 'A New American Approach to Asia? Maybe . . .' *Tokyo Business Today* 62, 8 (August): 36–9.

—— 1995. 'Clinton–Murayama Summit Will Reaffirm US–Japan Relations.' *Tokyo Business Today* 63, 12 (December): 18–21.

Fallows, James. 1989a. 'Containing Japan.' *Atlantic Monthly* 263 (May): 40–54.

—— 1989b. *More Like Us: Putting America's Native Strengths and Traditional Values to Work to Overcome the Asian Challenge*. Boston, MA: Houghton Mifflin Company.

—— 1990. 'How to Conquer Japan by Playing for Keeps Today: For Once, Short-Term Thinking May Be the Right Answer for American Business.' *Business Month* 135, 3 (March): 54.

—— 1993. 'Looking at the Sun.' *The Atlantic Monthly* (November): 69–100.

—— Chalmers Johnson, Prestowitz, Clyde, and van Wolferen, Karel. 1990. 'Beyond Japan-Bashing: The 'Gang of Four' Defends the Revisionist Line. *US News and World Report*, (May 7): 54.

Finnemore, Martha. 1996. 'Constructing Norms of Humanitarian Intervention.' In Peter J. Katzenstein (ed.), *The Culture of National Security: Norms and Identity in World Politics*. New York: Columbia University Press, 153–85.

—— and Sikkink, Kathryn. 1998. 'International Norm Dynamics and Political Change.' *International Organization* 52, 4 (Autumn): 887–917.

Flamm, Kenneth. 1996. *Mismanaged Trade? Strategic Policy and the Semiconductor Industry*. Washington, DC: The Brookings Institution.

Friedman, David. 1988. *The Misunderstood Miracle: Industrial Development and Political Change in Japan*. Ithaca, NY: Cornell University Press.

Friedman, George and LeBard, Meredith. 1991. *The Coming War With Japan*. New York, NY: St. Martin's Press.

Fukushima, Glen S. 1991a. ' "Revisionism" in US–Japan Relations.' *Business Japan* 36, 4: 42–3.

—— 1991b. 'Tales From A Trade Veteran.' *ACCJ Journal* 28, 1 (January): 19–25.

—— 1994. 'The Role of Government in High Tech Trade.' In Franz Waldenberger (ed.), *The Political Economy of Trade Conflicts: The Management of Trade Relations in the US–EU–Japan Triad*. Berlin: Springer-Verlag, 115–22.

Funabashi, Yoichi. 1989. *Managing the Dollar: From the Plaza to the Louvre* (2nd edn.). Washington, DC: Institute for International Economics.

Gephardt, Richard A. 1991. 'Toward a Better US–Japan Partnership in the 21st Century' (Address before the Center for National Policy December 6).

Gerlach, Michael L. 1992. *Alliance Capitalism: The Social Organization of Japanese Business*. Berkeley, CA: University of California Press.

References

Gilpin, Robert. 1981. *War and Change in World Politics*. Cambridge, England: Cambridge University Press.

Goldstein, Judith. 1993. *Ideas, Interests, and American Trade Policy*. Ithaca, NY: Cornell University Press.

—— and Keohane, Robert O. 1993. *Ideas and Foreign Policy: Beliefs, Institutions, and Political Change*. Ithaca, NY: Cornell University Press.

Haas, Peter M. 1992. 'Introduction: Epistemic Communities and International Policy Coordination.' *International Organization* 46, 1 (Winter): 1–35.

Hall, Peter A. 1989. *The Political Power of Economic Ideas: Keynesianism Across Nations*. Princeton, NJ: Princeton University Press.

Hatakeyama Noboru. 1996. *Tsūshō Kōshō: Kokueki o Meguru Dorama*. Tokyo, Japan: Nihon Keizai Shimbunsha.

Hills, Carla. 1993. 'Targets Won't Open Japanese Markets.' *Wall Street Journal* June 11: A10.

Horvat, Andrew. 2000. *Reviewing Revisionism: Judging the Legacy of an Era of US–Japan Acrimony*. Tokyo: The Asia Foundation.

Huntington, Samuel P. 1993. 'Why International Primacy Matters.' In Sean M. Lynn-Jones (ed.), *The Cold War and After: Prospects for Peace*. Cambridge, MA: The MIT Press, 307–22.

Irwin, Douglas A. 1994. *Trade Politics and the Semiconductor Industry*. Cambridge, MA: National Bureau of Economic Research.

Ishihara, Shintaro. 1991. *The Japan That Can Say No: Why Japan Will Be First Among Equals*. New York, NY: Simon and Schuster.

Jacobsen, John Kurt. 1995. 'Much Ado About Ideas: The Cognitive Factor in Economic Policy.' *World Politics* 47, 2 (January): 283–310.

Janow, Merit E. 1994. 'Trading With an Ally: Progress and Discontent in US–Japan Trade Relations.' In Gerald L. Curtis (ed.), *The United States, Japan, and Asia: Challenges for US Policy*. New York: W.W. Norton, 53–95.

Jervis, Robert. 1970. *The Logic of Images in International Relations*. Princeton, NJ: Princeton University Press.

Johnson, Chalmers. 1982. *MITI and the Japanese Miracle: The Growth of Industrial Policy, 1925–1975*. Stanford: Stanford University Press.

—— 1988. 'The Japanese Political Economy: A Crisis in Theory.' *Ethics and International Affairs* 2, 2: 79–97.

—— 1989a. 'Rethinking Japanese Politics: A Godfather Reports.' *Freedom at Issue* 111 (November 1): 5–11.

—— 1989b. 'Their Behavior, Our Policy.' *The National Interest* 17 (Fall): 17–27.

—— 1990. 'Trade, Revisionism, and the Future of Japanese-American Relations.' In Kozo Yamamura (ed.), *Japan's Economic Structure: Should It Change?* Seattle, WA: Society for Japanese Studies, 105–36.

Johnson, Sheila K.1995a. *Japan: Who Governs?* New York, NY: W. Norton & Co.

—— 1995b. 'Needed: A Japan Strategy.' *JPRI Critique* II, 8 (September). Japan Policy Research Institute, University of San Francisco.

—— 1995c. 'Tom Clancy's *Debt of Honor.*' *JPRI Critique* II, 4 (April). Japan Policy Research Institute, University of San Francisco.

Kaplan, Eugene J. 1972. *Japan: The Government–Business Relationship.* Washington, DC: US Department of Commerce.

Karube, Kensuke. 1996. *Political Appointees: Clinton–Ryū Tai Nichi Sensaku No Kokui-tachi.* Tokyo, Japan: Free Press.

Katz, Richard. 1997. 'Japan's Self-Defeating Trade Policy: Mainframe Economics in a PC World.' *Washington Quarterly* 20, 2: 153–81.

—— 1998a. 'The System That Soured: Toward a New Paradigm to Guide Japan Policy.' *The Washington Quarterly*, Autumn.

—— 1998b. *Japan: The System That Soured.* New York: M. E. Sharpe.

—— 1989. 'USTR Advisors Propose Negotiations on Market Share.' *Global Business* (February).

Katzenstein, Peter J. 1996. *The Culture of National Security: Norms and Identity in World Politics.* New York, NY: Columbia University Press.

—— Keohane, Robert O., and Krasner, Stephen D. 1998. ' "International Organization" and the Study of World Politics.' *International Organization* 52, 4 (Autumn): 645–85.

Kearns, Kevin. 1989. 'After FSX: A New Approach to US–Japan Relations.' *Foreign Service Journal* (December).

Kennedy, Paul. 1987. *The Rise and Fall of the Great Powers: Economic Change and Military Conflict From 1500 to 2000.* New York, NY: Random House.

Kim, Chulsu. 1990. 'Super 301 and the World Trading System: A Korean View.' In Jagdish Bhagwati and Patrick, Hugh T. (eds), *Aggressive Unilateralism: America's 301 Trade Policy and the World Trading System.* Ann Arbor, MI: The University of Michigan Press, 253–6.

Kissinger, Henry and Cyrus Vance. 1988. 'Bipartisan Objectives for American Foreign Policy.' *Foreign Affairs* 66, 5: 899–921.

Klotz, Audie. 1995. *Norms in International Relations: The Struggle Against Apartheid.* Ithaca, NY: Cornell University Press.

Komiya, Ryutaro, Okuno, Masahiro, and Suzumura, Kotaro. 1988. *Industrial Policy of Japan.* Tokyo, Japan: Academic Press Japan, Inc.

Krasner, Stephen D. 1987. *Asymmetries in Japanese–American Trade: The Case for Specific Reciprocity.* Berkeley, CA: Institute of International Studies, University of California, Berkeley.

Kunkel, John. 2003. *America's Trade Policy Towards Japan: Demanding Results.* London: Routledge.

Kuriyama, Takakazu. 1997. *Nichibei Dōmei: Hyōryū Kara No Dakkyaku (The Japan–US Alliance: From Drift to Revitalization).* Tokyo, Japan: Nihon Keizai Shumbunsha.

Kuroda, Makoto. 1990. 'Super 301 and Japan.' In Jagdish N. Bhagwati and Hugh T. Patrick (eds), *Aggressive Unilateralism: America's 301 Trade Policy and the World Trading System.* Ann Arbor, MI: The University of Michigan Press.

Kuttner, Robert. 1991. *The End of Laissez-Faire: National Purpose and the Global Economy After the Cold War.* New York: Alfred A. Knopf.

References

Latham, Scott. 1996. 'Market Opening or Corporate Welfare? "Results-Oriented" Trade Policy Toward Japan.' *Policy Analysis* (No. 252). Washington, DC: Cato Institute.

Layne, Christopher. 1993. 'The Unipolar Illusion: Why New Great Powers Will Rise.' *International Security* 17, 4 (Spring): 5–51.

Lincoln, Abraham. 1992. *Selected Speeches and Writings*. New York: Vintage Books/Library of America.

Lincoln, Edward J. 1999. *Troubled Times: US–Japan Trade Relations in the 1990s*. Washington, DC: The Brookings Institution.

Lindsey, Brink. 2001. 'Good Riddance to Managed Trade.' Cato Institute, Center for Trade Policy Studies (http://www.freetrade.org).

——and Lukas, Aaron. 1998. *Revisiting the 'Revisionists': The Rise and Fall of the Japanese Economic Model*. Washington, DC: Cato Institute.

Mason, Mark. 1992. *American Multinationals and Japan: The Political Economy of Japanese Capital Controls, 1899–1980*. Cambridge, MA: Harvard East Asian Monographs.

Mastanduno, Michael. 1991. 'Do Relative Gains Matter? America's Response to Japanese Industrial Policy.' *International Security* 16, 1 (Summer): 73–113.

——1998. 'Economics and Security in Statecraft and Scholarship.' *International Organization* 52, 4 (Autumn): 825–54.

Maswood, S. Javed. 1997. 'Does Revisionism Work? US Trade Strategy and the 1995 US–Japan Auto Dispute. *Pacific Affairs* (Winter): 533–54.

Mendelson, Sarah E. 1998. *Changing Course: Ideas, Politics, and the Soviet Withdrawal From Afghanistan*. Princeton, NJ: Princeton University Press.

Milner, Helen V. 1992. 'International Theories of Cooperation Among Nations: Strengths and Weaknesses.' *World Politics* 45, 3 (April): 466–96.

MITI (Tsūshō Sangyōsho, Tsūshōkyoku, Beishinka) (ed.) 1997. *Nichibei Jidōsha Kōshō no Kiseki*. Tokyo, Japan: MITI.

Miyashita Akitoshi and Sato Yoichiro. 2001. *Japanese Foreign Policy in Asia and the Pacific: Domestic Interests, American Pressure, and Regional Integration*. New York, NY: Palgrave.

Moravcsik, Andrew. 1997. 'Taking Preferences Seriously: A Liberal Theory of International Politics.' *International Organization* 51, 4 (Autumn): 513–53.

Neff, Robert and Magnusson, Paul. 1989. 'Rethinking Japan: The New, Harder Line Toward Tokyo.' *BusinessWeek* (August 7): 44–52.

Odell, John S. 1982. *US International Monetary Policy: Markets, Power, and Ideas As Sources of Change*. Princeton, NJ: Princeton University Press.

Office of the Federal Register. 1993. *Public Papers of the Presidents of the United States* (Books I and II). Washington, DC: National Archives and Records Administration.

——1995. *Public Papers of the Presidents of the United States* (Books I and II). Washington, DC: National Archives and Records Administration.

Okimoto, Daniel I. 1989. *Between MITI and the Market: Japanese Industrial Policy for High Technology*. Stanford: Stanford University Press.

——and Raphael, James H. 1993. 'Ambivalence, Continuity, and Change: American Attitudes Toward Japan and US–Japan Relations.' In The Aspen Strategy Group (ed.), *Harness the Rising Sun: An American Strategy for Managing Japan's Rise As a Global Power*. Lanham, MD: University Press of America, 117–63.

Okimoto, Daniel, Sugano, Takuo, Weinstein, Franklin. (eds.) 1984. *Competitive Edge: The Semiconductor Industry in the US and Japan*. Stanford, CA: Stanford University Press.

Orr, Robert M., Jr. 1990. *The Emergence of Japan's Foreign Aid Power*. New York, NY: Columbia University Press.

—— 1993. *Clinton Through Japanese Eyes*. Washington, DC: Economic Strategy Institute.

O'Shea, Timothy. 1995. 'The US–Japan Semiconductor Problem' *Pew Case Studies in International Affairs* (No. 139). Washington, DC: Georgetown University.

Patrick, Hugh T. and Rosovsky, Henry. 1976. *Asia's New Giant: How the Japanese Economy Works*. Washington, DC: The Brookings Institution.

Pekkanen, Saadia M. 2001. 'Aggressive Legalism: The Rules of the WTO and Japan's Emerging Trade Strategy.' *The World Economy* 24, 5 (May): 707–37.

Pempel, T. J. 1978. 'Japanese Foreign Economic Policy: The Domestic Bases for International Behavior.' In Peter J. Katzenstein (ed.), *Between Power and Plenty*. Madison, WI: University of Wisconsin Press, 139–90.

Prestowitz, Clyde V., Jr. 1987. 'US–Japan Trade Friction: Creating a New Relationship.' *California Management Review* 29, 2 (Winter): 9–19.

—— 1988. *Trading Places: How America Allowed Japan to Take the Lead*. New York: Charles E. Tuttle Company.

—— 1993. 'Japan and the United States: Twins or Opposites?' In the Aspen Strategy Group (ed.), *Harness the Rising Sun: An American Strategy for Managing Japan's Rise As a Global Power*. Lanham, MD: University Press of America, 75–98.

—— 2002. 'The Japan Model and Trade Policy: Interview with Clyde Prestowitz.' *GLOCOM Interviews* (October 23) (http://www.glocom.org).

Romberg, Alan D. 1990. *Same Bed, Different Dreams: America and Japan—Societies in Transition*. New York: Council on Foreign Relations.

Ruggie, John G. 1998. 'What Makes the World Hang Together? Neo-Utilitarianism and the Social Constructivist Challenge.' *International Organization* 52, 4 (Autumn): 855–85.

Schoppa, Leonard. 1993. 'Two Level Games and Bargaining Outcomes: Why Gaiatsu Succeeds in Japan in Some Cases and Not Others.' *International Organization* 47, 3 (Summer): 353–86.

—— 1997. *Bargaining With Japan: What American Pressure Can and Cannot Do*. New York, NY: Columbia University Press.

—— 1999. 'The Social Context in Coercive International Bargaining.' *International Organization* 53, 2 (Spring): 307–42.

Searight, Amy E. 2002. 'International Organizations.' In Steven K. Vogel (ed.), *US–Japan Relations in A Changing World*. Washington, DC: Brookings Institution: 160–97.

References

Smitka, Michael J. 1991. *Competitive Ties: Subcontracting in the Japanese Automotive Industry*. New York, NY: Columbia University Press.

Stokes, Bruce. 1990. *The Inevitability of Managed Trade: The Future Strategic Trade Policy Debate*. New York, NY: Japan Society.

Stone, Laura. 1999. 'Wither Trade and Security? A Historical Perspective.' In Michael J. Green and Patrick M. Cronin (eds.), *The US–Japan Alliance: Past, Present and Future*. New York: Council on Foreign Relations, 247–67.

Suzuki, Takaaki. 2000. *Japan's Budget Politics: Balancing Domestic and International Interests*. Boulder, CO: Lynne Rienner Publishers.

Tilton, Mark. 1996. *Restrained Trade: Cartels in Japan's Basic Materials Industries*. Ithaca, NY: Cornell University Press.

Tyson, Laura D'Andrea. 1991. 'Managing Trade by Rules and Outcomes.' *California Management Review* (Fall): 115–43.

—— 1992. *Who's Bashing Whom? Trade Conflict in High-Technology Industries*. Washington, DC: Institute for International Economics.

Uriu, Robert M. 1996. *Troubled Industries: Confronting Economic Change in Japan*. Ithaca, NY: Cornell University Press.

—— 1999. 'Refuting the Revisionists: Japan's Response to US Trade Pressures During the Clinton Administration.' *Proceedings of the International Symposium on Japan and Its Neighbors in the Global Village*. Nagoya, Japan: Nanzan University.

US Congress Joint Economic Committee of the Congress of the United States (1985). 'United States–Japan Trade: Semiconductors.' Hearings before the Joint Economic Committee of the Congress of the United States and the Subcommittee on Trade, Productivity and Economic Growth, 99th Congress, 1st session, August 6.

US House Committee on Foreign Affairs (1993). 'The New Framework for US–Japan Trade Relations.' Hearings before the Committee on Foreign Affairs and the Subcommittees on Economic Policy, Trade and Environment and Asia and the Pacific, 103rd Congress, 1st session, July.

—— Committee on Government Operations (1994). 'United States–Japan Framework Talks on Trade.' Hearings before the Committee on Government Operations and the Subcommittee on Commerce, Consumer and Monetary Affairs, 103rd Congress, 2nd session, February 23.

US Senate Committee on Finance (1993). 'United States–Japan Trade Policy.' Hearings before the Committee on Finance and the Subcommittee on International Trade, 103rd Congress, 1st session, July.

Van Wolferen, Karel. 1986/7. 'The Japan Problem.' *Foreign Affairs* 65, 2 (Winter): 288–303.

—— 1989. *The Enigma of Japanese Power: People and Politics in a Stateless Nation*. New York: MacMillan.

Vogel, Ezra F. 1979. *Japan As Number One: Lessons for America*. New York, NY: Harper and Row.

Waltz, Kenneth N. 1993. 'The Emerging Structure of International Politics.' *International Security* 18, 2 (Fall): 44–79.

Wendt, Alexander. 1992. 'Anarchy Is What States Make of It: The Social Construction of Power Politics.' *International Organization* 46, 2 (Spring): 391–425.

Whalen, Richard J. and Whalen, R. Christopher. 1990. *Trade Warriors: The Guide to the Politics of Trade and Investment* (expanded edn.). Washington, DC: The Whalen Company.

White, Theodore. 1985. 'The Danger From Japan.' *New York Times Magazine* (http://select.nytimes.com) July 28.

Wiseman's Group (The Japan–United States Economic Relations Group). 1981a. *Report of the Japan–United States Economic Relations Group* (January). Tokyo, Japan: Dai Nippon Printing Co.

——1981b. *Supplemental Report of the Japan–United States Economic Relations Group* (October). Tokyo, Japan: Dai Nippon Printing Co.

Wolff, Alan Wm. et al. 1985. *Japanese Market Barriers in Microelectronics: Memorandum in Support of a Petition Pursuant to Section 301 of the Trade Act of 1974, as Amended*. San Jose, CA: Semiconductor Industry Association.

Woods, Ngaire. 1995. 'Economic Ideas and International Relations: Beyond Rational Neglect.' *International Studies Quarterly* 39: 161–80.

Woodward, Bob. 1994. *The Agenda: Inside the Clinton White House*. New York, NY: Simon & Schuster.

Yamaguchi, Nancy. 1994. 'The US–Japan Framework Talks and the Politics of the Japanese Press.' *ESI Translation Series on the Japanese Political Economy* 1, 4 (November): 1–47.

Yamamura, Kozo. 1982. *Policy and Trade Issues of the Japanese Economy: American and Japanese Perspectives*. Seattle, WA: University of Washington Press.

——1990. 'Will Japan's Economic Structure Change? Confessions of a Former Optimist.' In Kozo Yamamura (ed.), *Japan's Economic Structure: Should It Change?* Seattle, WA: Society for Japanese Studies, 13–64.

Yasutomo, Dennis T. 1995. *The New Multilateralism in Japan's Foreign Policy*. New York, NY: St. Martin's Press.

Yee, Albert. 1996. 'The Causal Effects of Ideas on Policies.' *International Organization* 50, 1 (Winter): 69–108.

Yoffie, David B. 1988. 'How an Industry Builds Political Advantage: Silicon Valley Goes to Capitol Hill.' *Harvard Business Review* 66 (May–June): 82–9.

Zoellick, Robert B. 1995. 'Who Won the Trade War?' *The National Interest*, 41 (Fall): 78–81.

Index